"Mark McCormack, one of the smartest executives in the country, has come up with another bestseller—a 'must read' for anyone who has any interest in how to function in the business world."

—Herbert J. Siegel, Chairman and President,
Chris-Craft Industries, Inc.

"McCormack strikes again! Illuminating, interesting, and an entertaining read."

—Christie Hefner, President,
Playboy Enterprises, Inc.

"Regardless of whether you are buying or selling, Mark's reminders are meaningful and add up to a ton of sense."

—Russell W. Meyer, Jr., Chairman and CEO,
Cessna Aircraft Company

"After having had the pleasure of working with Mark McCormack for more than a decade and after having read his ten commandments in his 'Harvard II' book, I can state that Mark is one of the very few preachers who not only tell us what to do but also live up to their own commandments. His advice is useful not only for tough sportsmen and hardheaded and street-smart businessmen but for everyone who has to make decisions, get these decisions accepted by other people, and also wants to have a good relationship with his partners after the deal has been made."

—Baron Stig Ramel, President,
The Nobel Foundation

"Another 'must-read' book for anyone in business! Filled with common sense and a lifetime of successful salesmanship. Who but Mark McCormack can advise 'How to Manage the Boss' and make sense?"

—Frank A. Olson,
Chairman of the Board and CEO,
The Hertz Corporation

What They *Still* Don't Teach You at Harvard Business School

What They *Still* Don't Teach You at Harvard Business School

by Mark H. McCormack

Bantam Books
New York • Toronto • London • Sydney • Auckland

WHAT THEY STILL DON'T TEACH YOU AT HARVARD
BUSINESS SCHOOL
A Bantam Book / November 1989

Library of Congress Cataloging-in-Publication Data

McCormack, Mark H.
  What they still don't teach you at Harvard Business School : more notes
from a street-smart executive / Mark H. McCormack.
    p.   cm.
  ISBN 0-553-05748-0
  1. Success in business. 2. Management.   I. Title
HF5386.M474   1989
650.1—dc20   89-15097
                                                                   CIP

Published simultaneously in the United States and Canada

Bantam Books are published by Bantam Books, a division of Bantam
Doubleday Dell Publishing Group, Inc. Its trademark, consisting of the words
"Bantam Books" and the portrayal of a rooster, is Registered in U.S. Patent
and Trademark Office and in other countries. Marca Registrada. Bantam
Books, 666 Fifth Avenue, New York, New York 10103.

PRINTED IN THE UNITED STATES OF AMERICA

DH   0 9 8 7 6 5 4 3 2 1

To my wife Betsy Nagelsen,
my most important success secret of all,
with many thanks for her continued support
and inspiration

I would like to acknowledge the help
of Mark Reiter, the editor-in-chief
of my monthly newsletter.
Without his help this book
could not have been written.

Contents

CONTENTS

2

NEGOTIATING   49

..

3 .

MANAGING   91

4

5

GETTING ORGANIZED 203

6

COMMUNICATING 227

What They *Still* Don't Teach You at Harvard Business School

Introduction

The Ten Commandments of Street Smarts

I wrote *What They Don't Teach You at Harvard Business School* in 1984 not to take swipes at a great business school or to brag about my triumphs in twenty-five years of corporate warfare. Frankly, the book was born because I wanted to write down ideas I had been thinking out loud for years in lectures at places like the Harvard Business School and in the course of doing business.

Since the book's appearance, hundreds of people have let me know where they agreed and where they begged to differ with my business stratagems. Their comments have confirmed, and, in many cases, fine-tuned my thinking about being a street-smart executive. But certain ideas, I think, are universal and beyond discussion. I consider them the Ten Commandments of Street Smarts:

1. Never underestimate the importance of money.

I have always been grateful to my mother for cleverly letting me know that it was really all right to be concerned about money. It is, after all, the way most businesspeople keep score.

2. Never overestimate the value of money

Cash is by no means the only currency in business. There is much to be said for a job well done, the respect of others, or the thrill of building something from nothing. Pursue these goals as well and let the profits follow.

3. You can never have too many friends in business

Loyal friends who derive as much pleasure from your success as you do are the best leverage in business. Given the choice, people always prefer to do business with a friend, even if they sometimes can make a better deal elsewhere.

4. Don't be afraid to say, "I don't know"

If you don't know something, say so. There's no shame in not knowing everything. In fact, there is a subtle form of flattery and ego-stroking at work when you plead ignorance and ask the other person to educate you. If you're going to bluff, do so out of strength, not ignorance. I will very often say I don't know even when I do know—to find out how much the other person really knows.

5. Speak less

You cannot blunder or put your foot in your mouth if you are not speaking. More important, while you're busy talking, you are probably not reading the constantly shifting rhythms of your audience and your situation. Flapping gums dull your two most important senses—your eyes and ears.

6. Keep your promises, the big ones and the little ones

Few things in this world impress me as much as someone who does what he says he will do. Likewise, few things depress me more than someone who doesn't keep his word. This person is breaking an unwritten code of business. The starting point of any relationship is trust, not suspicion.

7. Every transaction has a life of its own

Some need tender loving care, some need to be hurried along. Once you figure that out, be adaptable. Go into a negotiation with as few preconceptions as possible. Whether you get less or more than you really wanted, it will always be more than you started with.

8. Commit yourself to quality from day one

Concentrate on each task, whether trivial or crucial, as if it's the only thing that matters (it usually is). It is better to do nothing at all than to do something badly.

9. Be nice to people

Not because you'll need them on your way down (as the cliché goes), but because it's the most pleasant route to the top. Being sensitive to other people's feelings always pays off; it has an uncanny way of (1) alerting you to their business needs, (2) sharpening your sense of timing, and (3) getting you out of awkward situations. All things being equal, courtesy can be most persuasive.

10. Don't hog the credit

Share it with your colleagues. If you have to tell the world how smart you are, you probably aren't.

Are these rules the last word on business success? Certainly not. But keep them in mind as you read the success secrets in the chapters that follow.

No matter what good and bad situations confront you in your business career, consciously adopting these ideas—and putting them to use every day—will always give you the edge.

1 | Selling

What Makes a Salesman?

I 've never met a salesperson who didn't have a personal sales slogan. The bromides seem to come with the territory. One of the most enduring is this fifteen-word sales course, authorship unknown:

> Know your product.
> See a lot of people.
> Ask all to buy.
> Use common sense.

Wise as this ancient advice may seem, I believe it needs some updating in today's fast-paced, global economy.

1. Know your product

More important, know your industry. It's no longer enough to memorize the items in your sample case. You have to know the competition as well. Information is gathered so quickly these days that customers, whether they are buying a toaster, a car, or a mainframe computer, feel compelled to shop around. Knowing your industry is a preemptive strike against this. You'd be surprised how trusting and appreciative busy customers can be when you have done the shopping around for them.

One connection between product and salesman, though, will never change. You must believe in your product.

Arthur "Red" Motley, the American magazine publisher, once recalled his rise and fall as a zither salesman in 1919. Motley was working as an iron miner in northern Michigan to save money for college. He hated the grime and the danger, so when a well-groomed zither salesman offered him a job, Motley jumped.

The zithers sold like hotcakes. Motley bought them for $5 a piece and never got less than $10 down. Even if he never collected another dime, he was ahead of the game. He gave away thirty sheets of music with each instrument. But when the customers came back for more music, he realized that his zithers only played in the key of C. They were useless for songs in any other key.

Motley continued to sell zithers right up to his first day at college. "But," he recalled, "I never sold as many per day or week after I found they played only in the key of C."

2. See a lot of people

This is good advice—but misleading if it lulls you into believing that selling is strictly a numbers game, determined by how many doors you knock on and how often you go back. Unless you work as hard at determining the quality of those doors and figuring out when to knock, you will be wasting your time and theirs.

3. Ask all to buy

I'm a great believer in this. Things go astray, though, when people use this as a license to be aggressive, intrusive, and overbearing.

Asking "all to buy" works fine 90 percent of the time, but not if the customer isn't ready to buy or needs time to think it's his idea.

4. Use common sense

This in itself is the ultimate common sense. Yet I've known people who, even if they had these words taped to their wrist, would find a way to misread the message. They are the ones who call a hot prospect at five o'clock on a Friday afternoon, who see the customer's interest wandering but deliver their sales pitch anyway, who believe that every thought that enters their head must be verbally exorcized.

Common sense is nice at all times, but you need it most when you think you need it the least—in the so-called easy sale (whatever that is!).

I remember meeting with a CEO in his office several years ago on a Saturday morning. He warned me that our meeting would be interrupted for twenty minutes by the arrival of a commercial real-estate broker who was a signature away from selling him on moving to a new office park. Since it was more or less a formality, he said I could stay.

The realtor arrived with final floor plans and cost projections and clearly had the CEO convinced. And then he turned stupid.

He had recently signed up the CEO's chief competitor as a tenant and, perhaps flushed with this success, proceeded to tell the CEO how he had made the sale. He extolled the virtues of the competition, literally congratulating them for having the wisdom and vision to lease his space. I guess he intended to flatter the CEO for doing the same.

The CEO stood up, thanked him for the presentation, and said he wouldn't be moving right now. As the stunned realtor turned to the door, the CEO said, "By the way, we happen to think we have some creativity and vision in this organization. But we don't think it comes from following in the footsteps of our competition."

The realtor was so proud about making the sale, he forgot to consider the customer's pride in making the buy.

What Makes a Supersalesman?

What qualities do you need to be a good salesman?

1. Believe in your product.
2. Believe in yourself.
3. Work on your timing.
4. Develop a sense of humor.
5. Realize that what your customer wants isn't necessarily what he's telling you.

Having listed these self-evident truths of salesmanship, I'd like to elaborate on a few qualities that make *super*salespeople.

1. Knock on old doors

I'm a firm believer in the 80/20 rule: 80 percent of your business is derived from 20 percent of your customers. That's because a customer you've sold and satisfied once is more likely to buy from you again. You see this in corporate life so often—giant defense contractors as well as upstart advertising agencies sustain the bulk of their payroll with three or four important clients—that it amazes me when people don't realize their old customers are their best prospects.

The 80/20 rule is equally important for individual salesmanship. For example, the number one salesman among the 75,000 Century 21 real-estate brokers in the US is a Rumanian emigrant named Nicholas Barsan. He sells a house *every four days* in the Jackson Heights area of

Queens, New York. More remarkable, a third of all Barsan's $1.1 million in annual commissions come from repeat customers. Barsan literally knocks on old doors and asks the homeowners if they're ready to sell.

2. Make your obsession their obsession

One thing I've learned in sports marketing is that it's a lot easier to sell participation in a sporting event to someone who shares my enthusiasm for sports. Yet even with people marginally interested in sports I keep trying—on the off chance that with careful exposure my obsession can be infectious.

I saw this work years ago with an antiques dealer in upstate New York who displayed his wares in the fifteen rooms of his landmark house. People would come in to browse and he would insist on giving them a tour of the rooms. Along the way he would make an interesting remark about each object—noting its origins or a design detail or even how cheaply he found it at an auction. Each item bore a tiny price sticker, but the dealer never mentioned money. As you wandered deeper into the house you became immersed in his world of beautiful things.

By the fourth room, the dustiest trinket took on an aura of significance—because it was important to him. His obsessions became your obsessions. And when he escorted visitors back to the front door, making sure they revisited each room, they invariably paused to purchase an item or two that they suddenly couldn't live without.

3. Choose little ponds to catch big fishes

Just as I counsel young executives to get a job in a company's international division (because that's where you can make the most impact with the least amount of competition), I also believe that supersalespeople tend to thrive in uncrowded territories.

Ever notice how often a company's top producers show up in the most improbable places? For example, one of the largest Steinway piano dealerships in the country is run by Michael Yeager in Waterford, Connecticut (population 18,000). Waterford is a suburb of New London, which ranks 146th among the top 150 US metropolitan areas.

Yeager succeeds because (1) his pianos are the best (although this doesn't explain why other Steinway dealers aren't doing as well); (2) his territory, though small, is heavily concentrated with wealthy people who can afford $35,000 pianos; and (3) there's no competition.

To use a golf analogy, you can win a golf tournament more convincingly if you play against a weak field. Of course, in golf this sort of easy victory is not very gratifying, but I guarantee that in business it is.

4. Bring something new to each party

A lot of salespeople are great at first impressions. They dress right, have a sense of humor, use all the right catch phrases and buzzwords. They even have something to sell. But on the second meeting, if they're back with the same patter the customer may sense that they lack substance—and walk away.

The best salespeople know instinctively that they have to keep the deal moving forward on the second meeting, if only in tiny increments. At each new sales opportunity they bring something new to the party.

If you're selling cars, you don't take customers on their second visit for *another* test drive. You talk about financing or fancy options or trading up. If you're selling a giant computer system to a company, you don't show up at the second meeting with the same pie-in-the-sky promises or glib swipes at your competition. You bring along a cost analysis and an articulate engineer or two.

5. Backpedal aggressively

There's nothing more refreshing than a salesperson who honestly says, "This is probably not right for you. Let's defer it for another time."

The best salespeople know that aggressive backpedaling in many cases is more important for long-term success than pushing forward full throttle to close a sale. Not only will customers trust you when you say, "Forget this for now," but they'll be more receptive when you ask, "Is there anything else we can do for you?"

6. Remove objections gently

It is said of good salespeople that they anticipate (and have an answer for) every customer objection. To them the selling process is like a Socratic dialogue or political debate whereby they wear down the customer through their powers of persuasion and their logic. Of course, they always run the risk of offending the customer or making him feel stupid.

Supersalespeople remove objections without the customer's noticing—often by learning to live with the objections or by letting the customer remove them himself.

I don't know how many times I've heard a customer object to a proposal for reasons that I know are illogical or factually incorrect. Demolishing the customer's position might be the easiest thing in the world for me to do. But why bother? Customers don't buy because you're one point up in a debating contest—and they certainly don't buy when they're angry or humiliated.

Instead, I bite my tongue and wait and gently make my point another day in another context.

7. Follow up after the sale

One of the best salespeople I ever met could sell anybody anything. He had wit, charm, substance, practicality, and a

British accent. He genuinely knew what customers wanted. Unfortunately, he had no follow-up and rarely delivered what he sold. After closing a sale, he would zip out of town and you'd never hear from him again. He's now using his selling skills to extricate himself from some very messy agreements.

The Offer They Can't Refuse

I have always contended that a great way for young people to land the ideal job is to work for nothing. If they have something to offer, they'll get on the payroll soon enough.

The same approach works wonders when you're selling your company's services.

Suppose that you feel very confident that you can do a good job for somebody and you have clearly established a benchmark amount for a particular service—say, a $10,000 monthly fee. It can often be to your advantage to tell a potential customer, "Look, I'm so confident that this will work out well, that I'll work on the project for six months and then, after the fact, you can pay me anything you wish, *including nothing,* if that's what you think it's worth."

This is a bold statement, but not a rash one. If you're providing a first-rate service and if you're dealing with an honorable person, I think your exposure is minimal. And the advantages are at least fourfold:

1. The client can't say, "We don't have the budget"

Quite often the people you are dealing with are not at the highest decision-making level. Thus, even if they are positively inclined toward hiring your company, they might not have the authority or budget to do so. At your rates, however, they can't use budget as an excuse.

2. The client can silence any objections by peers

Executives at every corporation have peers or superiors questioning their decisions. Projects get stalled not only for budget reasons but because of turf wars that you as an outsider might not be aware of. You will have gone a long way to helping an executive overcome such peer objections if he is able to go back to them and say, "Not only do I think we should go ahead with this, but they're willing to work for nothing."

3. It introduces you to all levels of a company

Working for nothing is a great way to meet a company's second tier of executives, often on a mystical level because these executives are not exactly sure of your relationship with their boss. The more you mingle among the second and third tiers of executives, the more likely you are to make allies instead of enemies.

4. It simplifies the chairman's life

In some companies, we have found that the work-for-nothing approach is best done at the level of chairman or chief executive. For one thing, there's no confusion about which person—rather than which committee—will be judging our work and fixing our fee after six or twelve months. Also, we find it's convenient to have the top decision maker on our side in case of surprises.

But dealing directly with the chairman is tricky—and certainly no guarantee of success. Chairmen can dictate anything, but they can't follow through on everything. The chairman who doesn't stay close to a project on a day-to-day basis is at the mercy of subordinates. This can complicate a project but need not endanger it.

We have used the "work for nothing" approach, carefully and selectively, for years. In all that time I can recall only one instance when someone treated us unfairly. This happened with a leading sports personality—not a corporation— who paid us a ludicrously low fee at the end of the year. I have to believe this told us more about him than about the job we did.

How to Prepare for a Sale: Five Overlooked Questions

I know of organizations that prepare for a sales presentation as if it were a D-day invasion. The boss commands dozens of lieutenants to conduct research, to file reports, to prepare impressive charts and slide shows. The staff then scurry around, often at cross-purposes, unaware of one another's assignments, hoping that a persuasive idea will emerge from this round-the-clock frenzy.

While I agree that it's better to overwhelm than under-whelm a prospective client, sometimes in all that military maneuvering critical questions are overlooked. For example:

1. Why are we making the sale?

Sometimes we want to make a sale just to make a sale, even if we don't show a profit immediately. There are strategic reasons for this: (a) the sale could be important as a *defensive measure*, to prevent the competition from doing business with the customer; (b) in *planning for the future* we might accept a loss on the sale for the opportunity of much greater long-term returns; (c) the sale may be important to *establish our credentials* as we enter a new field.

2. Is the proposal short enough?

I recently read about an executive who, when an associate handed him a three-inch thick book of numbers and graphs on a possible transaction, dumped the book in the wastebasket and told the associate, "Come back when you know what you're talking about." If your idea is good, you don't need charts and visual aids to sell it. If your idea is bad, all the bells and whistles in the world won't improve it.

3. What questions can I expect?

Customers and clients have a knack for asking perfectly reasonable questions that seem to catch salespeople off guard.

For example, when we are selling the international television rights to a sports event, we should not be surprised if the sponsor wants to know what time of day the show will air live, say, in Australia. Fumbling for an answer or giving the wrong one to this vital question would not enhance our position. After years of marketing international sports events, we have found it much more impressive to be ready with a piece of paper that lists air times around the world.

4. How are the payments timed?

Failure to consider timing of payments can turn a money maker into a money loser.

If we agree to put on a tennis tournament in twelve months for a $100,000 fee plus $75,000 in expenses, we do not want to carry the costs of staging the event for those twelve months. We prefer a schedule that pays us the fee in quarterly installments and covers our expenses on an as-you-go-basis.

You can't underestimate the importance of cash flow. It's pleasant to bask in the big round numbers of a transaction, but don't forget that *when* you get paid is just as important as how much.

5. Have I established clear lines of communication and authority?

After I've personally negotiated a transaction with a client company's chairman, the worst thing that can happen is for some unidentified person from our organization to call that chairman about implementing the sale.

The chairman is puzzled: who is this caller, what's his authority? I would understand if the chairman, slightly miffed, called me for an explanation.

Business relationships can fall apart over such misunderstandings. This is more than a matter of peers (in this case, chairmen) wanting to deal with peers. It is a matter of etiquette and respect for the chain of command. Near the close of every sale it is crucial that all parties establish who is reporting to whom. This avoids bad decisions (and bruised egos).

Taking Your Clients as Seriously as They Take Themselves

A friend at another company found out the other day that one reason his organization had met some resistance at Federal Express in past years might very well be because they once sent Federal Express an urgent proposal—via DHL.

(I can just imagine the DHL package arriving at Federal Express's Memphis headquarters, winding its way from the mail room to the intended recipient as if it were contaminated material, with everyone wondering, "What idiot sent that?" Whatever the merits of the proposal, I'm sure the method of delivery destroyed them.)

I mention this because I think it's important to *take the client seriously in every respect,* especially about the little things.

You don't drive an Avis rental car to a meeting with Hertz or fly American Airlines to Chicago to meet with United Airlines. You don't order Pepsi at a luncheon with Coca-Cola. You don't keep up the "Thank You for Not Smoking" signs when executives from Philip Morris come calling.

Unfortunately, many people don't appreciate how easily a client or customer can feel slighted. They think it's no big deal that they drive an Avis rental car to a meeting with Hertz. "The Hertz people will never know," they reason, "and why would they care?"

Believe me, this is the kind of situation that Murphy's Law ("If anything can go wrong, it will") was written for. The Hertz people will somehow find out. And with archrival Avis in the picture, they will certainly care.

One of our executives was recently scheduled to fly to the Midwest to meet with the executives of a major airline. He wisely booked passage on one of their planes. But at the last minute, the flight was cancelled. Eager to be on time for the meeting, he scrambled to get a seat on a rival carrier.

When he arrived on time at the airline's headquarters, the client was livid. They didn't care about his heroic efforts to be punctual. In fact, they said, "We'd prefer that you re-schedule the meeting before you patronize a competitor."

Perhaps the client was overreacting. But a street-smart executive would have anticipated it. He would have known that:

(a) It's the little mistakes, not the major screwups, that linger and fester in the client's mind; and

(b) Sensitivities are heightened by a factor of ten when a competitor is involved.

Unlike the company with the Federal Express fiasco, I like to think our people have developed some savvy about not irritating potential customers.

Like the advertising agency executive I know who drives one client's cars, brushes with another account's toothpaste, and uses another account's laundry detergent, being hypersensitive to a client's whims and desires is becoming second nature for us.

For example, one of our executives who regularly deals with a major wine and spirits company now makes it a practice to serve only the client's products when the client visits our offices. (That's common sense.)

Before a lunch meeting, he also warns his colleagues not to order beer—because the client regards all beer as competition. (That's a little more than common sense.)

At a recent hospitality program that we organized for the client at a resort hotel, this executive restocked the entire hotel—restaurants, bar, and minibars—with the client's products. (That's uncommon sense.)

Did the client appreciate or even notice all the work our man had done? I don't know. But I have a pretty good idea how the client would have reacted if our man had not bothered.

Buying: The Forgotten Half of the Sales Equation

Selling is such an important part of most people's business day that many otherwise shrewd people forget the other half of the sales equation—how to buy, how to be a good customer.

Figuring out why otherwise shrewd business people aren't as good at buying as they are at selling is complicated. But mostly it's a matter of perception. Buying is not perceived as glamorous; the honor of saving the company money rarely matches the glory of bringing it in (even though a poor purchase could affect profits more than a great sale). Nor has buying accrued the mystical qualities attributed to selling. It is not a skill that requires its practitioners to put their ego on the line with each call. There is not much fear of rejection involved in offering to buy someone's product.

Perhaps there should be.

If selling means systematically creating a need for your product or service and finding ways to enhance that need, then buying means consciously denying or postponing that need—until you find the right terms. Unfortunately, many people forget how much leverage they have as purchasers. Buying a computer system, for example, is a common task in many companies today. It is also expensive and tricky. Choosing the right equipment, the best vendor, and the right financing can take months. In the midst of all that research and maneuvering—and, perhaps, in their eagerness for instant gratification—buyers sometimes forget to get the best price.

I know one businessman who was so impressed (or perhaps intimidated) by how many hours a computer company spent writing proposals and counterproposals that he felt uneasy about asking them to cut their list prices. In effect, he was paying them a premium to sell to him.

There is nothing sacred about list prices or standard vendor's contracts. They cry out to be negotiated, especially if you use the power of leverage. Money is the greatest leverage—you have it and the seller wants it—but other factors can increase your leverage. For example:

1. How big is the order and the seller's profit margin?
2. Are you paying cash in a lump sum or installments?
3. Does your order represent the beginning of a long-term relationship?
4. Are you an industry leader the seller will eagerly claim as a customer?
5. Are you a technology leader who may help improve the seller's product over time?

6. Have you found an alternative supplier more agreeable to your demands?

The problem with leverage is that it's worthless in hindsight.
You can't spend your leverage once you've spent your money.

Even the most desperate seller will resent being bullied by
a large customer. If you break down your position into
"essential," "important," and "nice" points, you'll find it
worthwhile in the long run to let the seller win a few of the
latter.

The art of salesmanship is telling the customers what
they want to hear. The art of customership is hearing the
salesman's pitch and getting it down on paper. The simplest
way to do this is to keep notes on every one of the seller's
promises, incorporate them into an agreement, and then ask
for his signature. If he wasn't willing to negotiate before, he
will now.

Secrets of the Information Trade

In most corporate sales, half your time is spent trying to
obtain the right information. Before you can create a desire
to buy, you have to find out what the customer really wants
(which, as noted previously, is not always what he says he
wants) and what price he's willing to pay.

In my ideal world, potential customers would start out
every meeting by telling us exactly how they want to be sold.
Until then, however, the following strategies for gathering
hard-to-get information will have to do:

1. Ask questions you already know the answers to

If the other party is wrong, you will have identified someone
who (a) is wasting your time or (b) needs your product or
service more than they know.

2. Repeat questions at subsequent meetings

Not only is it fascinating to compare the contradictions, but they can tell you a lot about the person supplying the answers.

I once knew the CEO of a public company who on one particular occasion gave a glowing report about a certain key executive. Two months later, when I asked how that executive was doing, the CEO was violent in his scorn for the person. That told me a lot more about the CEO giving the report than the executive he was evaluating. It was also the first instance that made me think the CEO was losing it a little bit.

3. Give as much as you can afford

Since it generally doesn't cost you anything, information is the purest form of quid pro quo. To get a little, you have to give a little.

Preferably your information should sound like it's "confidential" even if it's not. I often go into negotiations armed with a few bulletins that I can afford to give away—because, like anyone else, I have certain proprietary information that I take for granted which another party might be dying to know. After I've shared my secrets, it's pretty difficult for them to keep theirs.

4. Consider the source

The level of people you're talking to and where you're talking to them can influence the kind of information you're getting.

Senior people, I have found, tend to reveal more the farther you get them from their office or yours. They're less likely to wear their "game face" during a pleasant dinner or a round of golf. If business does enter the conversation (and it does in more ways than you think), it's like a politician dealing with a journalist "off the record." Be prepared for the unvarnished truth.

Junior people, on the other hand, are less reliable than you or they may think. They tend to offer more opinion than fact—and require constant corroboration.

5. Ask for information they won't give you

How people deal with information that's truly none of your business is a reliable indicator of their character and integrity.

The most ticklish situations in our industry involve customers wanting information about one of our clients. We always respond, "Ask the client yourself. If they want you to know that, that's their privilege. But you certainly won't learn it from us."

I don't know anyone who's resented us or refused to do business with us because of this.

6. The hidden meaning of numbers

Have you ever noticed the shroud of silence that falls on a meeting the moment you ask, "How many widgets are you selling?" or "What's your profit margin on that unit?"

That's because *numbers* are the information the customer never wants to share.

Many people, perhaps because they're afraid of offending the customer or not getting an answer, avoid questions about hard numbers.

But to me this is the most telling part of a sale. In effect, you are drawing a line and asking your customer to cross it. This is the surest sign of whether a potential customer is ready to deal or is just playing games.

What the Other Guy's Expenses
Should Say to You

When they think about entertainment expenses, most business people think about how much or how little they're doing for the other guy. They rarely think about the other side of the equation: how much someone else is spending to entertain *them*. It's an insight from reading people that could benefit or cost you.

I perk up when people go overboard to entertain me. Translation: They are easily swayed by nonbusiness considerations—and I can easily sell them by pushing the right buttons. They have exposed themselves as being vulnerable, for better or worse, to the same lavish treatment from me.

For instance, if a company's senior executive offered to fly me in the corporate jet somewhere, I would interpret that to mean I could reciprocate (if I wanted to) and get a very favorable result for doing so.

There's a dark side to this as well. To my way of thinking, if someone took personal advantage of their company to suit themselves and me—to impress me, for instance—I could reasonably infer that if I did something for them, something that would make them feel like a big shot, they might do the same for me, regardless of whether or not that action might benefit their company.

These are very dangerous people, and dealing with them can compromise you in ways you never imagined.

Don't Forget to Ask for the Order

Dozens of facts and factors go into making a sale. They are part of the strategizing that can make business life fun. But all of your gamesmanship and ability to push the right buttons are worthless if you can't close a sale.

Perhaps because closing is such a crucial part of selling, many people have the misconception that it is an art form. It isn't. In many situations closing a deal should be like a bank closing on a newly purchased house. If you've prepared well, it should be a routine, almost robotic function. The only thing you have to remember is to ask for the order. That's very important.

In the early days of our company, when we were first branching out into corporate consulting, we called on the Simmons mattress company to acquaint them with our services. It had taken months to set up the meeting with Grant Simmons, the company chairman, and his vice presidents.

The meeting went fine but I sensed that they weren't convinced or ready to commit. And who knew how many more months it would take to assemble this group again? So I laid all my cards out on the table.

I said, "I've just explained to you what I think the benefits would be of a Simmons relationship with our organization. And you seem to respond warmly to that. But when I walk out this door, you'll probably forget about me. That's understandable. You'll go back to your offices and there will be a stack of urgent messages on your desk and soon a small contract with my company will seem insignificant."

I was probably aware that they would not mind me telling them how busy they were. I also knew that Grant Simmons, the man whose name was on the building, was present, and he could give a definitive yes or no if only I would ask. I was determined not to leave that room without a deal.

Continuing with my closing pitch, I said, "It has taken us four months to set up this meeting. We all agree that it's a good idea. So I'm asking you, can you make a commitment now?"

Grant Simmons stood up, said yes, shook my hand, and left the room. It was as simple as that.

As I recall, people in our organization were stunned that

we came back from that meeting with a deal. I never told them how easy it was.

Never Leave a Sales Call Without Selling Something

A few years ago I made a sales call on a corporation, trying to interest them in a major sponsorship of a television project. It was an expensive project. But the circumstances were promising. The company was interested. All the right people were in attendance, including their top decision maker. Our presentation went well.

Nevertheless, they said no.

On the way back to the office, I turned to an associate and muttered, "I can't believe that I left there without selling them something, even a $2,000 film idea."

An associate reminded me of that remark the other day. He wondered if I really believe that you should never leave a sales call without selling something.

Frankly, I do.

I am always reminding our people not to be so tunnel-visioned on a sales call that they accept a customer's yes or no on the specific matter at hand and leave it at that. Tunnel vision—the belief that you call on someone only to sell them what you need to sell or what *they* think you came to sell—is one of the most pernicious fallacies of salesmanship.

Best time to sell

To my way of thinking, if the customer says yes to your proposal, that's the best time to sell them something else—because they're already predisposed to buy from you. (Auto dealers who first sell you the car—and then add on the high-performance tires, the rustproofing, and the extended war-ranty protection—have known this for years.)

Likewise, if a customer with whom we should be doing business says no to one of our ideas, I want our people prepared to go back at him on the spot with a new idea. Preferably, this will be a less expensive proposal, on the theory that customers are more open to a little idea after they have said no to a big one.

Easier sales

I don't care if we don't make any money on the sale. With the right customers, it's better to do some business than no business. The sale itself is a positive step. It's the start of a relationship. It keeps the door open and the lines of com-munication working. If we do our job well, they'll buy much more from us in the future.

I have always believed, especially in the early days of our business, that it's easier to make a million dollars by selling a hundred $10,000 ideas than selling two $500,000 ideas. Implementing those 100 ideas may be tougher, but the plain truth is *they are easier sales*.

As a manager, I think that people often forget that the bread and butter of any enterprise is in the smaller deals. The small deals pay the rent and electric bills. The small deals give your people the chance to learn and make mis-takes. The small deals, by definition, are the ones that have room to grow.

Should Your Friends Be Clients?

Yes, but there's a right way and wrong way to go about it.

The wrong way is to assume that since they're your friends, you can be totally candid with them. "Let's have lunch," you say. "I want to sell you something." This rarely works, since it confuses them about the change in your relationship, and confusion tends to create barriers.

A better way with friends is to practice the ultimate soft sell. You have to convince them that you're totally indifferent to whether or not they buy your product or service—even though they know you well enough to suspect you want to sell them. Let them think that it's not that big a deal, that you'd rather have them as a friend than a customer. That's the best atmosphere in which to have a business relationship.

There are numerous instances where I have gone about signing clients without trying to sign them—by just continuing to be their friend. The scenario is fairly simple and not at all Machiavellian.

Step one, I invite them to dinner or a golf tournament. Step two, I don't mention business. Step three, I entertain them again a few weeks later. Step four, I don't bring up business.

Eventually, many friends will go on the offensive, not because they "owe me one," but because I've exposed them through osmosis rather than a direct sales pitch to how I work and what our organization can do. They consider the things I have been doing with them a fringe benefit of a potential business relationship. And they like that. Suddenly, they *want* to become a client.

The key in all this is to "expose" your friends to what you can do. And let them think it's their idea.

BMW, the German automobile company, has used this friendly exposure with great success in Japan. The company literally gives BMWs to certain key Japanese business people and VIPs. They test drive the cars for a month and then decide. It's not that risky if you have a good product. BMW is now the most successful import in Japan.

My Favorite Sales Pitch

The chairman of a Big Eight accounting firm recently made an interesting comment about my selling technique.

His firm had just made a long-term and substantial financial commitment to be associated with one of our most prestigious institutional (and non-sport) clients.

On the day we finalized the relationship, he said to me, "You told me two things when we first met a few months back. First, you told me not to think of your organization only in terms of sports. Second, you said there are a lot of things that can be done for $10,000 rather than a whole lot more. Having bought a concept that has nothing to do with sports, I realize now that half of what you said was right."

We both laughed over this, but he had put his finger on one of the most important points in selling: Nine times out of ten, you'll have far more success underselling as opposed to overselling your product or service.

In our organization, where we sell multimillion dollar sports marketing concepts to corporations and have a reputation for asking big numbers, there's nothing more disarming to a prospect than hearing a small number. That's underselling.

Two steps

The first step is to paint a pleasant picture of the possibilities for the prospect. For example, if price is a question mark—in the prospect's mind and mine—I love using examples of what other companies are paying for projects. I'll point out that XYZ Corp. spent $2 million on an event and a competitor spent even more on another tournament. And I'll let those big numbers linger in the background.

The next step is the most critical. Having established the

high end of the cost spectrum, I'll propose a $10,000 idea from the other extreme. My risk is negligible. If the customer likes the idea, I've made a sale and gained a friend. More often than not, however, they tell me, "We had something more elaborate in mind."

That's even better! Not only have I learned their level of seriousness and commitment, but they are, in effect, telling me to sell them more. Somewhere between $10,000 and a whole lot more, we'll do business together to our mutual satisfaction.

There's nothing particularly wily or insidious about this approach. In a way, it's the lowest pressure sale you can make—and it should be used more often in any business.

Problems of overselling

For example, auto dealers are notorious oversellers. They're always trying to "upgrade" their customers. If a customer walks into the showroom with a $10,000 budget, the salesperson is instructed to steer him to a $13,000 automobile on the theory that (a) the customer might go for it, (b) there's more room to negotiate, and (c) there's always the fallback of a cheaper car.

To me that's overselling (and helps explain why many customers are so suspicious of auto dealers). It assumes you can persuade the customer to go higher against his or her wishes. In my mind, underselling represents a refreshing change from what most people expect. If a customer came into my showroom looking for a $10,000 car, the first thing I'd do is show him our full line, from high to low. And then I'd offer him a car that lists for $9,500.

If he likes the car, I've made a sale. If he wants to spend more, that's nice to know too. But it's much better for him to come to that conclusion by himself than for me to assume it from the start.

The Best Technique to Win
the Customer Over

I once called a business acquaintance who had just been transferred from Japan to run the Latin American operations of a major corporation. In Japan we had concluded some blockbuster deals together, but I knew that we were dealing with different price capabilities in his new territory. My proposals anticipated these constraints. It meant spending $800 here, $1,000 there, $3,000 in another area.

He was delighted. "I was afraid you were coming in here with a six- or seven-figure program like we used to do in Japan," he said. "This market simply won't sustain that kind of budget. We're looking for cost-effective ways to reach dozens of small markets."

(Incidentally, this points up one of the biggest mistakes in selling: equating the size of your proposal with the size of the company you're approaching. The tendency is to think that huge corporations—an IBM or Ford Motor Company, for example—only respond to huge proposals. We've found the opposite to be true, perhaps because big corporations are very serious now about cutting fat, or they're relying more on in-house staff, or they see so many overpriced proposals. In our business at least, you're more likely to sell a big proposal to a smaller company.)

Cost, of course, isn't the only customer anxiety. In almost every transaction there are emotional considerations that, coupled with a good idea and fair price, can prove irresistible.

For example, we frequently do business with major automobile companies. We know they're all intensely interested in their dealer organizations. So we often try to put a favorable topspin on any proposal by including a dealer element in it.

Let's say we want a major automaker to sponsor the Tournament of Roses Parade for several hundred thousand dollars and all the television exposure that implies. In addition, we suggest that the company bring fifty top dealers and their spouses to sit in the VIP section at the Parade and the Rose Bowl game. That's an element the marketing chief will surely not regard with disfavor.

It makes our proposal look buttoned-up and suggests to the automaker that we know a little bit about his business *and* his problems.

The Power of Being "Reasonable"

In almost every negotiation, there are certain issues that cannot be quantified—and yet people insist on attaching a number value to them.

In our business of athlete representation, for example, one of the thorniest issues that begs to be quantified—but shouldn't be—is the number of days an athlete can commit to a sporting equipment company with whom he or she has a professional affiliation.

As agents we are very sensitive to this issue, because time is an athlete's most precious commodity. We believe an athlete spends his or her time most effectively on the playing field rather than in photo studios or making in-store appearances. On the other hand, we are not insensitive to the fact that a company spending large sums promoting an athlete's connection with their product would be concerned about getting the most exposure for their dollars.

In the past, we could almost predict the pattern of the negotiation. The company would demand a specific number of days of the athlete's time. And then the negotiations would bog down in a surreal discussion of how you interpret a "day." Is it 24 consecutive hours? A business lunch? More than half of a working day between 9 A.M. and 5 P.M.? After a while, this line of negotiation becomes very counterproductive.

A reasonable solution

More often than not, we have resolved this deadlock by simply agreeing to "a reasonable number of days" instead of a specific number. Rarely have our customers complained.

I remember dealing in this area with Allstate Insurance on behalf of Arnold Palmer in the early 1970s. Allstate was insisting Arnold commit to five days a year to them.

I told them, "Arnold Palmer is the kind of guy who will go out of his way to be a spokesperson for Allstate all of the time. What you don't want to do is get him into a mindset where you are forcing him to be your employee for five days a year. If you do, you'll get your five days—and nothing more.

"You'd rather have him do whatever you reasonably request consistent with his schedule. That way, he can be working for Allstate every day of the year if possible. But don't go into this agreement counting the minutes and subtracting the travel time to calculate an official 'day.'

"Let's get this going and at the end of the year see if Arnold has been reasonable."

If you know that your client is going to perform brilliantly, that he will become a great friend of the person on the other side of the table and make him look like a hero—in other words, if you know your client will be *more than reasonable*—then promising to be "reasonable" is one of the most effective words you can use in a negotiation.

Suddenly, the person on the other side of the table is your ally rather than your adversary. You will spend the year working together to see how much Arnold can reasonably do.

Of course, you have to be very careful with this approach. If your client isn't reliable, you can end up looking very bad. Not only have you failed to deliver, but you've lost an ally.

In my experience, the beauty of promising to be "reasonable" is that it forces the other side to be reasonable too.

Timing Phone Calls for Maximum Effect

People don't pay enough attention to the timing of their phone calls. They get the urge to call and the message goes directly to their dialing finger, bypassing their brain. They forget that *when* you call is no less important than *who* and *why* you're calling—and usually determines whether your call ever gets through.

In the early days of my business, when Arnold Palmer, Gary Player, and Jack Nicklaus were our major clients, as a matter of efficiency and self-preservation, I quickly figured out their phone habits. The obvious exercise is to get someone when you're not waking them out of a sound sleep and also when they're not just about to run out the door. After learning about all of their respective habits, it worked out that I always would call Arnold at eight o'clock in the morning, Gary at nine, and Jack at ten. In those days, if I phoned earlier there was a good chance I'd wake them and if I phoned one hour later there was a good chance they'd be gone.

Learn their patterns

Getting to know people's habits is invaluable, especially the people you deal with on a regular basis. You should regularly be fine-tuning your insights into their business patterns and life-style habits. The clues are everywhere.

A CEO I know once needed to speak to someone at a major corporation. The executive in his organization who normally dealt with that company advised him to call Ms. So-and-So at precisely four o'clock.

"Why that hour?" the CEO asked.

"I had a stack of phone messages from her once and

noticed that she called at four o'clock each time. That seems to be her slot for us."

Find out what's convenient

In any business there are people you have to reach whom you don't know too well, whose habits are impossible to fathom, or who are genuinely as busy as they claim to be. They may take your calls but they never have time to talk.

Be very frontal with such people. Ask them, "When is a convenient time to call you?" (That's a fair question and, politely phrased, hard to resist.) And then be sure to phone precisely at the appointed hour, no matter how inconvenient it might be for you.

Calling people on the road

The best time to call someone who travels a lot is between 8:00 and 9:00 A.M. at their hotel (unless you know something about their habits that would indicate to call even earlier). The cocktail hour is also good because people usually return to their hotel between 5:30 and 7:30 P.M. to rest or get ready for a night out.

Of course, you always run the risk of catching someone who's tired or aggravated. If I sense my call is ill-timed, I always apologize and ask, "How early can I call you tomorrow morning so as not to wake you up but to catch you before you leave?"

When to call to NOT get through

Occasionally, you may *have* to call people whom, for various reasons, you really don't want to talk to. A rudimentary knowledge of their work style should tell you when to call so you won't get through. For example, if they arrive at work late, call at 9:00 A.M. If they leave early, call at 5:30 P.M. The perfect time for such a call, obviously, is at lunchtime, in which case you get credit for making the call without actually having to complete it.

I don't necessarily endorse this sort of "telephone tag" but it's better than being considered totally unresponsive.

Making an Impression Through the Kids

I'm a great believer in doing something for a client or customer's children. I also think it is a vastly underused gesture in business, perhaps because most people don't have the time or inclination to find out about a client's family.

Indirectly including the kids in a business relationship is almost always impressive; it is remembered, appreciated, and in the long run, usually reciprocated.

Years ago when my son Todd was in grade school and crazy about football, a business associate of mine arranged for Todd to meet the Minnesota Vikings' quarterback Fran Tarkenton. Todd was absolutely thrilled—and *I* never forgot it.

There are all sorts of variations on this gesture. As long as the favors are genuine, not part of some elaborate quid pro quo, I think they are appropriate in selling.

In 1987 I was the "beneficiary" of a sales approach that involved—once again—my son Todd. The following story is proof that selling through the kids works—because I was the buyer.

A twenty-four-year-old entrepreneur named Mark Goldstein from Philadelphia was marketing a computerized business game developed at the University of Pennsylvania. It was called a "business simulation" whereby people using a personal computer could test the impact of any decision within their company in seconds on the screen. Big companies using million-dollar mainframe computers and six-figure software programs had been doing such simulation for years.

But Goldstein's company, Reality Technologies, was offering the first sophisticated, inexpensive simulation software for consumers and their PCs.

Goldstein's idea was to blend the stories and advice in my book *What They Don't Teach You at Harvard Business School* into his company's simulation model and market them in a software package using my name and title. Goldstein's only problem was getting through to me.

Goldstein's first step was to call my secretary in New York—about fifty times. In fairness to my secretary, I was out of the country at the time and she had no idea what a "business simulation" was.

(I hasten to point out that I am not by nature unresponsive to good ideas. In fact, because of our company's visibility, we're deluged with unsolicited ideas, the kind that come in envelopes marked "confidential" or "proprietary." But for assorted legal reasons, we are extremely cautious. We simply won't look at an unsolicited idea without a waiver or release from its creator. This "paranoia" is what Goldstein was up against.)

Eventually, Goldstein persuaded my secretary to see him. He arrived the next day at our New York office with a portable computer. He commandeered a conference room and gave my secretary a dazzling demonstration of his computer program. Afterward, my secretary apologized for not knowing all that much about computers but casually mentioned that my son Todd, teaching up in Boston, did.

Goldstein, to his credit, pounced on this information. He immediately flew up to Boston and gave Todd the same impressive demonstration. The next time Todd and I spoke, he mentioned Goldstein. He said, "I think you should take a look at what he's proposing, Dad."

That was all I needed to hear. Anybody smart enough to try to sell me through my son is someone I might want for a partner! We concluded a software deal a few months later.

"No Brainers" I Have Known

Business-school graduates, I've noticed, are fond of the buzzword "no brainer." It's become a catchall phrase to describe concepts and deals where the upside potential is so obvious and the downside so negligible that it literally takes "no brains" to say yes.

No brainers worry me—and not just because I can think of more flattering sales pitches than, "You don't need any brains to see this will work." The fact is, no brainers don't comport with reality. They rarely take into consideration that, first, people and circumstances change, sometimes more rapidly than anyone can predict; second, the numbers that guide and shape a decision may simply be wrong; and third, no matter how well the two of you may polish and fine-tune your deal, there are aggressive third parties outside your cozy circle who might not agree.

I get very suspicious whenever someone tells me it takes no brains to say yes. I immediately know I'll need all my brains to find a way to say no. Among the many "no brainer" situations that should put you and your colleagues on "special alert," the following three are especially dangerous.

When there's too much of a good thing

As the saying goes, if it sounds too good to be true, it probably is. You might have a hard time accepting this—especially when you and the other party do everything you say you'll do only to find that the more you succeed the more you fail.

Consider, for example, a recent no brainer that the people in charge of increasing circulation for the newspaper *USA Today* created with General Mills. The basic idea was simple: consumers would buy several General Mills products (such as Cheerios, Bisquick, Hamburger Helper), send in proof of purchase, and receive a free six-month subscription to *USA Today*. General Mills sells merchandise. *USA Today* gains readers. Everybody wins, right?

USA Today even covered themselves. They got General Mills to agree to pay for the first 52,000 subscriptions. The only problem would be if, say, 300,000 people sent in their proof-of-purchase coupons. But the newspaper circulation experts laughed this off as impossible.

Of course, the impossible happened. (That's the one certainty with no brainers.) The first week of the promotion 40,000 people sent in coupons for free subscriptions. By the twelfth week, 512,000 people wanted their free paper. The unprecedented response overwhelmed the company's computers and printing plants, not to mention slightly denting the treasury. Total loss: $12 million.

Lesson: If the upside goes on forever, you can be sure the downside does too.

Dealing with the 800-pound gorilla

I'm sure there are thousands of small and medium-sized companies that would kill for a contract with an American Express or General Electric. The decision is a no brainer. Giant companies mean giant volume. They are collectible. And you can leverage your association with them into contracts with other giants.

Unfortunately, it doesn't always work out that way. Doing business with a giant company reminds me of the joke about the 800-pound gorilla. (Where does the gorilla sit? Anywhere he wants.) At every step of the way, you're at the giant's mercy.

An instructive example of this is Sears, Roebuck. Years ago most manufacturers desperately wanted to do business with Sears. Getting products in the Sears catalog or stores meant instant huge volume. Companies would price themselves close to break-even or lower in order to hook Sears.

In the end, Sears hooked *them*. Sears would order a

million units at $1 a unit, and companies would crack open the champagne. They'd increase staff, machinery, and overhead to fill the order. Then Sears would pounce. They'd ask these captive companies to lower their price to 91 cents a unit—to increase Sears' profit. Small suppliers would either give up the business or get by on 91 cents.

There was a time when Sears bankrupted many suppliers by acting like an 800-pound gorilla. Happily, Sears soon realized that everyone deserves to make money and that building a network of happy, prosperous suppliers was a better long-range bet than squeezing them for every nickel of profit.

When you think you're all alone . . .

The most devastating no brainer is the deal that lulls you into thinking you're the only one left in the game.

This happened to Fuji, the Japanese film manufacturer, at the 1984 Summer Olympics. As part of its aggressive campaign to grab market share from number one Kodak, Fuji paid millions of dollars to become the official 35mm film of the Los Angeles Olympics. In one stroke, thought Fuji, they had shut out Kodak from the year's premier sporting event.

Remarkably, Fuji never considered that Kodak would—or could—fight back. Kodak asked our company to figure out ways to blunt Fuji's "coup."

The most interesting point, among many we found, was that Fuji's "exclusive" was not all-inclusive. Fuji had basically locked up *the two weeks of the Games*. But what about the rest of the year?

So we recommended that Kodak focus its marketing efforts on the six months of frenzied interest *leading up to the Games*. Kodak sponsored the US Track and Field Team, retained potential gold-medalists Edwin Moses, Mary Decker, and Alberto Salazar as spokespersons, sponsored the Olympic Trials in Track and Field, and saturated the Los

Angeles market with print, television, and billboard advertising.

By the time the Summer Olympics arrived, many sports-marketing professionals thought that Kodak, not Fuji, had sponsored the Games.

Signals You Should Be Reading When You Walk Into the Room

I have two objectives when I make an initial sales call: I want to impress the prospect favorably *and* I want to see what, if anything, the prospect does to impress me.

The first part is easy, assuming you're civil, presentable, and have something to sell. The second requires a little more thought. Here are some questions you should be asking yourself the moment you walk into the room:

Where are you sitting?

The offices of most decision makers can be divided into two areas: power desk or nonpower sofa. Where you're seated can determine the type of discussion that follows.

As a rule, conversations at the prospect's desk tend to be all business. The good news is that the prospect is often prepared to make a commitment. The bad news is that, if you're not careful, this face-to-face arrangement can turn "confrontational."

Discussions around the sofa tend to be more social, philosophical, or explanatory. Hosts subconsciously choose this arrangement when they (a) have no specific agenda or (b) are meeting someone at the suggestion of a mutual friend. While you probably won't close a deal at the coffee table, be prepared when the leisurely conversation takes some surprising and (in the long run) profitable turns.

Are you offered coffee or a drink?

A small point but surprisingly revealing. Offering coffee or a drink is a warm, social gesture, meant to relax and encourage guests.

Take such hospitality at face value: the prospect has a better-than-average predisposition to what you have to say. If nothing else, stay as long as it takes to finish your drink.

What's going on with the phones?

How your host handles the phone says a lot about him and what he thinks of you.

Your best prospects will tell their secretary to hold all calls during your meeting. This tells you they're (a) polite, (b) sensitive, and (c) sincerely interested in your proposal. They're the kind of people you want to deal with—the kind who've already told you they're willing to be sold.

Your next best prospect will take a call, but warn you about the potential interruption ahead of time. These people are thoughtful and obviously well organized.

The worst prospects will take any call. Listen carefully and you'll quickly know if they're trying to impress you or get rid of you.

What's on the wall?

Photos and works of art on an executive's wall won't tell you much. But the executive will. The trick is to get him talking by commenting on something he hasn't heard before or doesn't expect.

One of our sales executives had occasion to call on a

notoriously difficult record-industry executive. The man's office was vast and intimidating, with one wall literally a photo gallery of every rock star and musician he'd ever met.

Our salesman had no idea who the musicians were, but he noticed that the executive was much heavier in the photos. On the theory that everybody worries about their weight, our salesman boldly brought it up. "Before we discuss anything else," he said, "I have to know how you lost forty pounds."

Within minutes, the two of them were soul mates, sharing diets and exercise routines.

So, the Client Wants to Cut Your Commission?

There's nothing more maddening and frightening to a sales or service organization than when the client wants to cut your commission or, worse, cuts you out altogether because he thinks he can do the job better himself. Variations on this theme happen hundreds of times every day.

It happens to real-estate brokers who take a 6 percent fee when they sell a $200,000 home but have to claw and scratch to earn a 2 percent commission on a million-dollar property. Someone always thinks brokers earn too much for too little.

It happens to salespeople in the field who develop a barren territory into a goldmine, only to see their commission structure cut in half or their territory divided. Someone at headquarters always forgets the lean years—and the hard work—before it all paid off.

It happens to advertising agencies that create a successful campaign and add staff to service the account and nurture its growth, only to watch helplessly as the client slashes their commission from 15 percent of billings to, say, 11 percent. Someone always thinks your profit margins are coming at their expense.

These situations are a good argument for maintaining trust in business—because the start of any lasting relationship is trust, not suspicion. Unfortunately, there will always be people with short memories who can't help putting you between a rock and a hard place, no matter how much you deserve their trust.

What can you do when a client or customer or boss wants to cut your commission? Not much, even if you follow these three points:

1. Get assurances in writing

Ideally, when you sign on to do a job for someone, you should be asking them, "Once I've built this for you, will you take it away?" If they give you verbal assurances, ask them to put it in writing.

Unfortunately, this is the one contract point you frequently can't get. And even if you can, you're vulnerable at renewal time.

For example, consider this scenario. We approach a major American sporting event about selling its TV broadcast rights in a previously untapped market such as the United Kingdom. Since they have nothing to lose, the event's directors gladly give us our 35 percent commission. They even give us a three-year contract.

In year one, after working very hard to establish the event, we extract $100,000 for UK rights from the BBC. In year two, they pay $150,000. In year three, as the event catches on, the rights shoot up to $300,000.

You'd think everyone would be happy. But as year four approaches and our contract expires, the event directors begin to change. They stop enjoying all the benefits they're getting from the deal—and start worrying about the benefits we're getting.

In their eyes, the potential revenues in year four are a

windfall we had nothing to do with. Not only is the money higher than they ever imagined, but we don't have to work as hard to earn it! That's when they try to cut us down to 20 or 15 percent.

And that's when we have to decide if we can live with that—or walk.

Unfortunately, once the client starts slashing, it's a little like Vietnam. You cannot win the war of attrition. You can only delay the inevitable. And hold on to your dwindling share.

2. Keep them posted—often

It's ironic that you're more likely to face this problem when you do great rather than mediocre work. Great work produces greater-than-expected results—for the client and for you.

Fewer clients will resent your "healthy" commissions if you continually remind them of the efforts you're making, and subliminally indicate that you're eager for more, not less, work.

3. Call their bluff

If you have the leverage, call the client's bluff.

This worked successfully years ago for an American businessman I know who started out as the exclusive distributor for an auto parts manufacturer in three midwestern states: Illinois, North Dakota, and South Dakota. Within a few years he was registering phenomenal sales in heavily-populated Illinois and had built a customer network in North and South Dakota that, considering their sparse population, was encouraging.

The parent company was impressed. So impressed, in fact, that they called him in, congratulated him, and told him they were taking Illinois off his hands. It was a big territory, they said, and they could serve it better with their own people. This redistribution plan, he calculated, would cost him 70 percent of his sales and nearly all of his profits. So he called their bluff. "If you like Illinois so much, you can have the Dakotas too," he told them.

Within a week the company changed its mind.

Obviously, this cut-your-nose-to-spite-your-face tactic is less risky if you have assignments or relationships in other parts of the client's business.

The Best Closing Technique Might Be No Technique at All

Get a group of salespeople together in one room and inevitably they'll talk about deals they've done and how they closed them. Closing is the salesman's Holy Grail—the treasure at the end of the long arduous process of identifying prospects and transforming them into customers.

To many salespeople closing is a matter of technique. All you have to do is match the right method with the right buyer. For example, there is:

• The *deadline closing,* where you imply that the customer's great opportunity may vanish in the near future: "We'll have to get started soon."

• The *conditional closing,* where you ask, "If we can deliver by this time and that price, will you commit?" thereby forcing the customer to virtually sell himself.

• The *"Congratulations!" closing,* where you praise and flatter the customer for having the insight to buy from you. (I don't recommend this, but it works with certain indecisive or insecure personalities.)

• The *ambush closing,* where you surprise the buyer with an altered concept or inject a new personality into the sales equation at the last minute. For example, an auto salesman may spend hours selling a customer on the virtues of a car but it's often the sales manager (a totally new face) who comes in to mop up with the patented feel-good pitch about warranties and guaranteeing the customer's happiness.

• The *foot-in-the-door closing,* where you submit to the customer's terms just to get the relationship started.

And so on. There are dozens of closing techniques, equally indirect and, under the right circumstances, equally effective.

But nothing beats the direct approach where you confidently ask for the order.

My most successful sales have usually happened when, at the appropriate moment, I appeal directly to the customer's intelligence and logic.

"You're here. I'm here. And here's our proposal," I say. "Can you make a commitment now? If not now, when?"

It takes courage to force the customer to make a decision that can go against you. But there's no better way to find out whether he intends to spend money or just waste your time.

"Okay, that's one"

Actually, the greatest closing technique might be no technique at all—where the sales pitch seamlessly leads into the purchase and the buyer doesn't know the difference.

This was suggested to me a few years ago by a savvy sales executive in a funny green suit.

"The greatest salesman I ever met," he told me, "was the man who sold me this suit.

"The minute I walked into his store, he put five suits on the table. I didn't like any of them, and he starts arguing with me. He tells me to take off my jacket and try one on. He's smiling and joking as he says this, so I don't resist.

And, in fact, in the store with all the mirrors and wood paneling, I have to admit the suit looks good.

"That's all he needs to hear. He sets the suit aside and says, 'Okay, that's one.' That was his closing technique: *Okay, that's one.* It had a ring of finality that was very persuasive.

"Then he'd move on to the second suit. If I liked it, he'd say, 'Okay, that's another.' To this salesman, liking an item was the same as buying it. He refused to acknowledge that there was a difference.

"Within a half hour he knew what I thought about each suit. Then he'd start on shirts and ties. At the end, we had this complete *menu* of clothes to choose from. And this salesman knew that I couldn't leave his store without buying at least one item. I was so impressed I bought them all."

Find the Person Who Buys the Balloons

Several years ago the consulting division of our company was conducting a sports marketing "audit" for Coca-Cola. Our assignment was to pull together all the activities that Coca-Cola's vast array of companies, bottlers, and divisions were doing in sports to analyze if they were cost-efficient.

The president of Coca-Cola told me that he had a gnawing fear that the company's promotions were out of control or at least not synergistic.

"As a matter of fact," he said, "our system is amazing. Once a decision gets approved and into the system, it's very hard to get it out. Because nobody knows who made the decision in the first place, nobody short of me or the chairman knows how to undo it."

He then told me about "the balloons." Somebody at some point sold the company on the concept of huge balloons emblazoned with the Coca-Cola logo. The balloons would travel all over the world, like the Goodyear blimp, and hover over sporting events or any place where there were crowds.

"You know," he continued only half in jest, "I'm always seeing the balloons. And I have no idea who bought them. Or why they bought them. Or how we can unbuy them. Or even who to talk to about them. And I run this company!"

Fascinated as I was with this description of Coke's purchasing apparatus at the time, I found it instructive for an entirely different (and slightly selfish) reason.

I wanted to meet the person who bought the balloons! Here, I told myself, is someone who knows how to get things done. Here is someone who can push things through the bureaucracy. Here is someone I could sell to.

I periodically retell this story to our company's executives. You cannot overestimate how important it is to find the person who buys the balloons. Every company has one. He or she might not have a fancy title or prestige office. But he or she can do more for you in the long run than you can imagine in your wildest dreams.

2 | Negotiating

"Match-Tough" Negotiating—And How to Get There

There's a tennis phrase, "match-tough," that refers to the competitive edge players get after they've played several opponents who've pushed them to the limit. It's the reason a talented player like John McEnroe can lose to an unknown after a six-month layoff even though he's in great shape and has been practicing daily.

The same thing happens in business.

I don't know how many times in a negotiation I've seen people back down at the crucial moment when they should be fighting. Instead of bracing themselves and harnessing all their energy and insights, they retreat. Perhaps they are saying to themselves that they'll be tougher, more commanding *the next time*. Unfortunately, the next time never comes.

Being a street-smart negotiator isn't something that happens to you one day because you wish it to, or have memorized a set of rules. You have to practice. And you have to show your stuff when it counts—under game conditions, so to speak.

Staying street smart, like staying in shape or at the top of any game, requires daily exercise—and constantly trying to do more. It also means reminding yourself of the fundamentals. When Bjorn Borg was the world's number-one tennis player, he still went through his daily four-hour routine of the basic strokes. His brain was match tough, but his muscles had to get the message as well.

To me, the "basic strokes" of negotiating are silence, patience, sensitivity, curiosity, and showing up.

1. Bite your tongue

I've been telling myself this for so long that you'd think it would be automatic. But it's not. There is nothing more excruciating—and more important—than a protracted silence in a tense negotiating session. I still have to remind myself not to be the one who breaks that silence, no matter how awkward it seems.

2. Wait a minute. Or longer

I never cease to marvel at how the simple passing of time can alter a situation. And so I wait—for people to cool off, for problems to solve themselves, for bad deals to self-destruct, or for a better idea to come along. Waiting is tough to do. A dynamic executive is trained to act decisively. Yet in many crises, doing nothing is the most constructive thing you can do. Whenever I don't believe this, I remember that the bulk of our successes have somehow involved the exercise of patience and the overwhelming majority of our failures the lack of it.

3. Be sensitive to the other guy's point of view

American executives have been dining out for years on stories about the late Charles Revson, the legendary founder of Revlon. Revson had a reputation for being shrewd to the point of ruthlessness. But he was remarkably sensitive to other people's point of view (if not their feelings).

Several years ago when advertising executive Edward McCabe of Scali, McCabe, Sloves, Inc. was trying to win the Revlon account, he went to meet Revson for the first time at Revlon headquarters. The cosmetic tycoon's office was ostentatious to the point of intimidation.

According to McCabe, it "looked as if it had been built for Mussolini and shipped to New York piece by piece." There were marble columns, oversized nautical maps on the walls, a 25-foot conference table surrounded by black leather chairs dotted with gold studs. At Revson's place at the head of the table sat a solid gold phone.

When Revson entered the room, recalls McCabe, "I expected him to belch lava." But Revson's first words to McCabe were, "Do you think this room is ugly?"

McCabe wasn't ready for this, but he managed to mumble something about having different tastes in interiors.

"I know you think it's ugly," Revson insisted. "That's okay. But I'm looking for someone who also understands that many people would think it's beautiful."

4. Look for insights in unexpected places

Over the years I've learned as much about people outside the office as inside. That's one reason it's nice to dine out or play golf or tennis with "adversaries" or potential clients. People are easier to read in these fringe periods when their guard is down.

This applies in the most mundane situations. A woman I know, a very successful real-estate agent who spends hours showing suburban homes to husbands and wives, says, "I can tell by the way a couple gets in a car what's going to happen. If the man automatically gets in the front seat and the wife has to fend for herself in the back, then I know that he has the final say."

Most of this is common sense, but you have to remember to keep your eyes open. The clues are everywhere.

5. Show up in person

Nothing is more flattering to the other guy or more revealing about your opinion of him. It's the difference between visiting a friend in the hospital and sending a get-well card.

I once appeared on a late-night radio show, which is broadcast from a large office complex just outside Washington, D.C. As I arrived at the station a few minutes before 11 P.M., I noticed a man waiting in the dark by the studio door. He introduced himself and handed me his résumé. He had flown up to Washington from Miami that day when he read that I would be appearing on the show. He thought that meeting me in person would improve his chances of joining our company.

I didn't have an opening for him at that moment, but he certainly is several points ahead of everyone else when I do.

When in Doubt, Delay

Business people are encouraged to react quickly and decisively to situations. But this need to appear decisive sometimes gets in the way of sound decision-making. Not every point in a negotiation needs to be resolved on the spot. Sticky side issues have a way of gumming up the works. Sometimes it's wiser to step back, risk appearing indecisive, and hope the matter will fade away due to lack of interest.

I've seen this frequently in contract talks. Negotiations get bogged down, especially by lawyers (who, in fairness, are only doing their job), on a point of principle or a detail that has no business significance at all—for example, what someone's title will be when the transaction is in place.

Assuming both parties want the transaction to go through, I try to push such details into the background and urge everyone to go on to something else. I might offer to put some general language into the agreement suggesting the point will be worked out to our mutual satisfaction at a later date. My goal is to keep the selling process moving smoothly, not to make heroic efforts hurdling irrelevant obstacles.

Many times I actually prefer to get a deal going, with money and services changing hands, *before* the final contract is signed. It is a matter of self-protection to me. While I'm waiting for every issue to be resolved, circumstances could sour the transaction, my timing advantage could evaporate, or the other party could get cold feet.

Significantly, I have found that setting the wheels of commerce in motion without a contract often gives me a negotiating edge.

I learned this years ago with MCA, which owns Universal Studios and is a leading producer of television programming. MCA agreed to produce twelve golf shows a year for network television featuring my clients Arnold Palmer and Gary Player. We were into the second year of the agreement before we ever signed the first year's contract.

Being trained as a lawyer, I hadn't realized that this was how the entertainment industry sometimes worked. Then I got to thinking about the business implications of this practice. Here we were going through a standard 80-page contract, trying to get it all resolved, but MCA had already agreed to our gut issues. Palmer and Player would receive their fee up front for each program as well as a percentage of foreign rights. The remainder of the contract didn't make that much difference.

It seemed to me that MCA had outsmarted themselves. We made the programs. MCA paid Arnold and Gary. Meanwhile, MCA had its investment tied up in editing and post-production. If something went wrong, they had much more to lose than my clients. Thus, by getting the deal done (though not signed), we held all the trump cards.

There is nothing shady about this tactic. In fact, in an environment of complete trust, it is the best kind of leverage—the kind you never have to use.

The One Thing That Must Happen in Every Negotiation

Years ago, I happened to be present at a "confrontation" between the chairman of a large company and one of America's wealthiest men (I'll call him the Tycoon).

The Tycoon barged into the Chairman's office, enraged about a deal that was unraveling, and threatening to sue. (I found out later that the Tycoon didn't have a legal leg to stand on, but I think he expected to intimidate the Chairman through his wealth, prestige, and loudness.) I'll never forget how impressively the Chairman handled the situation, particularly the blunt but mercilessly brief way he stood his ground.

You could divide this hour-long meeting into three parts— of unequal yet instructive length. In part one, the Chairman asked the Tycoon about his various investments and basically told him what a great fellow he was. This went on for thirty minutes. Part two, the Chairman firmly told the Tycoon he was wrong, that the company had no intention of giving in to his demands. This took about three minutes. Part three settled into mollifying small talk. "Let's keep in touch," said the Chairman, "and stay on top of this." This went on for half an hour.

The Tycoon's problem soon disappeared, but I left that scene with two clear lessons about negotiating. First, there comes a point in every meeting where you have to look in the other person's eyes and commit to something—anything. You can ask the other party for their order or tell them they're full of baloney (as the Chairman did) or simply confirm a time and place for your next discussion. It doesn't have to be a major announcement.

Second, it doesn't require a lot of time. In most situations you can make your point in a few minutes. As the Chairman apparently sensed, if you're giving someone bad news—and hope to remain friendly—there's no advantage in prolonging that part of the discussion.

The seriousness of a topic is not related to how much or how little time you spend discussing it. I've seen executives commit to huge deals with a simple "Yes" in a matter of seconds. And I've seen executives waste twenty minutes playing tennis with their pocket diaries trying to schedule a phone call ("No, not Tuesday. I'm in London. How about Thursday?" "Can't. I'm in Singapore . . .").

Fail to commit to something in every meeting or negotiation and you have doomed yourself to an endless cycle of frustration. Unless you have a valid strategic reason for procrastinating, you are wasting your time and theirs.

When Money Is the Least Important Part of a Transaction

Everybody has a price. But many negotiators go wrong when they attach dollar signs to that price. They believe if they can just agree on how much cash should be passed across the table, then all parties will be happy. This logic (if we can call it that) ignores the noneconomic elements of a deal, the psychological needs that buyer and seller bring to the table.

In negotiations, I try to weigh the following four noneconomic elements carefully:

1. Quality

If unrivaled quality is your biggest asset, make that work to your advantage. People will frequently sacrifice money to have some of your prestige rub off on them. Such is the case with our client Chris Evert in her association with Rolex. Chris's popularity and championship career in tennis could perhaps guarantee her contracts with other watch companies for considerably more money than she makes with Rolex. But she wants to be associated with Rolex because it reflects supreme quality. In effect, Rolex has succeeded in paying less because its watches cost more.

2. The long-term view

The legitimate promise of great rewards in the future can outweigh big sums of cash in the present. Frequently, a company just entering a field is prepared to pay a lot less than an established company for the promotional services of one of our clients. But this new company might have an exciting idea that will make them stronger in the long run. They may offer to pay us $1 when they know the competition is willing to pay $20. If they're really smart, they'll add, "If our program works out the way we think it will, you'll make $50." If we believe them, they have a deal. It's a question of looking low today and high tomorrow.

Very often, a client of ours will have a choice between two offers. And we have to ask ourselves: where will we be five years from now with either of these approaches? We once had an opportunity to sign a huge clothing license for Wimbledon with a major US retail chain. A lot of money was involved. But we thought the longevity of that approach was not as good as going with a company that would build the brand and continue to grow with it over the years. So we turned down the money and went for tomorrow.

3. Tradition

The people you are dealing with often have an established, time-honored way of doing things. They are very loath to fly in the face of tradition. You have to be aware of that influence. Trying to change their habits may be impossible, or more than you can afford.

When we negotiated with the International Olympic Committee (IOC) for the US television rights to the 1988 Summer Olympics in Seoul, Korea, representatives from our company came up with a very sophisticated package to syndicate the Games over a network of independent TV stations. This package would probably have netted the IOC more than what was on offer from any of the three major TV networks. But the IOC (perhaps rightly) felt it was in the best interest of the Olympic Games to be on network TV. The tradition of being showcased on a network was more important than the money.

4. Privacy

Keeping a deal confidential until it is closed can save you money and heartaches. The best deals are made privately, one on one, and they're announced after they've happened. The worst thing you can do is negotiate in the newspapers or trade press.

The moment you leak your position to the press, then they're obliged to find out the other party's position. Suddenly, thousands of people in your community or industry are aware of both positions. You are no longer negotiating. You are trying to save face. Ultimately, one of you will look bad. And neither of you will be happy. You add all sorts of unnecessary ingredients by negotiating in public, whether it involves the Olympic Games or a labor-management agreement or an individual employment contract.

Your reputation for confidentiality can add to your value

as a negotiating partner. Likewise, your reputation for loose lips can steer many potential partners to your competition.

Three Reasons to Walk Away from a Sale (and One Reason to Stay)

Walking away from a transaction that "doesn't feel right" is an undervalued achievement in business. Companies don't encourage it; employees don't pursue it. After all, there are no commissions for avoiding a bad deal.

Nevertheless, it is a discipline that, with 20/20 hindsight, I have learned to appreciate. I don't know how many times in the past 25 years I wish we had had the wisdom to walk away from a deal.

From the buyer's perspective, this is obvious. If the price is too high, you walk away.

But if you're on the selling end, feeling the pressure of sales quotas and demanding bosses, the issues are not as well defined.

Here are three sales situations where I hope my salespeople would walk away—and one where I think they should keep selling.

1. When you can't deliver

There's nothing worse in the beginning of a relationship than to lead the buyer on, to promise something that you know you can't deliver.

Promising the world is one way to make a sale. But it's no way to start a relationship.

At any point in a business relationship, but especially in the beginning, you're always better off understating your ability to deliver and overdelivering on what you stated. If you can't do that, walk away.

2. When price and one other ingredient don't add up

Price alone doesn't usually kill a sale. It's price and one other ingredient.

For example, I've often found that if the price isn't right, I might still want to make a sale to establish a long-term relationship. But if the price isn't right *and* there's no chance of a long-term relationship, I'll walk away (or at least not make a price concession).

I remember years ago when the then-head of our West Coast television division got a multinational company mildly interested in a series of TV programs. The multinational said, "Let's make a pilot program."

Our executive was gung ho on the project. "Let's do this," he said. "In fact, let's lose money on the pilot and make it so good that they will want to do a continuing series."

That was a judgment call for him to make. Knowing the people involved at the multinational company, I didn't happen to agree with him. I thought we should make a profit on the pilot because that would be the last time we'd hear from them.

Although I've been wrong often in these situations, I was right that time. We went over budget on the pilot to impress them with our production qualities. But that's the only program they bought.

So we lost money *and* did not have a long-term relationship. We should have walked away.

3. When they demand you abandon your principles

Believe it or not, people will respect your principles. They will admire you for adhering to them rather than trying to slide around them to make a sale. Quite often, they'll see the light, follow you out the door, and agree to do things your way.

It's easy to pay lip service to this high-minded thinking. It's a lot more difficult to practice it, especially when there's a lot of money on the table, or you're under the gun to produce, or you're not being asked to do anything unethical or illegal.

Compromising your principles to make a sale is short-sighted. It's quick money. But bending the rules at the beginning of a relationship will affect everything else you do in the years to come.

4. When you've spent a lot of time and money

There's something to be said for pulling out of a sales situation after you've spent many months and many dollars trying to nail it down. With such a huge emotional invest-ment at stake, many people start making tremendous con-cessions in order not to come away empty-handed. They'll agree to any deal just to get it done.

I admire salespeople who can cut their losses and walk away at these crucial moments, who realize that they're emotionally vulnerable and they might not respect them-selves in the morning.

But many people take it too far. They think that walking away once means walking away forever.

As I've said, I'm a great believer in knocking on old doors—because a customer who bought from you once will probably buy from you again. That logic applies just as well to prospects who *almost bought*. Having invested months in courting a customer, regardless of the outcome, you have left certain seeds in their mind—so that going back to them in a few months is infinitely better than making a cold call on someone new.

In the real world, however, this is what usually happens: (a) the sale self-destructs; (b) the salesperson walks away confused, angry, and frustrated; (c) the salesperson writes that customer off.

Our company files are filled with instances of a sales executive withdrawing, for various reasons, from a transaction with the conclusion that "XYZ Corp. is not interested in sports." That information ultimately gets transmitted throughout our organization as, "Don't waste your time with XYZ Corp."

And then a year later we read that XYZ Corp. is doing a half-dozen projects in sports.

I continually remind our people: Go back in a few months, even if it didn't work out the first time. Usually, someone there will remember how hard you've worked. That someone will try to help you.

The Beauty of Barter

I am convinced that most companies don't maximize their barter possibilities. Instead of aggressively reducing costs by trading their services with those of their suppliers, they seem content to pay top dollar for everything.

The reasons for this are understandable, but inexcusable. One reason is companies forget to spend the psychological currency they've accumulated with their suppliers—for being loyal customers, large-volume buyers, or simply the kind of customer with whom people want to be associated. Also, they underestimate the demand for their particular product or service, particularly in situations that fall outside the normal buy-sell relationship. Most discouraging, I think, is when the company's top executives consider such "horse-trading" unworthy of their time and energy.

Any business organization, whether it deals in hard goods or intangibles, can increase its barter activities.

Consider a law firm with a terrific restaurant near its offices. The firm has nothing to barter—no widgets, no tickets to ballgames, no trips to Hawaii—nothing, that is, except its legal expertise.

If the firm's managing partner is as smart on the street as he is in the courtroom, he might say to the restaurant owner, "Look, we'll do all your legal work and your taxes for $5,000 worth of meals." The transaction is irresistible: both sides get to buy at wholesale.

The restaurateur should be pleased. He's getting $5,000 worth of expert legal work for $5,000 worth of steaks and drinks that probably cost him $1,500. Plus, he's guaranteed a steady stream of lawyers who, in turn, bring new customers to the restaurant. From a financial and promotional perspective, it's a nice arrangement. The lawyers, meanwhile, gain the same benefits. Their $5,000 worth of legal advice actually costs them $1,000 in time, plus they have acquired the good will of a fine restaurant where they are treated like royalty.

Executives in our organization are not timid or embarrassed about barter. Sometimes we have special arrangements with hotels in cities where we do a volume of business. In exchange for rooms at special corporate rates, we might give a hotel media benefits at one of our events, such as advertising pages in the tournament program or banners on the tennis court or golf course. We make similar proposals to airlines, restaurants, limousine services, and rental car companies.

In business you never get something for nothing, but barter arrangements come close enough.

If You Can't Make a Sale, Make a Buy— and Vice Versa

Sometimes the factors separating two parties in a negotiation are so infinitesimal that it doesn't matter which party does the buying and which the selling. In those situations it is essential to be very adaptable. A complete flip-flop from seller to buyer can be disarming and profitable.

This happens frequently in the licensing business, where rights and privileges rather than hard merchandise are up for sale. When we began representing Wimbledon, we approached Colgate-Palmolive (which owned Bancroft tennis rackets and also owned but was not using the license to the Wimbledon name) with the idea of manufacturing a Wimbledon tennis racket.

Bancroft didn't see much promise in our concept, but we were convinced it was a winner. So somewhere in the stalled negotiation, we switched tack 180 degrees: instead of selling them our idea, we bought the rights back from them and found someone else to make the rackets.

This "if you can't sell 'em, buy 'em" approach must be applied with great care. It doesn't work in many business situations—but it is particularly appropriate in the acquisition of talent. Sometimes the best executives you can hire are the people who come into your office selling or buying something. If I'm impressed with their concept or approach, I won't hesitate to turn the tables and sell them on *my* idea, even if it means their joining our organization.

I learned this in the late 1960s when I was approached by Jay Michaels, a vice president of MCA, the movie and television production company, about starting a leisure sports division for them. I declined the invitation, preferring to retain my independence, but I was very impressed with Michaels and his ideas about sports and television. Shortly thereafter, when we were ready to venture into television production, our first choice to run the new division was Jay Michaels. He accepted and succeeded beyond our expectations.

A useful variation on the buy-sell switch involves buying someone's product, then selling them your own. A few years ago the wife of an executive I know rejoined the workforce as an advertising salesperson for a local newspaper. Her first sales call was a pet shop from which she walked out a half hour later with a newly purchased $30 aquarium and $15 worth of fish (the owner was a very good salesman). The next day she went back to the pet shop and persuaded the owner to buy $600 worth of advertising. She's now the publisher of her own newspaper.

How to Get More Information Than You Give

Because so many of our sales efforts are aimed at large corporations, where the decision-making wheels grind slowly, we rarely expect to close a sale after one meeting. (When we do make a quick sale, it's usually because we've done business with the company before, or our concept is "hot," or we got lucky.)

As a rule, we need at least three meetings to close a deal: the first to pick up timing cues and information about the company's goals, its spending habits, and who makes the decisions; the second to present our proposal using that information; the third to restate our proposal to the right person.

Over the years, we've found that nothing is more important than the education process of that first meeting. Without it, you usually don't get a second meeting. So before we try to sell them, we let them tell us how to go about it.

Unfortunately, potential customers don't hand out fact sheets on how they can be sold. But they scatter valuable clues throughout their conversation. You should always be trying to get more information than you give.

1. People love to talk about themselves. Let them

Half the battle in getting rather than giving information is consciously deciding to do the first and not the latter. I've known executives who, before sales calls, literally budget two minutes of a meeting to talk about their company and twenty minutes for customers to talk about theirs. Lopsided as this ratio may seem, very few customers are offended by it.

Most people can't wait to tell you how successful they are. So don't make them wait. As they are boasting about their unit sales, marketing budgets, and profit projections, you should be recalculating your terms—upward.

2. Get them used to answering questions

I have never seen a sales effort fail because the seller asked too many questions. And I have never seen one succeed when the seller did nothing but answer questions.

To get information you must lull the prospect into your question-and-answer rhythm—without sounding like a prosecutor.

Look around the office. Comment on the furnishings, the view, a trinket on the desk. Preface each question with a compliment. It can be innocuous ("That's a beautiful picture. Are those your kids?") or pointed ("Your XYZ tennis racket has really helped my serve. How many people have bought the model?") But it should be genuine flattery, not false. Obligingly framed, the toughest questions tend to get the most obliging responses.

3. Take advantage of their discomfort

No matter how well you prepare for a sales presentation, there's no guarantee that the prospect has prepared for you.

At some point in a career you will walk into a prospect's offices and face a roomful of people who (a) have no idea who you are, (b) have "only a few minutes," (c) simply don't care, or (d) have no authority even if they do care.

Such slights should not go unmentioned or undisciplined. Tell people you're disappointed and, in most cases, the person with authority will be the one who apologizes to you. That's valuable information.

One of our executives recently flew several thousand miles for a sales presentation. From the start, nothing went right. Several attendees claimed they had other appointments in twenty minutes. The conference room video machine couldn't show our videotape. Worse still, it wasn't clear who was in charge.

Our executive quickly surveyed the scene and got up to leave. "This isn't right," he said. "I've traveled four hours to see you. I won't waste my time—and yours—rushing through this."

"You're not wasting your time," said a young woman who identified herself as the associate director of marketing. "I make the decisions here."

That was precious information. Armed with this knowledge, he suggested a smaller meeting that quickly resulted in a sale.

4. Look for the hidden commitment

Some customers really want to buy but have a lousy way of telling you. They browbeat you with numbers or argue with you to show how smart they are. Fortunately, the strongest adversaries often have the strongest interest.

Another of our executives offered the sponorship of a major sports event to the marketing vice president of a multi-billion-dollar company. After we presented the cost figures for the program, the marketing vice-president, who had clearly done his homework, countered with his own set of much lower figures.

He told us: "We're willing to work with you on these terms—and only these terms!"

An inexperienced executive—with a fixed dollar amount in his head—might not have heard the vice-president say, "We're willing to work with you . . ." An experienced one would seize upon it.

We soon obtained a commitment from them on their terms. But as the program succeeds and their involvement grows, they will eventually come very close to our terms.

Handling Questions You Can't or Don't Want to Answer

I once knew an executive who would break out in a nervous laugh whenever you asked him a tough question he was reluctant to answer. It got to the point where his laugh tipped me off that things weren't going well. I would innocuously ask, "How's business?" and he would giggle. No matter what he subsequently said, I already knew the answer.

When I pointed out that this nervous habit made him an open book, he told me, "The thing that gets me is that I'm aware I do this and yet I can't stop."

Obviously, the solution for this fellow was to stop laughing. But that's like telling someone to stop blushing when they're embarrassed. It's easier said than done.

What's really sad about his situation is that there are at least four ways to handle any question you don't really want to—or simply can't—answer.

1. Deflect it

Preferably with humor. I once spoke at the Wharton School of Finance in Philadelphia where the students bombarded me with probing, fairly personal questions. One student wanted to know what I would do if I had only twenty-four hours to live.

Now, even if I knew the answer to that "desert island" question, an overheated hall filled with several hundred young people is probably not the proper setting to expound on my most private thoughts.

Choosing my words carefully, I said, "Of course, that would depend on where I was." They laughed. I continued, "And I won't say who I was with." They laughed again, which was my cue to change the subject. "Seriously, though . . ." I said, and then proceeded to avoid the question completely.

2. Praise it

There's a show-off element in many questions that can work to your advantage—if you recognize that your questioner (a) already knows the answer or (b) is only trying to score points at your expense.

When people pose a question clearly designed to demonstrate their cleverness—and nothing more—praise them for it. Tell them "That's an excellent question" or "You raise a very important point." They'll be so busy congratulating themselves they'll never notice that you've moved on to another subject.

3. Rephrase it

This is the classic politician's dodge: field a hard question and duck it by saying, "What I think you're really asking me is . . ."

There is nothing wrong with rephrasing a question to fit your agenda. If you can finesse your way out of a tight spot, most people will respect (and secretly admire) you for it.

4. Bounce it back

An executive I know has a maddening habit of responding to tough questions by bouncing them back to the questioner.

I've heard salespeople ask him, "What's your budget on this project?" and he simply responds, "You tell me."

Initially, I thought he was being shifty and too clever for his own good. But it's amazing how many people fall into his trap.

Sometimes bouncing the question back to the other guy is a clever gambit. For one thing, it gives this particular executive more time to consider his position while forcing the other person to reveal a little bit of his. Second, it's a fairly friendly gesture, suggesting that he will deal fairly with you if you're fair first. In a quid pro quo relationship, this executive literally gives as good as he gets.

I'm not suggesting that these evasive tactics are standard operating procedure with me or with most executives I know. Evasion should be used sparingly and only in the most sensitive circumstances. Actually, absolute candor is generally the best tactic. When people ask me tough, intrusive questions, I try to disarm them with a frank, unequivocal answer. It's usually the last thing they expect to hear.

How to Avoid the Violent Objection

There are many reasons why negotiations break down. Egos get in the way. Emotions flare up. Phrases like "deal breaker" and "that's non-negotiable" get tossed around cavalierly. But in one form or another, stalled negotiations usually boil down to the issue of price.

As the seller, you have a closing dollar figure in mind. And the buyer only has so much money to spend. How the two of you come to a mutually satisfying agreement is what negotiating is all about.

That's why it's important to explore all the peripheral issues—e.g., timing, delivery, exclusivity, financing—before you name your price.

If you want a sure-fire way to draw a violent objection

from potential customers, try naming an outrageous price that they do not expect.

An executive I know has an interesting theory about how to handle the other side's violent objections at such moments. He ignores them and moves on to something else— on the theory that the objection was so quick, so resolute, that at that instant there is no way you can change their mind or argue your case successfully.

I wish I could agree with that theory, but in practice I've found that once people dig in their heels on a position, no amount of spade work will get them out. You're not really negotiating anymore; you're finding a way for them to save face.

The best way to handle violent objections is to avoid them altogether. I never mention a dollar figure until I know the other party is cushioned to hear it. I like to smooth my pathway into the price discussion rather than charge in like a bull in a china shop.

If I'm selling the sponsorship of a golf tournament to an automobile company, I might educate them about what a competitor is doing in the same sport. I'll say, "There are a lot of things you can do depending on how much impact you want to have and how much money you have to spend. Buick, for example, sponsors the Buick Open for x million dollars."

Then I pause.

If they object, "No way we would spend that much," at least I've elicited that fact without being confrontational or painting them into a corner. I haven't named my price but I've learned a good deal about theirs. And I have retained the option of adjusting what we have to sell accordingly.

This is a basic principle of selling. Most salespeople— whether they're selling home appliances or homes—have enough sense to first ask, "What can you afford?"

But in corporate sales—where salespeople look at big companies and only see deep pockets—this is the kind of common sense that is frequently forgotten.

Little Choices That Can Mean Much More

You always learn something about someone when they're forced to choose between option A or option B. Offer a child chocolate or vanilla ice cream and, if nothing else, you learn the child's flavor preference. This is dime-store psychology and worth about that much when it comes to children and ice cream. But in business, when the stakes are higher, it can be worth much more.

Devising A or B options for the other guy gives you a negotiating advantage. But sometimes A or B options pop up without any effort on your part—and without the other guy knowing he's made a choice!

I recently met with a top executive in London to discuss a wide variety of projects he was considering doing with us. We were in a hotel suite and one of his junior executives was present. As the senior executive was talking about a particular project, the phone rang. He answered it himself, made a few comments, and hung up. Then we moved on to another project, and the phone rang again. Only this time, the junior executive went across the room to answer the phone. A revealing choice has just been made and I don't think either of them realized it.

The insight I drew from this was that the conversation that was interrupted by the second call was far more important to their company than the first one—because the junior executive didn't want his boss to be distracted from this particular discussion but wasn't concerned the first time. Later on when we had moved on to other subjects and the senior executive answered a third phone call himself, that confirmed my impression.

Developing a Killer Instinct—Without the Blood, Sweat, or Tears

I frequently hear someone described as having a "killer instinct." But I'm never sure what that really means.

Some people compare a business person's killer instinct to that of a "great finisher"—say, a champion boxer or tennis player who can consistently put away an opponent. But that doesn't always apply in business, where it's usually more valuable to keep people *in the game* rather than dispose of them in an early round.

Some people think "killer instinct" means going for the jugular—finding the other guy's weak spots and exploiting them. That's useful in business, too, but not if the other guy is dealing from strength. I have much more confidence in an employee who hammers away at the other guy's strong points than I do in one who simply settles for the easy shots.

It seems to me that true killer instinct has a lot more to do with instinct than it does with being a "killer." I think the following are good instincts in business negotiations:

1. Time heals most wounds

In my early years, I tended to lose my cool when events didn't go my way. If a potential client signed with another firm, I sometimes would attack that person verbally for making a decision that had adversely affected me. Even though we lost the deal, I thought I could charge in and undo a *fait accompli*.

I didn't see that my frontal strategy only damaged my standing with the people I was trying to get—and that I should have held back, telling myself, "This is absurd. Wait a year or two. They'll come back." As I get older I appreciate that time rectifies most mistakes; it's the best weapon you have.

2. Sometimes it ain't the money

As the saying goes, "When people say it isn't the money, it's the principle, you can be sure it's the money." But a good negotiator will sacrifice money for certain nonmonetary benefits without giving it a second thought.

For example, we will often find that the organizing body of a major sporting event will concede some financial points in choosing which television networks around the world will best showcase their event. The good organizers are disciplined enough to know that broad exposure (ensuring the event's long-term growth) is usually more valuable than a little extra cash.

3. So what if it's not invented here!

We once had a fellow who was tenacious with his pet projects but woeful with those initiated by others. This is classic Not-Invented-Here Syndrome. He could kill outside projects with his enthusiasm—because he could never be counted on to follow through and his peers would always get the blame.

The executives I admire most love to sink their teeth into a project—whether it's their idea or someone else's. The killer part of them says "Don't let go." And instinct tells them it doesn't matter who gets the credit.

4. No guts, no glory

Most people are smart enough to know when they have leverage in a negotiation. But not all have the guts to use it.

I sat in on a Hollywood meeting a few years ago between a movie studio boss and three Europeans interested in buying foreign rights to several films. The studio boss quoted an astronomical price. The Europeans countered with an insulting offer. The studio boss said, "Gentlemen, we have nothing further to discuss," and very nicely threw them out of his office.

The meeting had lasted two minutes and eighteen seconds. But my friend said, "They'll be back when they get over the shock. They've flown too far to go home empty-handed." And the next day he was right.

5. "There must be some mistake, Mr. Morgan"

I can't think of a clearer distinction between killer and instinct than the following story involving a Morgan and a Rockefeller.

J. P. Morgan once wanted to buy a large iron-ore tract in Minnesota from John D. Rockefeller. Rockefeller sent his son, John D., Jr., to sound Morgan out.

"Well, what's your price?" Morgan asked.

"I think there must be some mistake, Mr. Morgan," said John D., Jr., "I did not come here to sell. I understood you wished to buy."

Morgan may have been a legendary "killer," but Rockefeller, Jr., had the right instinct.

How to Deal with Their Superiority Complex

In the course of a business life you will run across your share of pomposity and one-upmanship. As a general rule, you have three responses to blowhards and egomaniacs. One, you can avoid them (in which case you have probably cut yourself off from two-thirds of the business population). Two, you can compete with them, matching each of their boasts and exaggerations with one of your own. People get lured into this trap more often than they realize. And three, you can turn the tables on them, draw them out by stroking and flattering them (which beneath all their posturing is usually all they want).

I once had dinner with two of the most major superiority complexes on the face of the planet. These two very wealthy men spent the entire evening trying to impress each other.

When one mentioned his 28-room house in the south of France, the other brought up his 29-room villa in the Caribbean. When one of them described the improvements on his G-III Gulfstream jet, the other extolled the speed of his G-IV. If one donated $30 million to a hospital in South America, the other had given $35 million to a medical center in Tel Aviv.

This dialogue continued through five courses, until the perfect ending. After the brandy, megamillionaire No. 1 inquired, "Do you smoke cigars?"

"Yes," replied megamillionaire No. 2.

"Well, you must try one of mine. I just got it from President Marcos last week."

And with that—so help me!—megamillionaire No. 2 proudly reached into his vest pocket and said, "Have one of mine. I just got it from Castro."

Now each of those men probably thought the other guy was a jackass for trying to one-up him. But I can't help thinking that if one of them had adopted the mantle of humility and allowed himself to be impressed with the other guy's yachts and planes and hospital wings bearing his name, something positive and lasting might have resulted.

When you face one of those many people who've attained something in life (or think they have) and want to trumpet it, I think you're far better off encouraging them, playing accompaniment to their trumpet rather than trying to drown them out with your drums.

You Can't Say Yes Until You've Learned to Say No

People who know me well will tell you that I make decisions quickly, but that I sometimes take years to make up my mind. If that sounds like I'm talking out of both sides of my mouth, you're right.

When it comes to decision making, I do everything in my power to say no before I say yes. I attach too much importance to a "yes" commitment to be rushed or finessed out of my right to make an informed decision. But once I agree to something, I don't look back or second-guess myself.

Unfortunately, this hasn't made my decision making foolproof. Like everyone else, I'm still prey to the business fallacies and fuzzy arguments that can make a bad choice look like a good one. Here are five situations that often lead to flawed decisions:

1. Are you hearing what they're saying?

When I meet people, I never assume that they know who I am. If I have the slightest sense that they've forgotten my name, I extend my hand and say, "Hi. I'm Mark McCormack." I don't wait for them to ask. This gesture eliminates far more awkwardness and embarrassment than it creates.

The same thing happens in a business dialogue. People, perhaps out of timidity or a misplaced sense of politeness, allow themselves to be trapped in discussions where they have no clear idea what the other party is really saying. Worse, they go on to make decisions without ever taking time out to ask themselves, "Are we talking about the same thing?"

2. Are you being swayed by groupthink?

Group decisions are rarely good decisions. Something happens to people's skepticism when they're gathered in a room with the stated goal of achieving consensus.

They become too agreeable. They're intimidated by the boss and take positions they think the boss wants to hear. They're reluctant to challenge their allies. After a while, with everyone echoing the same opinion, a group euphoria that psychologists call "groupthink" takes over. This surreal euphoria often leads people to conclusions that fly in the face of reality.

This is why President Kennedy and his best and brightest advisers could believe that 1,400 Cuban exiles could invade the Bay of Pigs under impossible conditions and defeat Castro's army of 200,000. Or why a family decides to drive 300 miles to visit grandma; it's not because they like the seven-hour ride or need to see grandma but because each person thinks everyone else wants to go.

It's also why I listen to all points of view, but make my decisions alone—after everyone is gone.

3. How are the choices framed?

Forced to choose between a deal that has an 80 percent chance of success and an equivalent deal that has a 20 percent risk of failure, which would you choose? Most people choose the first, *even though the options are identical,* because they respond more favorably to choices that are favorably framed—that is, in terms of success rather than failure.

A good salesman will know how to frame his pitch in the most positive light. But a good decision maker will recognize what the salesman is doing—and explore his options from other perspectives as well.

4. Have you looked beyond the nearest available data?

In the same way that you should get to know the people two levels below you (because you'll get insights that your peers are missing), you should try to look two levels below the information on which you're basing decisions. When it comes to numbers, too many executives take the path of least resistance. They allow themselves to be swayed by the data at hand (especially if it fits their preconceptions) rather than insist on harder-to-get but more reliable information.

On the most rudimentary level, let's say I own a car dealership and ask my sales manager how we're doing. He'll say, "Great. We sold fifty cars this week." Now, that's up-to-the-minute data, but virtually useless. My sales manager is not telling me how many cars we sold in a comparable period the previous month or year, or how many of those fifty cars were big models (where the profit margins are bigger), or even how many cars were financed and at what interest rate. This is information I'd insist on before deciding to fire the manager or give him a raise.

5. Are you overrating your successes?

People can't resist associating a current problem with a previous success, especially if it lets them choose a course of action that's worked before. Keep this up, however, and you may start overrating your successes. You fall in love with your press clippings. You start measuring all situations by their similarities with your glorious past rather than looking for the new opportunities in their differences.

Sometimes your own people force you into this trap. One of our executives came to me with a client problem that's fairly common in our business: the boyfriend of a female athlete thinks he can manage her finances better than we can.

Now it would be the simplest thing in the world for me to outline how we handled this situation in the past. But what worked six months ago might not apply today. And given the wide range of personalities and emotions involved, it's risky to base a decision on it.

By all means, learn from experience. But keep in mind that your experience isn't always appropriate.

Make It Personal, or What I Learned from *The Godfather*

"It's not personal. It's strictly business," said Michael Corleone in one of the best business manuals ever written, *The Godfather* by Mario Puzo. The distinction is interesting because I think you usually have a negotiating edge if you can make it personal rather than business.

I learned this years ago in negotiating long-term contracts for our athlete clients. For example, given the choice of (a) a one-year contract with an option to renew for five years or (b) a five-year contract with an option to terminate after one year, which would you as a client choose?

We advise our clients to go for the latter, on the theory that it's much easier for the other party to passively ignore the renewal option than it is for them to tell you, "You're fired." Renewals, we've learned, are business; terminations are personal.

Injecting the personal element can improve your chances at almost any point in a negotiation, not just when the contract expires. I can't think of a more perfect illustration of this principle in action than *California* magazine's account of how Bert Fields, a powerful Hollywood attorney who represents some of the industry's biggest stars, settled a contract dispute involving—of all people—his client Mario Puzo.

After the enormous success of his *Godfather* movies, Puzo went on to write the original scripts for *Superman* and *Superman II*. Fields had negotiated a princely contract for Puzo, including a percentage of every theater ticket sold. However, the producer of the *Superman* series, a courtly gentleman named Alexander Salkind, was reluctant to pay Puzo his share of the gate. Using his battery of lawyers as mouthpieces, Salkind contended that Puzo's scripts had not met "the standards of the industry."

As Fields pursued the case around the world, taking depositions on several continents, he grew to admire Salkind and his personal style of doing business. He noticed that Salkind liked to kiss women's hands, was unfailingly polite, and took enormous pride in his relationships. He also suspected that while Salkind's lawyers treated the Puzo matter as just business, to Salkind it might be more personal.

Fields arranged to continue discussions with Salkind and his attorneys in a hotel in San Remo, Italy. The two men talked amiably in the hotel garden when—of all people— Mario Puzo strolled by. Salkind was surprised but instinctively rushed to hug Puzo, crying out, "Mario! My friend."

At that instant, Fields jumped in. "Mr. Salkind," he said, "was there anything Mario Puzo did not do in performance of his contract?"

Salkind hesitated. Could he insult his dear friend Mario to his face? He conferred with his lawyers. Fields repeated his question: "Mr. Salkind, was there anything Mario Puzo did not do in performance of his contract?"

Salkind smiled at Puzo and replied, "Not only did Mr. Puzo do everything that was required of him under the contract, he did it *superbly*."

Extreme as Fields's tactic may seem, I don't think it was abusive—since it added a personal element to resolve a situation that, in strict business terms, was going nowhere.

Conversely, I think there are times, particularly with close friends, when you can push the personal element too far. I don't know how many times I've seen business people approach friends at other companies with genuinely bad deals, expecting them to go along with it because of the personal connection. This is abusive. It's the business equivalent of your best friend asking to borrow your shiny new car for the day. You don't feel comfortable saying no, but a thoughtful friend would never have asked.

In dealing with friends, you're far better off negotiating on the merits rather than you-owe-me-one.

An executive I know was agonizing about whether to approach his friend, a decision maker at another company, with what sounded like a very good idea. He didn't want to put his friend in the position of having to say no or, worse, having to say yes against his better judgment. But he was convinced it was a great opportunity.

He eventually sold the idea to his friend by giving him the right to hear it first. "Look," he said, "I know I'm going to do this project with someone—because the concept is strong. But because of our relationship, I feel I owe you the first crack at it."

If a negotiation is all business, find a way to make it personal. If it's personal, keep it strictly business.

Beware the Dollar Anchor!

It's impossible to generalize about the most important factor in a successful negotiation. Circumstances vary widely and no two deals are exactly alike (no matter what you think). Success usually depends on the quality of the product or service on the table and a combination of timing, personality, and luck.

But there's one aspect of negotiating I'm sure of: the *first dollar figure mentioned* is the most dangerous. This is the "dollar anchor," the high or low number that frames and affects everything that follows. As a buyer or seller, you have to be very wary of the dollar anchor. Unless you're the one dropping it, you can't be sure where it came from or who made it up.

Dollar anchors are dropped on unsuspecting consumers all the time in everyday life, usually when a product has no "recommended retail price." Antique dealers, for example, notoriously overprice merchandise to allow for impressive on-the-spot markdowns.

But dollar anchors are less obvious in business situations. In a long, drawn-out negotiation, when numerous dollar figures are tossed up in the air and it's hard to distinguish the legitimate from the bogus, even the wiliest negotiator can mistake a floor price for where the ceiling should be.

Here are two negotiating situations where you're particularly vulnerable to errors in judgment.

1. Bait and switch in reverse

We're all familiar with "bait and switch" selling—the practice of enticing buyers with low prices and then persuading them to trade up. It's a popular and legitimate consumer sales tool. Where would department stores and supermarkets be without below-cost "loss leaders"?

But in corporate sales, where you don't stay in business for long by selling below cost, the bait and switch strategy is most effective *in reverse*. That is, you "insult" buyers with high prices and then persuade them to trade down (at a price still acceptable to you).

I noticed this reverse bait and switch several years ago— when I was on the buying end. An executive from another company approached us with a project that would fit perfectly with one of our client's marketing goals. Unfortunately, the asking price was $300,000. I told him that figure was way out of line.

Much to my surprise, the executive agreed with me. "You're right," he said, "it isn't worth it." And we parted amicably.

A week later, he called again. "It's too bad that project doesn't make sense at $300,000, because it certainly solves your client's problem," he said. "What if I can come up with a smaller $75,000 project that has nearly the same impact?"

With the $300,000 dollar anchor now firmly sunk in my mind, I was interested. How could I pass up a $300,000 deal at $75,000?

Only when more objective heads in our company (who had never heard the $300,000 figure) concluded that the $75,000 project was more fairly priced at $25,000 did I realize how his dollar anchor had clouded my judgment.

2. The nonconfrontational discussion

It's very easy in a *nonconfrontational discussion* to establish a high dollar anchor—because nobody is inclined to challenge it or, among "friends," even properly evaluate it.

For example, your neighbor casually tells you that he was offered $600,000 for his home. This is astonishing news, because you know it's worth closer to $450,000. Your neighbor, of course, assures you that he isn't selling.

But, in fact, the sales process has already begun. It started the moment he dropped the $600,000 anchor in your lap. Believe me, should you (or whoever else he told) steer a prospect willing to pay anywhere near $600,000 to his door, he'll sell.

My point here is not that you should be manipulating numbers in business. But be aware that other people are prone to do this to you.

Getting Your Money's Worth from a "Mediocre Deal"

Experienced negotiators tell me there are three types of deals in business—good, bad, and mediocre. In a good deal both parties are happy. In a bad deal, one party is much happier than the other. In a mediocre deal, neither party has much to complain about—but they do anyway.

This sort of dissatisfaction, and the way it can lead to bitterness and ultimately poison a healthy business relationship, is one reason I think the mediocre deal is the most dangerous deal of all.

I noticed this years ago with a consultant I know. A small but rapidly growing company needed his expertise but could only pay a fraction of his usual monthly consulting fee. Reluctantly, he agreed to the reduced fee but, human nature being what it is, started giving the client reduced service. In his mind, the lowered fee made the account a low priority. He didn't return the client's calls, handed in shoddy reports, missed deadlines.

Inevitably, the client came to the conclusion that even a cut-rate fee was too much. As for the consultant, he lost on every count. He cut his rate, sullied his reputation, and lost the goodwill of an attractive client. He would have been better off doing nothing at all than doing something badly.

Let them know it's mediocre

If you're involved in a mediocre deal, it's important to put your displeasure on the table rather than into the job you do.

I don't know how many times I've heard people complete a deal and then privately complain that they don't like it. These are probably the same people who go to restaurants and call the headwaiter over to complain about the food *after* they've picked their plate clean.

The only way to let the other party know you know it's a mediocre deal is to tell them!

There have been many occasions when companies have approached us about hiring one of our athlete clients to make an appearance for, say, $5,000 where we would normally receive four or five times that amount. We do not automatically dismiss these overtures. We might say, "Look, our client will do this for $5,000, even though he's never done this for less than $20,000. He will because (a) he likes you and (b) he thinks we can do more business in the future. But you have to understand two things: One, at $5,000 this is not a good deal for us. Two, this is the last time we'll accept $5,000."

That sort of candor not only places them in your debt but also exposes them to the concept of future deals.

Go in with your eyes open

The best advice about mediocre deals is to go into them with your eyes wide open and think of them as the first step of a long series of improved deals.

The international expansion of the National Football League is a case in point.

When we began selling the international television rights to NFL games several years ago, the indifference to American football overseas was overwhelming. We knew that we would have to put up with years of mediocre deals before a big payoff, but we decided to grin and bear it.

In 1982 we put the Eagles-Raiders Super Bowl game in closed-circuit theaters in England. It was a fun event—slightly tongue-in-cheek but very British. Men wore black tie. The house lights went up during commercials so British cheerleaders could spur the teams on. After that, we approached Britain's Channel 4 about presenting a Game of the Week. Channel 4 was a small, newly formed, independent television channel that desperately needed unique programming, but even so, the deal we got was worse than mediocre.

Our plan was simple: Edit a Game of the Week into a tight one-hour show and hope the British public goes for it. That in turn would result in greater public acceptance of the sport, which would lead to nonmediocre deals in the future. This is loss-leader thinking, pure and simple. But you have to remind yourself—and the other guy—that it won't go on forever. Now, of course, the NFL is in the next phase of expansion—namely, live games overseas.

We're using a similar approach in Japan. The NFL and Coca-Cola sponsored a closed-circuit Breakfast at the Super Bowl in Tokyo. In Australia there's Monday Night Football (on Tuesdays, actually, because of time zones). In Italy, 72 teams in three divisions play American football. There's even an event called the Eurobowl to decide the European football champion.

Eventually, there may be NFL franchises with names like the Paris Panthers or Tokyo Tigers.

But this sort of success is hard to imagine in the beginning when you literally have to give the product away. You have to swallow a lot of mediocre deals before you can feast on the good ones.

What Makes a World-Class Negotiator

What qualities do you need to be a good negotiator? A good negotiator knows:

1. What he's negotiating for.
2. How long the agreement will last.
3. Who it involves.
4. Who it excludes.
5. How much money will change hands.

These are the basics of negotiating. Nail them down and, even in a protracted and tense negotiation process, you will do at least as well as the other side.

But negotiating is more than memorizing some rules about what, who, how long, and how much. Having listed the nuts and bolts, I'd like to elaborate on a few qualities and instincts that make a world-class negotiator, the kind of negotiator who can get his terms without compromising himself, his client, or the transaction—and without the other side feeling that they've been compromised.

1. Avoid confrontations

Too many people confuse the idea of being a tough negotiator with the ability to be confrontational. Not true. Confrontation is a necessary part of negotiation, but it's vastly overrated. It has nothing to do with toughness or machismo and everything to do with timing.

As a general negotiating rule, I save all confrontations for last. If some issue threatens to be a source of controversy, I'll table it until all the other points of the agreement are resolved.

This has a double-edged benefit. First, it gets you on the proper footing at the *beginning* of a negotiation. After all, if you start off taking a hard line with someone, you can't expect them to concede many points afterward.

Second, it smooths your path at the *close*. After weeks or months of hard work, people seem to be more compliant, more willing to resolve one issue—no matter how thorny—if it's the only one left on the table.

2. Cast carefully

The best negotiators are very careful about who they bring to the negotiation.

For example, in many negotiations, absenting myself from the process is the smartest thing I can do. When the other side is pressing for a decision on a delicate matter, my surrogate can always say, "I like this, it makes sense to me, but I have to check with Mark." This delaying tactic may irritate the other side, but the opportunity to discuss the issue privately later on may improve our position.

Likewise, if I bring everyone in our company who matters to a negotiation, I have cut off my ability to check with someone who isn't there. In my experience, *not* having all the right people in the room is a great advantage.

3. Check your baggage

Everyone brings some "baggage" to the negotiating table—a track record, a personality defect, a boss looking over his shoulder. A world-class negotiator determines ahead of time whether the baggage he's bringing is something the other side is willing to carry.

An associate once suggested that I step aside from a negotiation because of my reputation as a tough negotiator. His reasoning: The other side would be overcompensating; they would be more obstinate and demanding in order to beat me at my own game.

Flattering as this "fastest gun in the West" theory was, I declined his suggestion. I didn't see any reason to walk off the field simply because the other side respected me and intended to try harder.

It reminded me of what Bjorn Borg once said about being the top seed at Wimbledon.

I asked him, "What do you think of your draw?"

"What difference does it make?" he said. "I'm number one in the world. I'm supposed to beat everybody."

4. Remember the competition

The other side's competition is the unseen (and most under-appreciated) factor in any negotiation. All companies worry about what their competitors have done, are doing, or will do. It stimulates them, consumes them, and from the standpoint of ego, goads them into making extraordinary gestures.

If you are sensitive to these rivalries, you can often negotiate terms that exceed your wildest dreams.

I remember some years ago when the entire senior management of the United Artists film studio resigned on the same day. The problem for the newly installed management at UA was obvious: Convince the film community that UA was still a major player.

The solution: Quickly make a major statement, which in Hollywood usually means—"Spend a lot of money."

The beneficiary of this development happened to be journalist Gay Talese, who was selling the film rights to his book *Thy Neighbor's Wife*. The book was a bestseller, but it was nonfiction and salacious and, in the opinion of many, virtually unfilmable. But Talese's agent, Martin Bauer, recognized that UA was bringing their checkbook *and* their ego to the negotiating table. They had a need to be seen as a big spender.

United Artists ultimately paid a record $2.5 million for the film rights to *Thy Neighbor's Wife*—because they needed to make a statement to the competition, and Talese's agent played on that need. To this day, the book remains unfilmed.

Admittedly, Hollywood plays by different rules. But the same competitive dynamic exists in every business, whether it's Ford versus General Motors, Pepsi versus Coke, or two groceries slugging it out in the same neighborhood. A world-class negotiator develops an instinct for this, and profits by it.

5. Use candor

A world-class negotiator is candid rather than devious—because the quality is so rare and disarming.

Candor is particularly effective when negotiations get tense or are about to fall apart. An honest statement such as "I really want this to go through," or "This is important to me" has a refreshing way of ending the gamesmanship, clearing the air, and educating the other side about your priorities.

The area where candor is most effective, I've found, is the one where many people are coy: Price.

Too many people are afraid to quote "big numbers"—perhaps because they're afraid of sounding like they're making too much profit. I don't share this fear. I'm willing to ask for big numbers because I'm willing to be candid about my costs and my profit.

We recently asked a television network to pay us $10 million for a project. They liked the idea, but the negotiations stalled. It turned out they were negotiating under the misconception that we were making a $5 million profit on the deal—which they found unconscionable.

In many cases, this is where the deal would die. One side wants to know how much money you are making. The other side gets huffy and defensive, contending "My profit is none of your business!"

But this is precisely where candor is most disarming. We took the network step-by-step through our budget and convinced them that a 10 percent profit margin wasn't excessive. "In fact," we argued, "we probably deserve more."

They wisely didn't pursue this final point, but the negotiations went smoothly thereafter.

3 | Managing

The Importance of Building Value, Not Profits

In 1987, when Ted Turner, the flamboyant American entrepreneur, was scrambling to save his broadcasting and cable empire after a period of almost reckless expansion, he paused to explain his entrepreneurial philosophy and why he took such big risks. "You have to understand," he said, "I've never been too concerned with profits. My goal is to build value."

Turner's point is too important for any entrepreneur to ignore. Profits in and of themselves are important only on Wall Street. In private companies they're practically irrelevant—because all you do with excess profits is share them with the government.

As Frank Bennack, the chairman of the Hearst Corporation, once told me, "In a private company, you don't try to build profits. You try to manage cash." And the best thing you can do with cash is pour it back into the company or share it with your employees.

I suspect most small business owners with a decent accountant know this intuitively. But maybe they don't act on it as efficiently as they should. I'd guess there are thousands of small business owners out there who, without realizing it, turn small-minded the instant their business turns "profitable." They put the newfound cash into bank accounts and contingency funds for a rainy day that make them feel secure. While security is a legitimate goal, in a rapidly changing economy steady growth is even more important. They'd be better off buying the store next door to keep expanding. At the end of ten years they'd not only have a healthy bank statement but an operation that's fifty times more valuable than the day they started.

Why doesn't everybody see this? For one thing, not everybody wants to be "big." Others aren't keen on risk. But most often, I think, the real problem is that people don't clearly see what phase of growth their business is in.

When it comes to building a business, entrepreneurs generally go through three phases:

Phase One. In phase one, when you start out, all you think about is income. Not "profits" or "net revenues" or "return on investment," but sales, receivables, cash in hand. Your entire mindset is "I have to make money to pay my overhead and keep things going."

Phase Two. Eventually you find out that despite your success at generating cash, you're not making profits. Because you're spending too much. So you become a little more disciplined about cutting costs—in order to make your income productive.

Phase Three. Finally, you realize that a private company is neither income (phase one) nor cost-cutting (phase two) but a carefully calculated combination of the two. This is when you start managing cash, making capital investments, increasing your asset base, and as Ted Turner says, building value.

Even the most skillful entrepreneurs get confused about which phase they're in. Many get so caught up in the start-up phase mentality of "We need income!" that they don't realize they're already in phase two or phase three. You see this repeatedly with entrepreneurs who are very sales-oriented but cannot administrate. Likewise, others plunge so deeply into the cost-cutting economies of phase two that they don't realize that they're in phase three and need to spend for the future.

If you've done all this properly, there probably is a phase four. This happens when you decide to sell your company—and you need to create an attractive pattern of profit growth for potential buyers.

For example, if you've been very disciplined about keeping profits in line and you decide to sell your company three years out, you might want to show $2 million profit in year one, $6 million in year two, and $11 million in year three. And then you sell. If you've done phases one through three correctly, you can almost write your own ticket.

Growing for the Right Reasons

"Intrapreneuring" has become a fashionable phrase in American business. It means turning your employees into entrepreneurs *within* the company.

I tend to be suspicious of terms that glamorize what entrepreneurs actually do (mostly, it's a lot of risk and hard work). Also, I doubt that you can translate the entrepreneur's independence and passion into corporate life simply by coining a buzzword.

The term really describes something that solid businesses have always had to do—namely, keep growing. In that sense, I suppose intrapreneuring should be encouraged, but not if it inspires companies to grow in the wrong direction or for the wrong reasons. I can't help but wonder how many of these so-called intrapreneurs, in their eagerness to gain a power base and a little autonomy, have the company's best interests at heart—or their own.

Growth is very important in our organization. But, to use another buzzword, we try to handle our horizontal expansion in as synergistic a manner as possible. If one of our executives has intrapreneurial urges, we hold him or her to one rigorous standard: does it make sense for us and will it make money?

Virtually all of our business expansion derives from the following growth formula: we stick to what we do best but apply it in areas no one has considered before.

When our financial people got very good at investing and tax planning for the likes of Jean-Claude Killy and Bjorn Borg, they came to me and, in effect, said, "Hey, we're really good at what we do. We'd like to have our own profit center. Why can't we sell our financial services to executives and other busy professionals in the US and abroad?" I agreed and offered to help them with our corporate contacts. That is how we developed a financial management operation that *Money* magazine described as "arguably the most extensive in the financial planning field."

Our entry into classical music is another case in point. We began representing classical musicians because we found that all the things we were doing, all our managerial, pro-motional, and financial talents, could be used in another field.

The reasons were compelling: (1) classical musicians need tax advice on an international level just like our ath-letes do; (2) their art can be performed without considera-tion of language, same as with athletes; (3) their career longevity is impressive, more than most athletic careers; (4) companies that sponsor sports are increasing their sponsor-ship of art and are looking for creative, imaginative ways to accomplish this; and (5) the income opportunities for clas-sical artists have increased tremendously.

The only thing we didn't have was expertise in the classi-cal music business itself—so we acquired that. That was the easiest part.

What to Do After "That's a Great Idea!"

An idea is never more vulnerable than in the critical mo-ments after somebody says, "That's a great idea!" That's when most people decide how they can resent it, resist it, misrepresent it, misuse it, lose it, neglect it, or love it to death.

A few careful responses can minimize the damage:

Check your ego at the door

It's easier to resent a good idea than to embrace it—especially if it's not your own. This is human nature.

Many people want to be the first person to come up with a winning concept. So when they hear something really new, they get defensive. They wonder, "Why didn't I think of that?" and then use their excuses and self-justifications to attack the idea.

As an executive you have to be aware of this all-too-human tendency—in yourself and others. Amid the excitement of a new idea, it's often hard to tell the difference between the grinding of axes and the sound of applause.

Don't go by the book

People often react to a good idea by trying to figure out what it has in common with what they've done before. They'll do this even though the product, the market, the timing, and the people involved are completely different. The real opportunities, I've found, usually lie in the differences.

This was never more evident to me than in the legal squabbling several years ago between the New York Yacht Club and our client, the Royal Perth Yacht Club, over who owned the licensing rights to the America's Cup.

For years the New York Yacht Club had generated considerable revenues—for itself and the sport—by licensing the Cup name and logo. When the Australian sailors defeated the Americans in Newport, Rhode Island, in 1983, ownership of the Cup went to the new host, the Royal Perth Yacht Club. And with it, we contended, went the fees and royalties traditionally associated with the Cup. The New Yorkers disagreed—and put up legal obstacles to Perth's every effort to market the event.

Our company had faced this problem many times before in other arenas. The standard solution was to file for trademarks, fight the legal battles, and patiently wait for justice to prevail. But patience didn't appeal (or apply) to Perth, which had an expensive race to host in less than two years and needed hard cash more than hard-won legal victories.

So we focused on the differences.

Accordingly, at a meeting in Australia late in 1985, we suggested to Perth that they call off their attorneys and write a simple letter to the New York Yacht Club (which was spending millions to recapture the Cup) and to all other competing parties. The letter essentially said that if anyone did anything to hamper the Royal Perth Yacht Club's efforts to market the 1987 defense *in exactly the same way that it had been marketed in years past by the New York Yacht Club*, that party would be barred from racing at Perth. Period.

No one challenged the letter. They all came to race. And the licensing rights sidestepped the courts and landed in Perth.

Be ruthless about profitability

I keep a mental file of all my "good" ideas that never make money and the "bad" ideas that always do. It's the only way I can remind myself to be ruthless about profitability.

To me, surviving in business has always meant balancing the risks versus the rewards. And no matter how elegant or seductive the idea, I always keep my eye on the rewards.

For example, one of our executives once suggested that we get involved in marketing what he called "College Videos." Our company would produce film documentaries about several dozen popular American universities, then market them on videocassettes to prospective students and their parents as a low-cost alternative to an on-campus visit.

Major corporations, who have a vested interest in higher learning, would probably fight to sponsor many of the videos.

On the surface, that's a good idea. It involves young people, affluent parents, and the corporations trying to reach them. Furthermore, it would play to our company's experience as a film producer and marketing consultant to corporations.

But precisely because of our experience, I realized that distributing videocassettes to every high-school student in the US was virtually impossible. Regardless of whether parents would base a $40,000-to-$60,000 tuition investment on a thirty-minute video, there was no cost-efficient way to get the tapes into parents' hands—and back.

The project would take so much money, time, and manpower that by the time we got our rewards out of it (if we did), all we would be doing is building blueprints for competitors to do the same at other schools. The idea may be good, but it's neither protectable nor profitable.

Management by Federal Express

A friend of mine once visited the weekend home of the CEO of a large and very successful investment bank. Throughout the Saturday morning the two of them spent together, my friend watched Federal Express vans pulling into the driveway. A few moments later the package would be delivered to the CEO's study. And he would toss the envelope onto a slowly mounting pile.

"What's in those envelopes?" my friend asked.

"Progress reports, deal memos, notes for the Monday morning management meetings, things like that," said the CEO.

"Are you going to read any of them?"

"No," said the CEO.

"Then why have them rushed to your home on a Saturday?"

"Because my people don't know I won't read them," said the CEO.

I've heard of far more costly ways to let employees know that (1) their work is important, (2) they shouldn't miss deadlines, and (3) they shouldn't hand in something that's less than their best.

Why I Prefer Winners to Heroes

Every business person at some point in his or her career has to come to grips with the fundamental question: do you want to be a hero or a winner? This applies to employees and employers alike.

Heroes are the men and women on the glitzy front lines who get their names in the papers whenever they hit a home run for their company. Winners perform their jobs just as well as the heroes, but (to continue the baseball analogy) they rarely come up to the plate in dramatic, bottom-of-the-ninth, game-winning situations. Instead, they're terrific fielders and steady singles hitters. They get the job done without the fireworks and tightrope antics. They're the frequently forgotten base runner who just happened to score the winning run that the hero drove in.

A successful organization needs its share of heroes and winners, but on the whole I prefer winners, people who know their roles and do them well. I work hard to motivate them, to give them their proper recognition, and to stifle some of their "heroic" urges.

In our organization, we have a lot of people who are talented at one thing—investing, accounting, taxes, contract law, computer systems—but it amazes (and troubles) me when these expert role players want to be something else. They're winners at what they do. But because of various quirks in their personality, they feel that they're not heroes in the company unless they see their name in lights.

As a result, they fight to get involved in high-profile, glamorous projects only dimly related to their expertise. Suddenly, you have accountants who want to produce televised sports events, money managers who want to hobnob with the athletes they occasionally advise, lawyers who try to sign up team sport athletes. This is very counterproductive for them and our company.

This need to be in the spotlight is understandable. A brilliant financial analyst who can come up with creative tax schemes for the world's leading sports personalities, for example, will not grab headlines in the press, not like one of our team sports executives who had just signed a multi-million dollar contract for a major-league ballplayer. But this financial analyst should be smart enough to know his value to me and our company. If he doesn't know this, I remind him.

I point out that it is easier to find people to handle the glamorous jobs that bring in the profits than it is to hire expert technicians who know how to maximize those profits. This fact tends to increase the value of a technician in my scheme of things and diminish the "indispensability" of some of my higher profile executives.

For example, setting up a computer system in our financial department is very complicated, but it may turn out to be the most important project we can get done *well*. Outside of our financial group, there will be very little recognition or appreciation for our in-house computer wizards. But I think it's important to honor these people who are less visible than others, even if it only means paying them very well. They should be thought of as winners. I think that's much better than being a hero.

P.S. As someone who has been written about in nearly all the major publications, I can assure you that a little bit of celebrity within your industry can help you in business. But trying to get your name in the papers is a trivial pursuit, especially if it turns your attention from actually doing your job well to having people think you do your job well. Don't forget who signs your paycheck; it isn't the local newspaper.

Drawing the Career Curve

I recently read an article by sports psychologist George Leonard that described the four learning curves that recreational athletes follow on their road to mastering a sport.

There is the Dabbler, whose closet is filled with golf clubs, tennis racquets, running shoes, and dumbbells—evidence of all the sports he started but soon abandoned when his progress slowed down or his enthusiasm waned.

There is the Obsessive, who starts out by making tremendous progress and pushes himself mercilessly to maintain that growth. Eventually, he's burned out by injuries.

There is the Hacker, who becomes adequately skilled at a sport—and then is satisfied to maintain that plateau. He often relies on one strength and works around his many weaknesses.

Then there is the Master, who realizes that excelling in sport is a constant tug-of-war between progress and frustration—and that you can't improve unless you go back to the drawing board and patiently work your way through those down-cycles when your game seems to be falling apart.

I bring this up because I've always believed there are parallels between success in sports and success in business. Taking a cue from Leonard's categories, I think the careers of most business people tend to follow similar curves. Here are four common career curves—and how they should be managed:

1. Champions

The champion's upward curve is not as smooth as it might seem. The glitches and plateaus make champions interest-

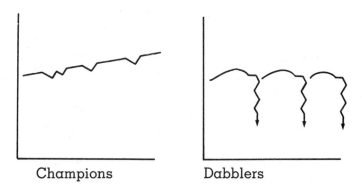

Champions   Dabblers

ing. They represent the little defeats—the misguided projects, lost clients, missed quotas—champions have to overcome. They also represent the champion's true secret: his
willingness to take risks. The singular quality of a business
champion is his ability to learn from his mistakes and never
repeat them.

How to manage champions: First of all, recognize that
there are degrees of champions. There are the heroes who
consistently bring in the big deals and maintain your company's winning streak. And there are the winners who excel
in small but vital areas that are just as crucial to maintaining
your company's day-in day-out commitment to quality. Both
are champions and should be treated equally.

Second, do all that you can to identify and develop new
champions—even by trial and error. Over the years we've
had several executives who, either by choice or by structure,
have been very suppressed in one part of the company. Yet
once we move them to another division, a totally new dimen-
sion to their abilities surfaces. They exceed our expectations
and theirs.

2. Dabblers

A lot of people spend two or three years at one job, one year
at another, and so on, never recognizing the stop-and-go
pattern in their careers. They have enough brains and skills

to land good jobs, but they're not disciplined enough to keep growing in them or, for that matter, to hold on to them.

How to manage dabblers: The dabbler is someone who always gets excited about something new and then loses the excitement. You see this everyday with people who go on diets or start new exercise programs. They don't see dieting as a way of life. They dabble with a diet, then revert back to their old ways, then start again. The same with exercise. Instead of starting slowly and increasing through moderation, they overexert themselves at first—and within a few weeks stop.

In business there are many areas where the dabbler's personality can turn him into a champion.

Our event implementation division, for example, is custom-made for the dabbler's bursts of enthusiasm. The dabbler gets excited about setting up the World Ski Championships for three weeks, and by the time he's ready to lose interest, the event ends. By then the dabbler is already hard at work on next week's golf tournament.

3. Plodders

The plodder is the straight 9-to-5 employee. He can be a very accomplished professional, but has other interests outside the company. As the company grows, so grows the plodder but never with the meteoric speed of a champion.

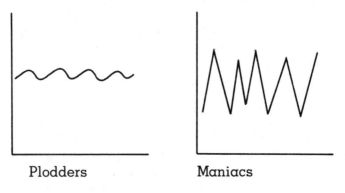

Plodders   Maniacs

How to manage plodders: I had a lot of trouble dealing with plodders when I was younger. I was ambitious. I wanted to do all the "mores"—create more, earn more, satisfy myself more, impress other people more—and I found it hard to believe that other people weren't as excited about their work or these objectives as I was.

I realize now there is a need for plodders in most companies and that, given the right circumstances, they can become champions. It's a manager's job to create those circumstances for plodders and keep them plodding in the right direction.

I'm sure there are very valuable plodders at many pharmaceutical or computer companies. Their minds are brilliant and their personality is such that they can work nine-to-five for years on a new drug or microchip design without getting bored. Eventually they develop a product that is brought to market and becomes a multimillion dollar enterprise. That's when the plodder produces the results of a corporate champion.

4. Maniacs

Maniacs have volatile highs and lows—in their personality and their performance. Everything is either/or with them. A project is either all-consuming or irrelevant, never in between. A colleague is either with them or against them, never indifferent. They never settle for second best and, as a result, give up too soon on valid concepts that may not measure up to their high expectations.

How to manage maniacs: The problem with maniacs is that they are unpredictable. You can't plan for the future based on their performance. They can hit brilliant highs that make you as a manager look very good. But their lows can tax your spirit and drain your company's resources.

Maniacs require more monitoring than anyone else. Someone must keep an eye on them to protect the company during their low points and take full advantage during their highs.

Some Kind Words for "Corporate Cultures"—And How to Get One

Remember the term "corporate culture"? It was an important buzzword a few years ago. The concept was simple: a company's culture—its shared values, goals, and rituals—can spell the difference between success and mediocrity.

Since then corporate cultures have been derided as a fad, a quick fix embraced to hide deeper managerial failings.

Business Week a few years ago mocked a chief executive who responded to a slick ninety-minute lecture on the value of corporate cultures by turning to his aide and gushing, "This corporate culture stuff is great. I want one by Monday."

I don't agree that corporate cultures are dinosaurs. The IBMs, the Proctor & Gambles, and the Morgan Banks of this world have profited handsomely (and held on to their talented people) with their strong corporate cultures. From dealing with them, and managing my own organization, I've learned how they do it. There are seven steps and they take years.

Step one. Raise your hiring standards and deflate theirs

Strong-culture companies want first-rate people, but not if they arrive with second thoughts. Thus, the hiring process is equal parts seduction and discouragement. Applicants are told about the company's strengths as well as the extraordinary hours and demands that will fall upon them. At Proctor & Gamble, for instance, line managers rather than the personnel department wean out the winners from the losers. They do it with candor, backed up by a series of tests and interviews. Candidates ultimately join the company with eyes very wide open.

Step two. Humble your new recruit and break their bad habits

Top companies wear down their new employees with an impossible workload. If the recruits can't take it, it's best to know early in the game. But the long hours have a hidden motive: they shrink an employee's self-satisfaction, increase his vulnerability, and make him more open to seeking help from others. This humbling process, plus the long hours working with equally dedicated people, creates a collegial ethic. The survivors are stars, and they are team players.

Step three. Let your future leaders get their hands dirty

Top companies, large or small, push their top people to master the firm's core business from the ground up. It's a timeless instinct. Just as a father who owns a bakery will push his children to learn how to bake bread, how to package, how to buy supplies, and how to sell to customers, a giant like IBM will put its managers through an inflexible program of training in the field. Employees at all levels of IBM know, and appreciate, this.

Step four. Tell people where you're going, and reward them for getting there

Corporate cultures are reinforced by (1) telling people how the company is doing and (2) paying them for a good job. (Keep the first part to yourself and you won't have to worry about keeping the second.) The key is to have consistent criteria for measuring success. If everyone knows that your company's overriding goals are, say, maintaining a 50 percent share of the market or achieving 20 percent annual growth, then that's the standard everyone must aim for. Without these hardline targets, you don't have a corporate culture, you have people hanging on to their jobs.

Step five. Motivate them one step beyond the profit motive

Making money is the result, not the means, of a strong corporate culture. Employees will commit themselves fully to a company where values transcend the bottom line. At IBM, employees believe in their bones that unfailing customer service is the source of their prosperity. At Sony, innovations that take the public's (and the competition's) breath away prevail over everything else. At Avis, employees came to accept the fact that being No. 2 was their unique advantage.

Step six. Develop a corporate folklore

All companies have in-house stories of triumph over adversity, but strong cultures repeat these stories until they achieve mythic dimensions. At one bedding company the tale of the sales manager who dragged a mattress across Moscow has set the standard for company showmanship. The message to their sales force: you have to wake up the customers before they'll sleep on your mattress.

Step seven. Prop up a few corporate heroes to prove the culture works

Nothing is more impressive to young employees than a role model clearly labeled a winner. Strong cultures make a point of identifying these role models and creating a hierarchy of mentors and protégés. This keeps the culture turning.

Break Their Life-Style, Make Their Career

When one of our executives visited a software developer in Florida, he came back marveling at how impressive the company was in all phases of its business. It had a tremendous reputation and earned 50 cents on every dollar.

"The first thing I noticed," he told me, "was how nice the receptionist was. I knew I was in a professional outfit." Then he noticed two marble bars to the side of the reception area where two people were answering additional phones so no caller waits more than two rings. He also noticed that the conference-room doors read Seville, El Dorado, and Fleetwood. When he asked the receptionist why the rooms were named after Cadillacs, she replied, "Because we consider ourselves the Cadillac of the business." The company sells computer software to banks.

It turned out that the founder-chairman of the company also handed out Cadillacs, in addition to bonuses, to motivate his sales force.

As a senior executive of the company explained: "The problem we find in motivating our salespeople is that they sometimes reach their quotas and meet their personal financial goals, and then they stall because they're comfortable with their life-style. The question we face is, 'How do we elevate the salespeople into a higher life-style level so they want to (and have to) sell more?' The Cadillac does the trick. Suddenly they're driving a big fancy car that looks out of place in their neighborhood. Before long they're moving into a bigger house—and selling better than ever just to carry the mortgage. Our motto is: 'Break the guy's life-style, make his career.' "

I'm not sure if this is cornball or genius. But considering

the company's 50 percent profit margins, there's no doubt it works.

The Mixed Blessing of Superstars

You can never have too many superstars in a company. But managing them can be a mixed blessing. They're hard to hold on to, they're even harder to replace, and the gaps they create with each promotion can wreak havoc on your organization. As a manager you have constantly to balance the superstars' justifiable demands for advancement with the impact they make on your existing talent pool.

Sometimes top performers simply get promoted beyond their usefulness. A common example: You promote your best salesperson to sales manager and suddenly sales drop because he or she is in the office rather than out selling.

The key in all this, I think, may be to stop thinking of promotions as a narrow ascent up some corporate ladder where the employee has to shed some responsibilities in order to keep climbing. A better way may be simply to pile on the work.

In our organization, for example, when we give executives new responsibilities, we prefer they continue with many of their old ones as well. If and when they need support, they know who to hire from the outside or who within our organization can help out.

We don't regard an executive's hard-earned expertise in one field as "baggage" that should weigh him down in a new position (or exclude him from it). On the contrary, we think expertise props people up. The executives who really are as good as they think they are seem to prefer an expanding power base to a rising star.

When Two Employees Disagree

Few things disturb a manager more than having to mediate between two feuding employees. Even to the most hard-boiled CEOs, intracorporate squabbles are unpleasant because (a) one of the warring parties must ultimately lose face and (b) the winner isn't always right.

Because the situation is so ticklish, I try to communicate to our people that they should settle disputes among themselves, like adults. If they want me to be the Supreme Court, they better go through the appeals process first.

When disputes require my attention, I have simple criteria to determine my level of involvement. First I ask myself, is this disagreement professional or personal? If I substituted two different people in the same situation, would they argue too? If so, then I know the conflict is professional—and I need to get involved. And second, I factor in the two combatants' rank within the company—because rank is so often at the heart of the matter.

Disputes between people perceived as equals are easy to resolve: you choose sides, explain your reasons (to show you're not playing favorites), and insist that both of them keep you posted. However, disputes between executives of different rank are tricky. For one thing, if a dispute between a ranking executive and a comparatively junior employee arrives unsettled in your office, more often than not it's because the junior employee is right. Resolving the situation calls for Solomon-like wisdom rather than a verdict based on just the facts.

To maintain the integrity of the organization, I will frequently let the senior employee have his way—even when I'm sure he's wrong. It might cost me a little time and money before the executive sees the light. But on the plus side, I haven't undermined his authority, he will remember that I supported him, and if he's really good, he'll change his ways (and think it's his idea, not mine).

I realize this runs counter to our notions of fair play and "blind justice." But corporate life isn't a courtroom, and when human emotions are involved, I prefer to let time rather than a snap decision heal the wounds.

As for personal disagreements, I see no percentage in getting caught in the middle. I recently had to "judge" a dispute ostensibly about corporate turf that was really nothing more than a personality clash between two executives. I let them air their charges and countercharges for ten minutes, and then I literally walked out of the room. I'm not sure what went on in the room after I left, but the warriors apparently came to their senses—because the problem disappeared.

Understanding the Turf Around Your Relationships

Protecting your turf is a fact of life in any company. There will always be people who covet or want to share in your success, whether that means they're after your spacious office, your sales territory, your staff, or ultimately your job. You can usually spot these people in time and if you're as good as *they* seem to think you are, you can usually fight them off.

However, many people grow careless when it comes to the turf surrounding their relationships. Every businessperson cultivates (or should be cultivating) friends as potential business contacts—and vice versa. The trouble is, this sort of turf is hard to define, even harder to protect, and is constantly vulnerable to people who use or abuse it.

For example, a CEO recently told me how he helped his secretary find an apartment in Los Angeles. He put her in touch with a friend, a businesswoman at another company, who he happened to know was selling her apartment. The women met, closed the deal, and as things turned out, became good friends.

Such good friends, in fact, that the CEO's secretary arranged to get the woman special rates at a resort the CEO was involved with.

"When the woman mentioned this to me, I didn't mind at first," the CEO explained to me, "but then it struck me that if someone's going to do favors for her with my contacts, I'd like to know about it. I might not want my secretary to use my 'capital' that way. I might not have that much 'capital' to spend! Yet here she was spending my markers and people were taking them because of her connection with me."

In many ways this situation is not much different from the standard two-men-and-a-woman scenario, where two buddies meet for lunch and one of the fellows brings a date. The other guy takes a fancy to the lady and the next day asks her out. Is he out of line?

He is, in my opinion, unless he first discloses his intentions to his friend to find out how serious the relationship is.

I'd expect the same sort of honorable behavior and candor in business. Most executives I know who are skilled "networkers" don't expect an instant payback—for example, a finder's fee—when they introduce friend A to friend B and the two of them start turning it into a business relationship. Being kept informed is usually all the "appreciation" they need. It certainly clears the air and avoids the mixed allegiances that can lead to bad deals and bad feelings.

Invariably, whenever I have felt "betrayed" by a friend or business associate, it is not because of something they did but because they never told me about it.

The Biggest Hiring Mistake You Can Make

The biggest mistake is failing to hire people who are smarter than yourself.

You'd think this would be obvious to any rational person. Or that the alternative (namely, hiring someone dumber than you) would obviously be self-defeating. But hiring decisions seem to bring out the worst insecurities in people. I've seen this happen high and low.

A top executive hires toadies and then wonders why they have no initiative. A small-business owner deliberately hires people who are "good, but not so good that they'll get ideas about stealing clients and going out on their own." A devoted secretary finds a substandard replacement so she will be fondly remembered and/or sorely missed.

Unless you hire first-rate people and lead them by example to do the same, you will doom your company to being second-rate.

David Ogilvy, the legendary adman and founder of Ogilvy & Mather, made this point vividly years ago at a meeting of his agency's board. Ogilvy placed one of those Russian dolls in front of each director's chair.

"That's you," he told the directors. "Open it."

So they opened the doll, and found a smaller one inside. They opened that and found another and another. Inside the smallest doll was a note from Ogilvy, which said: "If you always hire people who are smaller than you are, we shall become a company of dwarfs. If, on the other hand, you always hire people who are bigger than you are, we shall become a company of giants."

How to Pick the Right Talent

Over the years we've hired MBAs, lawyers, accountants, former athletes, and several escapees from the Fortune 500 to do jobs they were trained to do and some jobs that they never anticipated.

At first, we hired the best young people we could find to give our organization depth. We figured that the best people would do good work anywhere and eventually would gravitate to the right spot. Now that we have depth, we hire to meet specific needs.

Beware the familiar face

If there's one hiring lesson I've learned, it's this: beware the familiar face. Don't hire people just because they are well-known in your industry. You may find out they know their business but not yours.

When we signed up Jean-Claude Killy, the triple gold medalist in skiing at the 1968 Olympics, our first impulse was to find an avid skier to handle him, someone who could speak his language. But we soon realized that we didn't need someone who knew skiing to sell Killy to sponsors and corporations. We needed someone who knew how to sell a personality. (It's the same if you were marketing a new soap. Who would you hire to sell it? The chemist who invented the soap or a marketing expert who can sell anything?)

We learned to hire against the grain the hard way. We once hired a golf pro for our golf division. But it became quickly apparent that you can't take someone from the golf tour, put him behind a desk, and expect the golfers he used to compete against to accept him as the expert who's managing their careers and money. Inevitably, the clients would say, "He's just a golfer. What does he know?"

The same thing happened when we hired a former professional football player to run our team sports division. The football players, it turned out, didn't want someone who could relate to them. They wanted someone who was skilled at contract negotiations and money management.

This sort of problem may be unique to our business, but I think the "beware the familiar face" theory applies to businesses a lot less specialized than ours.

Someone to challenge the status quo

When Arnold Palmer started his first auto dealership, he knew nothing about the car business (and he was slightly preoccupied by golf). So he hired a division general manager from one of the major American automakers to run the business, figuring that this fellow knew the industry.

Unfortunately, he knew it as a manufacturer, not a dealer. He had never sold cars to customers. He was used to the luxury of being a division manager with a huge support staff. He was not accustomed to running a tight ship. Even worse, he was too willing to accept the factory's point of view. In the car business, where dealers have to fight the factory to get the biggest allocation of a hot model, this can be ruinous.

Arnold eventually hired a talented businessman from outside the industry. This fellow had run his own business, had dealt with overheads, loved to cut costs, and challenged people when they told him, "It's always been done this way."

I think that's our heavy hiring criterion now. We want someone who is a fighter, who doesn't accept the status quo. We don't expect them to flout tradition or custom, but at least they'll question it.

Why Good Employees Go, and How to Keep Them

There's no mystery to holding on to good employees.

1. Give them a lot of responsibility.
2. Don't insult them with their paycheck.
3. Tell them once in a while how they're doing.

Unfortunately, the simplicity of this approach hasn't eliminated executive turnover at most companies. Good people will always leave good companies. Here are some reasons they do and what you can and cannot do about it.

1. The surprise departure

It's a sign of poor management when a good employee leaves to take another job—and it's a complete surprise to his or her boss. Somebody in the company should have known and made an effort to turn the unhappy employee around.

The best managers are sensitive to what their people want, what motivates them, what irritates them. Employees leave clues all over the place. They come in late. They miss deadlines. They subtly let you know that their spouse or children hate the city they're in. Perhaps you won't always be able to solve what's ailing them, but you can recognize the symptoms and sympathize. Remarkably, sometimes that's enough.

2. Doing great—at the wrong job

An employee's performance isn't always a sure sign of how he feels about the company. Quite often, an employee, through sheer talent and discipline, may be doing great work in an area that holds no interest for him.

For example, we may have an executive breaking sales records in our licensing division. But his dream job is in our television division. As far as we're concerned, he should continue breaking records in licensing. But the truth is, if he really wants to get into television, and some outsider offers him a television job, then he'll soon be out the door.

Our solution for this problem—and it's worked frequently—is to let him do both. If he's good, and getting his feet wet in television won't hurt his performance in licensing and will broaden him or keep him on our team, then everybody wins.

3. Hating the boss

There are not enough pages in this book to go into why employees hate their boss. But whatever is behind the conflict, it can usually be resolved if the boss keeps an open door.

If it's a manager's duty to be sensitive to his associates' ambitions, then it cuts both ways. Employees have to tell their boss what's bothering them. Bosses can't read minds (though they should try), but they can make it easy for employees to open up.

Our company has long grown past the point where I know every employee by name. But I still will make time for anyone if they ask to see me and tell me how much time they need. Whether they need 15 minutes or three hours, I'll be there. I have a hunch some of our employees don't believe me, but if they're as smart as they think they are, they would try.

4. Faster than your fast track

On occasion you will be blessed with an employee who is so productive that his advancement through the ranks is a foregone conclusion. The question here is: How far and how fast?

You have to be very creative in how you promote this fellow, for he can wreak havoc on your organization chart. If you get it wrong, you not only risk losing him but offending those he leaves behind.

Admittedly, this is a high-class headache, but don't take it lightly.

We once hired a young man to work in our overseas golf division. Within months it was obvious that he was a thoroughbred in terms of ability, and his boss, by comparison, was a plowhorse. Promoting him to the job he deserved—namely, his boss's—would have damaged the integrity of our organization. Instead, we transferred him to run one of our foreign offices that needed his sort of skills. We literally promoted him three steps at once—and none of the people he leapfrogged either noticed or complained.

5. Young with great expectations

It's a fact of corporate life that your newly hired superstars, fresh out of college or business school, are the people most likely to leave you—usually within two years. They're the ones you've worked hardest to attract. They're the ones with the greatest expectations. And sadly, they're the ones that most companies neglect.

It doesn't surprise me that a smart, ambitious employee who's thrown into an entry-level executive position and left to fend for himself soon moves to greener pastures.

The solution: For the first 12 months, treat new hires as an investment. If you lose them, it really costs because you have to reinvest in someone else. Watch them. Train them. Expose them to your best people. Nudge them into projects a little beyond their experience. And like any investment for the future don't expect to earn your money back right away. The payoff increases the longer they stay.

6. More money

A bigger paycheck, of course, is the biggest reason people leave. There's not much you can do about this, especially if you are already paying them as much or more than you think they're worth.

You can go through the ritual of making a counteroffer, but this sort of Russian roulette with salary rarely pays off for the employee or the company.

I recently saw a study by Boyden International, a search firm, of 450 executives who had changed jobs. Of the 40 executives who received counteroffers, 27 accepted the pay hike and stayed with their old employer. Within 18 months, 25 of the 27 had either left or been fired. Money, it seems, wasn't the solution to their problem.

How to Fire People Fairly

One of the toughest CEOs I know once told me that he found firing people to be the most difficult part of his job. I was surprised. Was this normally thick-skinned executive getting sentimental?

But as he talked about "damage control," the integrity of the organization, and keeping customers happy and employee morale up, I realized it wasn't the emotions but the *mechanics* of a dismissal that made him uncomfortable. He wasn't losing sleep about sending incompetents packing. He was worried about what to do after they were gone.

There are as many *ways* to fire a person as there are *reasons* for doing so. But in my opinion, two factors—timing and the individual's loyalty to our company—determine everything that follows once I decide to let someone go.

Think about your company—and then the employer

The key to firing anyone is to do it when it suits you, not them. Whatever business you're in, if an employee controls certain clients or elements of the business, don't dismiss him until you have a plan to replace him. You might have to wait a couple of days or (in one instance that I can recall) a couple of years before you're ready to let an individual go—but patience pays off. Control the timing of a dismissal and you can contain the potential damage.

While you wait for the right moment, quietly work to minimize the fallout, both internal and external. Externally, you might want to alert an important customer that "We're having problems with Jones"—even before you fire Jones. This may endear you to the customer and signal to them that you're interested in the account long after Jones is gone.

Internally, you should be moving another executive into

Jones's place. This could mean throwing more responsibilities on Jones's assistant or acquainting an executive from another department with Jones's clients and responsibilities.

Let them resign

The best way to fire someone is to let them resign. If you treat them fairly on severance pay and help them find a new job you will have earned their goodwill forever. An ex-employee who has been fired "fairly" is less likely to bad-mouth his ex-employer.

Orchestrating a resignation is not complicated, but don't get too cute. I've heard of one CEO who calls doomed employees into his office, invites them to sit in his leather chair, and tells them, "Okay, what would you say in this situation if you were me?" I suppose that's one way to get people to resign, but I know several silver-tongued employees who could probably talk their way into a promotion from the boss's chair.

I find it much easier to ease an employee into the situation. I say, "This isn't working. I've decided that you ought to find another place to work. I haven't given much thought to the how or when, but why don't you think about it for a couple of days and then we'll talk." You can't believe how such a dialogue sharpens their attention and helps them come to the desired conclusion.

Let the competition "steal them away"

Over the years I have fired people without their realizing it. Instead I have found jobs for them with another company and silently let them slip from my grasp.

Disguise a demotion

Often you will have loyal people whose skills cannot keep up with your company's growth. You might have a public relations person who is very good at hand-holding clients but offers little else in the way of coming up with new ideas or products. Then it's not a case of dismissing or demoting these people; you just don't promote them. They usually settle into a segment of the business where they can do well—and it's your job to help them find it.

Fight fire with "You're fired"

The only time firing someone isn't painful is when they have been totally dishonest with you. We once had a brazenly disloyal employee who, we learned, intended to leave the company with everything he could lay his hands on—clients, files, confidential information. So we arranged a one-day business trip for him. While he was away, we cleaned out his office and changed the locks. When he returned, we fired him.

There's nothing devious or unseemly about this. You have to fight fire with fire. It happens in tiny companies and among the giants too.

I remember about ten years ago when a powerful division chief at a major broadcasting company committed some foolish financial improprieties. While he was being confronted with the evidence and summarily dismissed in the CEO's office, workmen appeared on his floor to remove his property and seal off his office. Abrupt and harsh as this may seem, it was probably the only way to end a messy situation.

Where you do it doesn't matter

Where you choose to fire someone—their office, your office, a neutral site—depends on your inclinations. There are no rules, since there are so many circumstances.

Some managers determine where and how they'll fire someone by the kind of message they want to send to other employees. I heard of one CEO who fired an executive in front of the whole company to set an example. He gathered his 100 employees in a room, knowing full well that during the course of the meeting he would single out the bad apple and fire him on the spot. It was a calculated move, but his employees didn't know that. I leave it to you to judge how this stunt would motivate the ninety-nine survivors.

Who's Driving the Company: Your Line or Your Staff?

The goal of any thriving organization is to stay lean rather than fat, hungry rather than satisfied.

But in a growing company it's often easy to lose your way—particularly in the area of corporate staff. As your business becomes more complicated, it's inevitable that you add support personnel such as accountants, data-processing experts, and facility managers. You need these people to supply information and maintain controls.

But keep in mind that, like any bureaucracy, corporate staffs have a remarkable capacity to self-perpetuate and swell. If you're not careful, they can usurp the powers of your line executives. Pretty soon your corporate staff is establishing procedures, setting policy, and creating forms—mostly to talk to each other—and requiring line executives to comply with *their* forms.

One sure sign that your organization is less lean than you think is the intracorporate memo. When our line executives start copying me on memos complaining about staff, I suspect we've lost our way.

That's when I have to remind employees that in the tug-of-war between line executives and staff, I will always be pulling for the people on the line. In our business, they are the ones knocking on doors, bringing in business, and maintaining relationships. They're in the best position to make decisions. And they deserve everyone's support.

As a manager, you have to constantly step back and ask yourself: are we line-driven or staff-driven? If you don't like the answer, you won't solve it by adding more staff.

In Search of the Perfect Meeting

It's not fashionable nowadays to admit you like attending meetings. There are too many of them. They take too much time. If they didn't exist, some real work would get done. And yet, have you noticed how the severest critics of the internal meetings are the same people who sulk and scheme and snoop around when they're excluded from one?

I must confess to having mixed feelings about internal meetings, whether I'm chairing them or someone else is. I realize that meetings are essential for intracorporate communication and decision making. But make them a regular event or give them a name and they tend to outgrow their usefulness. They can dissolve into forums of Olympic gamesmanship and self-justification. People score points by asking pointed questions rather than supplying good answers. People's egos swell or deflate according to who else has been invited.

Perhaps because of these mixed emotions, my meetings are mixed successes at best. Since I could be in meetings twenty-four hours a day every day of the year, I have definite ideas about who attends, how much time to allocate, and what points will be discussed.

As a result, my meetings are never long enough. I squeeze the meeting to satisfy my agenda, but then we get into a productive discussion about one point and there are twelve other points to go over and people are picking up their notes to make their other appointments.

Behavioral scientists divide the human dynamics of a meeting into four stages, which they cutely call forming, storming, norming, and performing.

In the first, attendees assess the group and assume their desired role. In the second, they argue about their goals. In the third, they agree on how to behave. Finally, they get down to business. I realize now that you need a lot of time for these dynamics to play out and pay out.

Keeping this in mind, the perfect meeting might be structured this way: I'd have our four or five top executives in a room, where each executive had a phone in the corner and in the middle there would be a big table. The meeting would be fairly open-ended in length, perhaps a week. Most of the time we would be talking at the table. But people could freely go to the phone and make their necessary calls, while the rest of us continue the discussion. I have a hunch that as we tackle the important issues, we would turn up numerous possibilities in the unimportant details too.

Actually, I've noticed that the best meetings are the ones that people fall into without an invitation. They happen in small groups of three or four in hallways or by the watercooler or as you're heading out the door.

Perhaps the perfect meeting is the one you never have to call.

Who's Who at Your Meetings

I've read that the President of the United States has a fairly complete seating chart of the reporters attending his press conferences and, more important, has been briefed on their quirks, interests, and the kind of questions each is likely to ask.

I often wish I had a seating chart and briefing before

meetings. No matter how closely you follow the standard rules for a successful meeting—be prompt, have a firm agenda, set a time limit, don't call it a "committee," invite some new faces, etc.—if you aren't well briefed about the cast of characters in attendance, you'll never know why your meetings take so long to go nowhere.

Some of the personalities (not all of them bad) to keep an eye on at internal meetings include:

The straight shooters. These are the people who are always honest in their opinions. They have no guile, no hidden agenda. They are valuable at any meeting. But you have to protect them. They tend to get smug about "truth being the best defense" and may create more arguments than they solve.

The martyrs. They're good at taking the heat and quickly accepting responsibility when things go wrong. The danger here is that they accept blame too quickly, perhaps before you've pinned down who or what is really at fault.

The poker faces. They keep their ideas to themselves. Or maybe they share them with the boss in private after everyone is gone. Whether their suggestions are on target or not, you have to wonder what game and on whose team they're playing.

The cheerleaders. They have learned the wonderful power of saying, "You're right. I never considered that." I like these people.

The orators. They begin speaking softly, gather momentum, and fifteen minutes later are still assaulting your ears and insulting your intelligence. They substitute emotion and rhetoric for insight. You get the impression they work harder to convince themselves than you. Handle them with care—or not at all.

The devil's advocates. Everything to them is debatable. The good news is that, like a tenacious prosecutor, they often get to the truth. The bad news is they take too much time and too many casualties. Invite only one per meeting.

The destroyers. They can't say no without destroying someone's idea, project, or ego.

The recliners. They lean back, prop up their feet, and hunker down for a nice long stay. They're in no hurry to settle the issues at hand. Meet them in a hallway or a room with no chairs.

The statesmen. They advance themselves or the meeting through shrewd handling of people. Theoretically, this should be you.

Taking Your Hidden Agenda Out of Hiding

Given the choice, I prefer a flexible rather than a fixed agenda in meetings.

Of course, I provide a broad outline of why everyone is there and what subjects will be put on the table. To do anything less would be manipulative and counterproductive. But as for specifically spelling out every item under discussion *in the order it is to be discussed,* that's one secret I prefer to keep to myself.

Not only have I found that a super-firm agenda tends to straitjacket candor and creativity, but I'm convinced that the sequence in which you discuss topics at a meeting can determine how well the discussion goes. The best meetings develop from how carefully you read people, not how carefully you write out the agenda.

I noticed this once in a meeting with an important executive (whom we'll call Mr. Jones) and a few members of his staff. There were two items on the agenda as far as I was concerned. Item A would be a relatively brief discussion in which I would be announcing that we had decided not to go ahead with a project near and dear to Mr. Jones. Item B would be a lengthy, open-ended discussion where I expected—and needed—considerable input from Mr. Jones.

Now, the logical impulse would be to start off with Item A, since it could be disposed of in a minute, and then settle down for the remaining time with the meaty issues of Item B. But such a sequence would have been disastrous. For one thing, I had a hunch that Mr. Jones would take the "no-go" on Item A hard. I also knew that he doesn't "compartmentalize" well; he lets his emotions spill over from one situation to the next and tends to shut down after a disappointment. The last thing I wanted was him to be sullen and noncontributory during the discussion of Item B.

So I kicked off the meeting with Item B and got the full benefit of Mr. Jones's expertise. (Mr. Jones, I'm happy to report, also took the bad news on Item A much better than I expected.)

Cynics might say that I do all this because I always have a hidden agenda, which I can spring on people in order to dominate them. But this completely misses the point. Frankly, I think everyone—even the most open and guileless among us—has a hidden agenda. But not enough people know how and when to take their hidden agenda out of hiding.

What Small Companies Can Learn from Giant Corporations

I run a relatively small company. We have thirty-seven offices around the world that generate nearly a billion dollars in revenues, but we have fewer than 800 employees. In the larger scheme of things, that makes us small. I know vice presidents who are responsible for ten times that many employees.

It's tempting for the heads of small, rapidly growing companies to be a little too proud of their diminutive size. They boast about being small but agile, disciplined but unstructured, well directed but free spirited. They make a fetish about being unlike giant corporations. They scorn the stifling, rigid policies that bigness seems to demand from big companies.

But as I've gotten older, I've realized that some big corporate policies are not all that bad. With their huge workforces, large corporations are very adept at handling personnel problems. I have found their ideas particularly useful in the areas of (1) salary structures, (2) bonuses, and (3) performance appraisal:

1. Salary structures

In our early years, we tended to give everyone annual raises as part of our company philosophy. In bad years we gave small raises, in good years big raises. The problem with this loose compensation structure is that after a while you have a lot of well-paid employees who (1) if they were run over by a truck could be replaced for half the money or (2) are quite mediocre and never should have been given raises in the first place but came along in the tide of good fortune.

This kind of chaos usually occurs in rapid-growth businesses where the chief executive no longer hires everyone personally. Here's where a compensation structure modeled on a large corporation can help.

Many large companies structure their salary levels into numbered categories, with a maximum/minimum salary level in each category. A "deputy assistant manager" in category 4, for example, knows that to earn more money he must get to "assistant manager" in category 5. He won't get a raise by chatting with his boss; he has to go through channels.

I've always hated this sort of bureaucracy. It reminds me of the federal government. But I've learned to be flexible.

Over the years our company's compensation structure has evolved into the shape of an hourglass. First, we hire people at a discount—often for a fraction of what they could earn in more conventional jobs. (Fortunately, we can do this because of the kind of company we are.) Once these people have proved themselves, usually within six months, we flow them to the center of the hourglass where their compensation matches what their peers are earning at other companies straight out of university.

Then comes the hard part. For these people to force themselves through the narrow part of the hourglass and come out on the high side of the compensation scale, they have to really perform. Otherwise they remain in the middle.

In the long run, I think, this system rewards employees as much as it does the company.

2. Supplemental compensation

Big corporations are particularly adept at spreading out executive compensation. From them I have learned how to space out payments over several years so a financial windfall—or disaster—doesn't drastically alter an executive's annual compensation.

I know a top executive at one of America's largest corporations who has received a $1 million bonus in a good year and absolutely nothing in tough times the next year. But fortunately for that executive, the corporation spreads out payment of that $1 million over five years so he doesn't have undulating valleys in his cash flow or life-style. There are tax benefits to this as well.

You can never cut an employee's salary, unless you're about to close down the office. So you must construct a compensation package that's flexible. As an executive gets more senior, I've learned that you have to increase the flexible part of the package. We call it supplemental compensation, others call it a bonus.

Unlike salaries, you can always cut supplemental compensation. People understand that supplemental compensation is linked to the company's and their performance. Thus, as an executive rises in our company, his compensation mix becomes higher in supplemental compensation and lower in salary. For example, if he or she is making $50,000 a year, $40,000 is salary and $10,000 is supplemental; $200,000 splits evenly into $100,000 salary, $100,000 supplemental; $300,000 is $125,000 salary, $175,000 supplemental.

As owner of a business, I like this concept of spaced-out payments and bonuses escalating faster than salaries. Not only does it add a little stability to my executives and prevent them from thinking they are richer than they are, but I can plow some of the delayed payments back into the business and perhaps guarantee everyone bigger bonuses in the future.

3. Performance appraisal

I have always been skeptical of personnel files in big corporations. An employee's file sits in a drawer to be pulled once a year so that Joe Smith's boss can ask him what he thinks he's doing right and what he's doing wrong. After this, Joe's boss usually tells him what he's doing right, what he's doing wrong, where he can improve, and what he should do over the next 12 months to look good the next time the file is pulled. An agreement then goes back in the file, often after both Joe and his boss have signed it.

That is a highly structured technique that most big companies use to control unwieldy payrolls.

With the executives reporting directly to me, I get along fine on salary, company objectives, personal goals, etc. They know going into a year where they stand and what's expected of them, and I'm always there to remind them.

Unfortunately, I've learned these executives are not doing the same thing with the 15 people reporting to each of them. Many of their people—good, medium, and bad—leave their performance reviews disappointed because no one has been telling them along the line what's expected of them, what they have to achieve. This doesn't necessarily mean just increasing profits. It could mean retaining a client, making a client like you, changing your work habits, or filing reports on time. The problem is that these uninformed employees get surprised at salary time—and irritated. (Employees, I have found, prefer all salary surprises to be on the upside.)

So we're becoming more like the big companies, using clearly stated objective standards and telling people how they're doing throughout the year.

Controlling Expenses: How One Dollar Misspent Can Cost You Two

As a manager I spend a good deal of my time worrying about how to contain costs. In the back of my mind, a one-dollar expenditure represents two dollars. That is, every dollar misspent is actually costing me another dollar that could have been well spent in another part of our company. This downside logic hasn't necessarily made me miserly, but it has made me cautious and very diligent about expenses.

"Nice to have" or "must have"?

I like to divide purchases into "nice to have" and "must have." For example, it might be nice to have eight more computers in our London office—and when we're in a growth mode, it's easy to say, "Let's buy them." But "nice to have" purchases have a pernicious way of turning into "musts" in everyone's mind—and they're not so nice when the company moves out of its growth mode. It also leads to the "me too" syndrome.

The "me too" syndrome

You see this in office decoration. A senior executive says he needs a couch ($2,000), a coffee table ($1,000), an easy chair ($1,000), and two lamps ($1,000). You approve. But this $5,000 expense can turn into a $100,000 nightmare. Suddenly, nine of his peers in different parts of the world announce that they too need a couch, table, easy chair, and lamps. And then the people one level below start making rumbling noises, on the theory that they don't need a couch but they ought to have a couple of chairs. And so on down the line.

Before long, a busy manager has to waste time putting out brush fires of ego and pride throughout the company— or paying dearly for them.

The back-end costs

"Back-end" spending is more dangerous than the ripple effect. You see it nowadays in computer purchases: on the front end, you have large but finite and controllable expenditures for a start-up computer system; but on the back end, you lose control paying for extras such as laser printers, modems, memory upgrades, etc.

I'm no expert on computers, but I sometimes feel like one after listening to the tribulations of a friend who owns a small business. He needed twenty desktop computers. To get the right models and best vendors, stay within budget, and get all employees in agreement, he formed a Computer Acquisition committee. The committee worked hard for four months to arrive at a consensus.

The day the personal computers arrived may have been the single most exciting day in the company's history.

Then all hell broke loose.

The staff loved the PCs. They were seduced by the technology and loved "improving" the equipment. Three people traded in their monochrome monitors for full-color screens (at $350 apiece). Two secretaries ordered laser printers (at $3,000 apiece). One manager bought a $500 shroud to muffle his noisy $400 printer. The accounting department needed a faster computer ($3,500) and customized software ($1,500). Within twelve months my friend had spent more on what he calls "support appliances" than on the system itself.

He now chairs the Computer Policy Control committee and signs off on every purchase.

Management by Phoning Around

One of the most popular business practices of the 1980s is "management by wandering around." This is where chief executives come out of their ivory tower and rediscover their employees. They do this by taking meals in the cafeteria, milling about the watercooler at midday, and regularly visiting the shop floor.

This is a good idea if (1) you don't wander around so much that you neglect your real job (a popular executive diary that actually schedules a daily session of MBWA, I think, is going too far) and (2) you talk to the right people.

A wise friend advised me a few years ago to get to know the people two levels down from me. "That's where your future is going to be," he said. I see his point. I already know what my top executives and their like-minded lieutenants think. But people one level below that, with their narrow but no less sincere opinions and prejudices, often surprise me. They're the ones who follow through on top management's promises and, in effect, maintain a company's standards. Talking to them, I can't think of a better way to learn the kind of face my company presents to the outside world. I can see firsthand how alert, courteous, responsive, and caring our people are to clients and customers.

Phone, don't walk

Given the choice, however, I prefer "management by phoning around." I learn just as much letting my fingers do the walking and, with executives in more than a dozen countries, it is infinitely more practical. I try to stay in daily telephone contact with many people, and I prefer short calls, rarely exceeding five minutes.

As a result, I rack up large phone bills but I reduce my toll of costly mistakes and missed opportunities.

I schedule phone calls to my executives as firmly as I do an important meeting. This helps me master my time while respecting theirs. It also makes the other person on the line very alert. Letting an employee know that I'll be calling for five minutes at 11:20 A.M. to discuss a particular project has a funny way of turning even the most rambling executive into a model of precision and brevity.

Great opener: "What's new?"

Quite often I will schedule eight phone calls in a row within a half hour. And I'll open each conversation with the same two words: "What's new?" What follows is usually a well-organized account of projects that executive is developing or pursuing or finishing up. Any subject he or she glosses over or neglects to mention usually pinpoints where both of us should be concentrating more of our time.

The phone is for getting and imparting information, not playing power games. I don't lose sleep wondering who called first or why someone won't take my calls. But the phone has a subliminal power that too many bosses overlook. The well-timed call can be a great management tool, forcing people to act, to get answers they've been avoiding, or simply to learn that they are not forgotten.

Most of my calls, for example, cross several time zones. I will place a New York-to-London call at 9:30 A.M. London time because it is most convenient for my executives and me. But I am not unaware that they might be impressed (and motivated) by the fact that I'm calling at 4:30 A.M. in my time zone. For them to know that I'm up and thinking about them and that our discussion is important is good.

I also place frequent calls to my executives because, frankly, I sometimes think I am better at organizing their time than they are.

The Hidden Costs of Profit Centers

When we were a young company, I was skeptical of budgets. I could see how, in a vague way, they let us control spending during a fiscal year. But I always thought budgets were slightly self-fulfilling—people would spend their limit even if it was unnecessary or imprudent. Conversely, I also thought budgets were self-limiting: how, in a dynamic industry, can you presume to accurately forecast your budget needs twelve months down the road? And what do you do if you're wrong?

For example, say we have a golf division consisting of one group head, an assistant, two accountants, and two secretaries. My experts tell me the division must have a budget. The group head, they argue, has to be in control of his people's salaries and travel and entertainment expenses. But, I wonder, what good does it do? What if by December the group head has spent his travel budget, but for $3,000 he could fly to Australia and sign up a top client. Am I going to say, "Don't go"?

I've been persuaded to institute budgets and profit centers in our organization, but I am not totally convinced. Profit centers are a two-edged sword to me. They certainly can tell a manager more or less how his or her group is doing and tell us at central management kind of how the various groups are doing. But they also create internal rivalries and jealousies. Group heads bicker about how much of "their" money is being charged to overhead or the legal department and why they should have to pay for a computer they didn't ask for. I spend so much time in that sort of dialogue that I wonder if profit centers, as a management tool, are worth it.

I also wonder who profit centers are supposed to benefit. When a big deal is in the works, rather than having two senior executives in agreement saying "Let's get this contract for the company," I find them more likely to say, "I want it for my profit center." Ultimately, they will start feuding over this, and the company always loses from this fight.

Flexing Your Humility, Not Your Ego

One of the most successful woman executives I know has all the earmarks of a champion CEO. She works hard. She is bright and creative. She uses her time well. She's ambitious and has a healthy ego. But having watched her over the years, I think her greatest virtue is her ability to stifle her ego for the sake of others, especially her employees.

As one person who has worked with her recently told me, "No matter who you are, when you're in the room with her, she acts as if you're the only person who matters. She makes you feel like her equal. She defers to you, cares about your opinions, gives you time to present your views. If there are other people present, even if you are a secretary or minor flunkie, she treats you like the chairman of the board."

That sort of talent can make up for a lot of other failings and speaks volumes about why she's so successful.

CEOs generally are not known for subsuming their egos. But I think that's unfair to CEOs. The best of them are a lot more adroit at flexing their humility than their subordinates suspect. You see this among CEOs who bring subordinates to important meetings or business lunches. The CEO doesn't have to do this, but the fact that he does adds immeasurably to the subordinate's standing.

I was recently in a meeting with a CEO and one of his vice presidents. I couldn't help noticing how carefully the CEO avoided taking credit for deals that I know he had personally done. Instead, he shared the credit with his associate, in some cases crediting him for successes to which I suspect he had contributed little if anything.

This sort of calculated humility isn't that big a deal (except perhaps to your employees) and doesn't usually call attention to itself. But it's one of the most effective tools at a manager's disposal, for three reasons:

1. It makes your employees feel good

There's nothing better for building morale than acknowledging that you value a colleague's contributions. It's even more effective when you go public with that praise. Great quarterbacks who tell TV interviewers, "I owe it all to the blocking of the offensive line," have known this for years.

2. It increases an employee's stature with outsiders

The CEO above could have described his company's successes in several ways.

If he had said, "I negotiated the leases on Project X," that would be a 3 on a scale of 1 to 10—because it's factually true.

If he had said, "We negotiated the leases," that's a 6 or 7

because it lets some of the glory rub off on his subordinate (although an outsider can't tell how much).

But, in fact, he said, "Joe and his group negotiated those leases." In my mind that's a 10, because the CEO has intentionally (and selflessly) tried to make his associate look more impressive to everyone in the room. And that, in the long run, does more for the CEO and his company than any momentary display of ego.

3. It makes you look better

Sharing the credit is not a zero-sum game, where there are a limited number of points that you must score at someone else's expense. In the ego game, you don't lose points just because you award them to someone else. In fact, you usually gain.

Besides, most people aren't fooled or impressed by a CEO who claims to do everything. After a while the monologue becomes tiresome—and even your own employees tune out. The next time you find yourself beginning all your sentences with "I," just change the pronoun to "we" and watch how everyone in the room snaps to attention.

What the Boss Brings to the Party (or How to Be a More Perfect Leader)

Most people think being the boss is a matter of *power*. The boss has it, the bossed don't. The boss gives the orders, the bossed obey.

I don't agree. To me, being the boss is more a question of *adding value* rather than exercising power. The most effective bosses are masters of restraining their power rather than abusing it. They don't regard every decision as another test of whether people jump when they wiggle their finger. They realize there's a difference between being the boss and being bossy.

The most effective bosses constantly ask themselves, "What am I, as the boss, bringing to the party? How does my presence contribute to the situation and add the most value to the organization?" If they sense that they are more valuable removing themselves from rather than injecting themselves into a situation, the best bosses can walk away.

Here are eight duties that may be more vital to your becoming an effective boss than how well you give orders to the troops.

1. Staying in touch with your expertise

Quite often, the boss simply has superior technical knowledge. He knows how to do things better than anyone else. The founder of a computer company is still a wizard in product development. The chairman of a giant record company still has the keenest ear for musical talent. An advertising agency CEO remains the best copywriter in the shop.

To "Peter Principle" yourself out of this expertise—that is, to abandon it for more bosslike duties—is a great disservice to your company.

I suspect Dr. Edwin Land, the founder and guiding genius behind Polaroid, realized early on that he could contribute more to Polaroid by staying in the laboratory and inventing great products than by worrying about administrative details or what Wall Street thought of him.

2. Eliminating duplication

Some organizations are so far-flung and decentralized that the boss is often the only person who knows what everyone else is doing. Functioning as the nerve center for subordinates is a crucial responsibility—and frequently a thankless one.

There have been times in our organization when I could see that two executives were on a collision course working on identical projects. I could foresee that ultimately they would realize this, exert their territorial rights, and come to me to resolve their dispute—at which point I would be expected to side with one over the other.

This sort of duplication of effort goes on all the time in companies. It's up to you as the boss to catch it early and resolve it as painlessly as possible so that neither party feels like a loser. You must be diplomatic rather than authoritarian. This may make you appear indecisive to both sides, but that's a small sacrifice for the good of the company.

3. Instruction

It's difficult for many bosses to give up the ego gratification of doing a job themselves. But a good manager ultimately derives even more satisfaction from instructing others and seeing them do a better job.

The worst thing you can say as a boss is: "It would take me five hours to explain this to a subordinate and five minutes to do it myself." And then use that as an excuse to do it yourself.

What this misses, of course, is that five hours of instruction now could save you hundreds of hours later, thus freeing you up for more important tasks and greater responsibilities.

Earn a reputation for training your people well and you'll not only make more productive use of your time but you'll end up with the most productive people. The star performers will gravitate toward you.

4. Leading by example

This may be the most important point of all. You can't demand from your employees anything that you aren't demanding from yourself.

I genuinely believe that a big reason for our company's growth is that our people know I work as hard as they do. I'm up as early as they are (if not earlier). I work as late as they do (if not later). And I'm as interested in all aspects of their business as they are (if not more so). In a healthy way, they are emulating and almost competing with me.

But role modeling goes beyond how many hours you put in. It's also a matter of work habits and style. You can't ask someone to be punctual or precise or courteous to a customer if you don't do so yourself.

Stanley Marcus, of the Neiman-Marcus stores, hit upon the essence of role modeling in a story about a small retailer in Oklahoma City who was selling huge quantities of $350 handknit sweaters while other stores in bigger cities couldn't sell any.

"What happened," Marcus told *Inc.* magazine, "is that this merchant liked these sweaters, he believed in them, bought them, and then got his salespeople together. And he said, 'This is the hottest thing that I saw on the market, and I believe our customers are going to like them. Be sure you show them, because they're not going to walk off the shelf and twist a customer's arm. You have to sell them.'

"The next day he was on the floor and saw one of his top salespeople waiting on Mrs. Porter and not showing her the sweater. And he went up to Mrs. Porter, presented the sweater, and Mrs. Porter decided to buy it. All of a sudden, the salesperson became a convert.

"That's what selling and sales training is all about—it's the only way I've ever seen it work."

5. Clear objectives

It's amazing to me how many otherwise competent executives are failures at telling their subordinates how they're doing and what's expected of them.

Simply put, a boss has a duty to tell his people (a) what a good job is and (b) whether they're measuring up. Getting this information clearly and regularly is an inalienable right of an employee.

As far as I'm concerned, if an employee thinks he's doing a great job and his boss thinks otherwise, and the scene ends badly, then the boss is to blame.

6. Praise and recognition

Praise and recognition occur in two situations: when the employee is present and when he or she is absent. The most effective bosses realize that it's essential to get both right.

A good boss doesn't take sole credit for a success if his entire group deserves it, nor does he attribute credit to the group if it rightfully should go to one individual.

A good boss also lets it be known to employees that he's saying the same nice things about them to others in public as he's telling them in private. You cannot underestimate how much employees worry about this.

7. Error avoidance

Bosses generally get to be bosses because they learn from experience and they don't repeat mistakes. They're paid to anticipate errors—and avoid them.

One of the worst things a boss can do is discount the value of his experience or assume that employees are as experienced (or jaded) as he is.

You see this in bosses who claim to have "seen it all before" and use this as an excuse to ignore or dismiss their employees' problems.

I'm constantly fighting this impulse. After 25 years in business, there are many client situations, negotiating snags, and administrative problems that, indeed, I have seen before. But the fact that a problem is familiar to me doesn't diminish its seriousness, especially among younger executives who have never faced it before.

One of the unsung virtues of a good boss is that he can impart the same attention and urgency to familiar problems as he does to the more immediate newer ones. When an employee seeks advice on a problem, a good boss may think, "Gee, I dealt with that 15 years ago. It's not that big a deal." But he never says it.

8. Ruthless streak

Obviously, there's a "tough guy" aspect to being the boss. Everyone faces moments when they must reprimand, re-motivate, or remove employees in the best interests of the company.

I don't know anyone who really enjoys these moments, but they're certainly less painful if you realize that no two employees respond to the same approach.

Some people respond to anger and threats. They need that jolt to get moving.

Some people require methodical rationality; they have to see the step-by-step logic behind your displeasure before they'll accept it.

Some people respond to humor or sarcasm. Some respond to constant nagging, while others hear your message instantly and then want to be left alone. There are even people who respond to wagers ("I'll bet you that you can't do that . . ."). Whatever method works, a good boss will find it.

4 | Getting Ahead

My Shortcomings

I f you've ever applied for a job, you've probably heard the interviewer say, "Now that you've told me all your good points, why don't you tell me your three biggest faults?"

This is a classic trick question. It's so familiar, in fact, that even marginally clever applicants have a trick answer for it.

"First," they say, "I probably work too hard. Second, I get very impatient when people mess up on the little details. Third, I take my job too seriously and can't tolerate people who don't."

Obviously, these hard-charging applicants are twisting their flaws into assets—and hope the interviewer either won't notice or will agree.

But I think there's something to be gained by being a little more honest about your shortcomings. If nothing else, you'll know where there's room for improvement.

Here are my shortcomings, the ones that worry me and have cost me in the past. (Believe me, I'm not boasting.)

---

1. I'm too time sensitive. If anything, I'm overorganized. I try to do too much and get frustrated or mad when I sense myself running behind.

2. I ruthlessly separate my personal life from my business life. This makes me appear impersonal and uninterested in human details that don't impact on my business.

3. I'm not detail-oriented. Given the choice, I prefer to oversimplify things rather than overcomplicate them. If I want to accomplish something major, I'll broadbrush any problems that could delay or destroy the deal. I'll get the deal done, recognize the side issues, and hope I have the weapons to resolve them when the time comes.

This has spared me from getting lost in the alleyways of irrelevant detail. But no doubt I miss a lot of opportunities and tend to get misunderstood more than I deserve.

4. I ask for too much money. Ordinarily I'd consider this a big plus. But it has probably scared away many people I should be doing business with.

5. I have no willpower around food. If it's in front of me, I'll eat it. And then I worry.

Now that you know my shortcomings, take a look at yours. Can you honestly pinpoint the weak spots in your personality, your attitudes, and your behavior? And do you realize how they are limiting your performance and holding back your career?

As you read the advice that follows in the various sections that make up this chapter, keep in mind that the chapter has a dual purpose. The first few sections intentionally pose tough questions in order to shed light on your blind spots and to help you identify where the likely problems are. The remaining sections provide some likely solutions.

Where Are You Now, and Where Are You Going?

It is a popular notion today that, like Shakespeare's "seven ages of man," there's a life cycle of the businessman.

In your twenties you learn the ropes and develop the work habits, friends, and contacts that, for better or worse, you'll probably keep for life.

In your thirties you assert yourself in what you now think of as a "career." You also become acutely aware of how you stack up against your peers.

In your forties, you shift into overdrive. You are giving orders instead of taking them. You are making decisions rather than preparing reports for other decision makers. Promotions don't come as fast, but when they do they mean more.

In your fifties, your career track is established though not necessarily finished. You consolidate your skills and play off your achievements. You accomplish more in less time and, as a result, earn more. People pay you for what you have done in the hope that you will do the same for them.

In your sixties, you either retire or continue as the gray eminence. Which it is depends on how well you did in the decade before.

If there is a make-or-break point in this cozy scenario, it probably occurs between your late thirties and early forties—when you're too old to be the boy (or girl) wonder but too young to assume the role of CEO.

There are many reasons why people run into trouble in this natural transition period, but two stand out in my mind. The first has to do with how you assess yourself, the second with how you reassess your business relationships.

1. What makes you special?

At any point in a career, but particularly in your mid-thirties when you are just a face in the middle-management crowd, you have to ask yourself what makes you special. What talent sets you apart? Answer that honestly, act on it, but don't let it confuse you.

I've often had discussions with people who have risen in their organization because of a special expertise—say, as a tax accountant. Around age thirty-five they begin to regard that narrow focus as a career liability that will confine them forever to a desk and calculator. Instead of congratulating themselves on how far they've come, they fear they have no place left to go.

It's ironic that they save their greatest envy for the people on the corporate fast track who are perceived as having unlimited choices. These are the people who move from division to division, developing a broad range of talents but never mastering a specific triumph or sticking around long enough to score a corporate triumph they can call their own. They have unlimited possibilities, but this may be the greatest liability of all. Around age forty they look around and see a glut of generalists just like them. Unfortunately, most companies have room for only one or two "generalists." And they're usually called chairman or president.

2. Who are your friends, and where are they going?

One of the nice things about having friends in business is that they grow with you—and vice versa. Yet it puzzles me how often people fail to realize this and use it to their advantage.

This is a common problem in sales and marketing organizations, particularly small entrepreneurial outfits where much of the business grows out of personal relationships developed by the founder.

I noticed this several years ago when a friend described his company to me. He was forty at the time, building up a young, energetic organization where the executives were, on balance, ten years younger than he was. He was constantly urging his people to develop contacts of their own.

They would complain to him, with some merit, that it was easy for him at forty, with his title and experience, to cultivate relationships with CEOs and division heads, but they were too young to do the same.

Now that his people are in their late thirties and early forties, many of them are still missing out on opportunities. They still don't appreciate that the friends they started out with have acquired clout, that their roommate in college is a decision maker. Their focus on relationships hasn't varied or expanded as they've gotten older. They continue to entertain their original business friends, not realizing that it's overkill, that one less lunch each month doesn't mean they've lost a friend.

If you really want to know where you are and where you're going, look at your friends or clients. Who are they? Where are they going?

Finders, Minders, Binders: Which One Are You?

An executive in our organization believes successful businesspeople in any service organization fall into three categories. They are either Finders, Minders, or Binders.

Finders are the "rainmakers," the people who generate the income stream—either by creating new products and services or finding new clients. Minders are the caretakers, the corporate accountants and go-betweens who make sure the idea is executed properly and makes a profit. Binders are the coordinators. They make the first two types of people feel good. They're usually the boss.

At a company like Polaroid, where this executive once worked, the finder would be the inventor of a new film, the minder would be the advertising manager in charge of letting the world know about it, and the binder would be the vice president of marketing who keeps them seeing eye to eye.

Perhaps these distinctions are contrived, but there's wisdom here—especially if you see yourself in any category.

Employees who are 100 percent finders can go very far and very fast in any organization. People who are 100 percent minders can go far too, but they take a slower route. The binders are usually blessed with a lot of the other two qualities; that's one reason the finders and minders trust them.

A final point: people who have a little of each don't go far.

Positioning Yourself Like a Pro

If you were a product, how would you position yourself?

Would you be up-market or down?

Would you be high-priced or low?

Would you advertise yourself as the "best" or the "best alternative"?

The "fastest" or the "longest lasting"?

The "most convenient" or the "most exclusive"?

These are not idle questions. If you were introducing a new product or service, you could easily spend months and thousands of dollars trying to come up with some answers to insure success.

That's why it amazes me when genuinely smart people don't apply the same principles to an even more important product—themselves.

The more I deal with businesspeople at the top, the more I appreciate how personal marketing—and more important, positioning—helped them get there. The most successful people not only do the right thing at the right time (or even the wrong time), but they know how to turn it to their advantage.

Ask them about their success and they'll tell you they not

only worked hard and did a good job but they were always positioned to have someone recognize (and reward) them for it.

This sort of "career positioning" requires neither brilliance nor distasteful scheming, just a little honesty and objectivity about the following questions:

1. Is your packaging appropriate?

While I have always believed that the contents were more important than the packaging, that's meaningless if the desired consumer is turned off by the package. Positioning, after all, is less about the product than how the consumer perceives the product.

A top tennis player who was *not* our client once told me, "The reason I did not sign with you is that the fellow I met from your organization looked too much like me—a little too disheveled and too much on the run."

While that comment might impel me to institute a dress code, I'd much rather have our people reexamining who they're trying to impress with their appearance and why.

In the old days we had people in our tennis division coming to work in their jeans and Ellesse shirts, trying to look like tennis pros. Part of that was understandable since relating to tennis players was an important element of their job. But on another level, they failed to see that when a tennis player is hiring a business manager to handle his money, he is really looking for someone who carries a briefcase rather than a racket and reads *The Wall Street Journal* rather than the comics.

2. Have you found your niche?

Products that claim to be all things to all people never succeed. They are always vulnerable to competitive products that do less but do it better or cheaper and are not afraid to exploit that difference.

It's the same with people. The salesman who can sell anything is not in demand as much as the salesman who can sell one thing well.

No doubt, there are a few geniuses in business who can master any discipline—who can design a computer, build it, sell it, and write the brochure to describe it. But chances are you are not that genius.

Even if you are, other people will not accept you as such. In a society where we put a premium on expertise and specialization, people feel comfortable pigeonholing their colleagues.

Don't expect others to position you correctly if you can't do so yourself.

3. Is your position accurately presented?

One of our executives is very bright and quick. He can take a situation involving A, B, and C and, with alarming speed, turn it into a brilliantly conceived geometric equation.

But this facility for problem-solving that has proved so valuable within our company is often perceived as something else outside the company. It makes him appear too sharp and too clever.

He recently met with a national governing body of a particular sport, a conservative group devoted to tradition and very slow change. He listened to their problems. But when he started rattling off one of his patented equations, he not only caught them by surprise but lost them totally.

He had presented himself as a quick study without first positioning himself as a thoughtful one. I think they would have been much more responsive if he had held back and returned a few days later with the solution that had been on the tip of his tongue.

4. Are you making the right mistakes?

People are known as much by the quality of their failures as by the quantity of their successes. So if you're going to make mistakes (and believe me, you will), make sure they are smart rather than dumb ones.

"Dumb errors" tend to be sins of omission—where you are expected to do something and, either through incompetence or forgetfulness, don't.

"Smart errors" tend to be sins of commission—for example, as your company's chief financial officer, you decide the dollar will go down, act accordingly, and then it doesn't. If you've done your homework, your career (like the dollar) will recover.

John Reed of Citicorp, the nation's largest bank, is a case in point. Some years ago, Reed was best known at Citicorp as the vice president who lost $175 million setting up the bank's credit card division. Reed's enormous error naturally caught the attention of his superiors. Big blunders always do.

But it also positioned him as a bold and decisive executive in their eyes. Reed's ability to handle that crisis and his division's eventual turnaround is a big reason he became chairman of Citicorp in 1984.

5. Do you have name recognition?

You don't want to be anonymous; that's bad positioning. But pushing your name so forcefully to the forefront so that people resent you is hardly an improvement.

The best way to avoid anonymity is to do such a good job that people want to talk about you. Great word of mouth is great positioning.

Conversely, the best way to avoid resentment is to use the pronouns *we, us,* and *ours* instead of *I, me,* and *mine*—even when *I, me,* and *mine* are more appropriate.

6. Are you riding the right horse?

Horse racing jockeys are quick to say that winning is 90 percent horse, 10 percent rider. This explains why the winningest (if not the best) jockeys tend to get the best mounts.

The same thing could be said of a business career. The most successful people tend to ride the best horses. In business, positioning yourself with the best horse can be anything from joining the right company to having a powerful boss to coming up with a unique idea.

Of all the positioning tools at your disposal, probably the best is having a great idea *that people associate with you*. This requires creativity and execution. Your idea will not remain yours unless you bring it to fruition over all the obstacles your organization and peers put in your way. This takes courage, but if you succeed your position will be unassailable.

The right company is the most overrated positioning tool. It's the one you can overcome most easily if it's not helping you (namely by joining another company) and it's the one that can really disappoint if you pin too much of your personal success on it.

Can You Be at One Company Too Long?

As an employer I've learned to live with the fact that you can't hold on to all your talented, young executives. No matter how well you train them or pay them, outside opportunities will lure some of them away. This is only natural. No organization can fulfill everyone's ambitions.

I once interviewed an executive in his early thirties who, of all things, felt guilty because he had been with the same company since college! During that time, he had watched many of his friends change companies every two or three years and, according to him, gain more money and responsibility with each move. He was wondering if his "stability" was a bad career move. Did it prove he was too safe, afraid of taking risks?

I couldn't help pointing out the irony of his situation. There are plenty of business decisions that you can feel guilty about, but being loyal to your employer isn't one of them.

In my experience, there are two equally valid paths to career advancement in corporations. In the first, you spiral your way to the top, jumping around from company to company. If you're quick, adept at making friends and leveraging what you learn at one company into a better position elsewhere, this path may be for you.

In the second, you grow within one company. This is hardly a life sentence to a desk. In fact, in large organizations with "fast tracks" for their promising executives, you may move among the divisions and regional offices more than you like. Whether you ascend the ladder gracefully or in violent fits and starts (there's no way to predict this), at least you're headed in the right direction.

Not enough people recognize the secret advantage to this cradle-to-grave approach: you succeed as much by *attrition* as by *achievement*. If you're good, there will come a point when you simply outlast your internal competition, when it's finally obvious to everyone that you're the right person for a top spot. There's nothing wrong with earning a promotion partly through patience. After all, companies no longer hand out senior titles simply because of seniority.

Whether you choose the first or second career path depends on personal preference. Ask yourself: are you looking for a house or a home?

Are You at Your Company's Core?

The more vital question you should be asking yourself is not "Have I been in one place too long?" but rather "Am I involved in the company's core business?" To get a senior position in the oil industry historically has meant you should be an engineer. In retailing, you probably should be making buying decisions. In a sales organization, you should be in sales, not accounting or customer relations.

Jeffrey Campbell, the former chief executive of Burger King, explained the turning point in his career as the moment he realized he was in the "restaurant" business.

It happened the day he was promoted to the number two marketing position and named an officer of the company. As he drove home in his new company car, Campbell realized the promotion was meaningless for his personal goals. He wanted to run the company, but he wasn't at the company's core. In his words, he was "only exposed to 15 percent of the pie." The core was in the restaurants, selling hamburgers to customers.

So Campbell gave up his title and ran a franchise for a year. He relearned the business from the bottom up. Within a year headquarters called him back to run the marketing division. Shortly thereafter, when Burger King's CEO accepted a job at another company, Campbell was tapped as his successor.

You may want to keep this in mind the next time you waver about your commitment to your job.

Incidentally, I don't buy the argument that people who move around a lot are somehow bigger risk takers. On the contrary, I sometimes think they are more "risk averse." They often jump ship just as their razzle-dazzle ideas are scheduled to pay off or fizzle out. They tend to leave a lot of unfinished business in their glorious wake.

Are You Resting Too Comfortably on Your Laurels?

Paul Austin, the late chairman of Coca-Cola, once told me, "The worst thing that can happen to a CEO is to *enjoy* his company's position in the marketplace—especially if it's the dominant position. Anytime you become content with where you are, that's like issuing a corporate decree to stand still."

I suspect something like this happened to the people who make Hershey bars. A man named Milton Hershey invented the chocolate bar in 1903. The bar was an instant success and the Hershey name virtually became a synonym for chocolate. Hershey products were so well-known, in fact, that for six decades the company took a smug, almost perverse pride in never having to advertise.

Only when American kids in the 1960s switched allegiance to competing brands such as Snickers and Three Musketeers did Hershey deign to advertise. Today, Hershey Foods Corporation is a big advertiser, a very sophisticated marketer, and incidentally, quite profitable. But I can't help thinking that those decades of self-satisfaction cost the company big chunks of market share and opened the door to many competitors.

This happened to me in the 1960s when we represented Arnold Palmer, Gary Player, and Jack Nicklaus. Frankly, we were small but really good. In terms of imagination, creativity, contacts, international scope, no one could touch us.

So I just sat back, thinking that any golfer with any potential would obviously *want* to come to us. Unfortunately, this wasn't obvious to other golfers. At the time I didn't appreciate the need to sell the company or even to go out and get to know the up-and-coming pros on a personal level.

A big reason for this attitude, I think, was that we had our hands full with Palmer, Player, and Nicklaus. Golf was exploding and we were the people lighting the fuse—literally making sales without selling. There were times would-be customers would race into my office and tell me they needed one of our clients to make an appearance and (being in a hurry myself) I'd say, "Fine, he'll be there. That'll be $15,000." Then I'd look at my watch to nudge my newest customer out the door.

This sort of thing catches up with you. Even though we had the best product, which we delivered professionally and efficiently, eventually people began resenting the lack of a personal touch. They didn't like the fact that I didn't seem to care about them. And when the time came for us to expand, we met some resistance at first.

It was humbling, but I learned that there's more to business success than getting the job done. Fortunately, we recognized this fairly quickly. And I think we've maintained our dominant position because we are genuinely more concerned about what we can do for our clients in the future than we are relaxed about all that we've accomplished in the past.

With hindsight, it's easy to see that a big corporation like Hershey erred in being too self-satisfied; the proof was right there on the bottom line, in slower growth and lost opportunities.

But the lost opportunities aren't as clear-cut in individual careers. People rest on their laurels and never notice that they're losing ground. I don't know how many times I've seen very talented people get short-changed on a promotion or new job because they rested on their laurels. They think that because they're doing a great job, it should be obvious to the people who control their future that they *deserve* success. This is the most dangerous type of complacency— because it leads to injustice.

I remember a few years ago when the No. 2 and No. 4 executives at a major corporation were jockeying for the No. 1 job. The No. 2 man had performed splendidly. Convinced he had earned the inside track to the presidency, he saw no need to campaign for it. He just continued working hard, assuming that his profit centers would speak for themselves.

Meanwhile, the No. 4 man, also an able executive, hired a publicist and a new tailor. He gave speeches, visited regional offices, courted individual board members, schmoozed with the chairman. A "presidential" halo gradually appeared above his head. Predictably, he won the job. As for the stunned No. 2, he resigned.

I am not sure that the No. 2 man did anything wrong (perhaps he didn't want the job enough to affect a new style). Nor am I advocating a world where everyone is a boasting self-promoter. But I'm convinced that, nine times out of ten, if you're resting on your laurels you probably should be building on them.

Are You Overestimating Your Strengths, or Ignoring Your Weaknesses?

I recently heard a middle-ranked American tennis pro compare the differences between playing in college and on the professional circuit. Unlike college, he said, where you can have decent skills and succeed simply by exploiting another player's weaknesses, on the pro tour strengths are more important than weaknesses.

There's something to that in tennis. A powerful serve—as Boris Becker, Kevin Curren, and Roscoe Tanner have proven—can compensate for many deficiencies in other parts of your game.

The same is true in business. The most successful executives get that way by identifying their one or two greatest assets and exploiting them fully rather than worrying about how they can correct their weaknesses.

Unfortunately, the subject of strengths and weaknesses is one area where people are most likely to delude themselves. People tend to overestimate their strengths and to underestimate the negative impact of their weaknesses.

I see this in myself on the tennis court. My wife, Betsy Nagelsen, who is a champion professional tennis player, chides me for thinking I'm a better player than I really am. She once said to me, "You actually think you're fast on the tennis court!" She was right. In my mind, I am fleet of foot, even though in reality I'm horribly slow.

Now, this self-deception is fairly harmless in recreational

tennis. But in business it can have serious career consequences.

Masters of self-deception

I know a sports entrepreneur who is an incredible stand-up salesman. He can fill any room with his charming presence and make people part with their money. This is his one strength; he has no others. He is not good at organization or handling money or motivating people, and he is disastrous on details and follow-up.

He is the type of person who should be a company's star sales executive, not an entrepreneur managing his own business.

And yet, he is a master of self-deception. In the last decade he has started up and lost several companies, because he thinks he is a much better manager than he really is.

In one final irony, he compounds the error by taking his extraordinary selling skills for granted. Because selling is so easy for him, he thinks everybody can do it well—and thus, he stays in the office to manage the business while his other executives are out selling. In effect, no one in the company is operating from strength.

I'm not sure there's any quick cure for what ails this fellow, but I do know this: In tennis or in business, you have a much better chance of success if you concentrate on improving your strengths rather than worrying too much about turning your weaknesses into strengths.

When Bjorn Borg started winning major tennis championships, it was clear that he had several strengths. On a scale of 0 to 10, his ground strokes, foot speed, and concentration were 10s. His serve was weak, and he worked to eliminate it as a liability in his game. I think Bjorn was sufficiently smart and disciplined to know that his serve would never become the dominant element in his game. It would have been futile and counterproductive for him to try; the rest of his game might have suffered.

But Bjorn did improve this weakness to the point where it didn't hurt him. Businesspeople who can face up to their strengths and weaknesses should do the same.

For example, if you are brilliant with numbers but have a personality that falls somewhere between wooden and obnoxious, there's no point in overexerting yourself to become Mr. Personality. But you can try to minimize the damage. On a 0-to-10 scale, you can certainly go from 0 to 5 in being less obnoxious (which is easier to do) and devote the rest of your energies to becoming a 10 with the numbers.

So, You Think You're Not Creative?

Over the years I've heard a lot of theories and myths about creative people. Creative people are flamboyant and funny. They're mercurial and temperamental. They thrive in chaos. They bristle at interference. They disdain other people's suggestions. They talk a lot and wander the hallways bouncing ideas off anyone who'll listen.

It's tempting to take much of this to heart because the profile, to some people, is romantic or appealing. Unfortunately, it has little to do with creative businesspeople in the real world.

The truly creative executives I've met are just as likely to be composed, buttoned-down types. They're well organized and disciplined and, in turn, more productive. They don't hoard ideas. They encourage, even demand, outside suggestions. They're team players because that's the best way to get their ideas to market. They're silent because they actually listen.

Obviously, it's dangerous to generalize about what makes a person creative. And there is nothing to be gained by dwelling on the "package" creative people come in.

The biggest myth about creativity, in my opinion, is that it is the exclusive property of an anointed few. Almost anyone can be creative—if they're smart enough to apprentice themselves to someone who already is.

Robin Cook, a surgeon by training, claims he learned to write novels by reading 100 best sellers and figuring out what they had in common. Then he started churning out best sellers like *Coma, Brain,* and *Sphinx.*

I doubt if this would work for writing the next *Hamlet* or *War and Peace.* But 90 percent of the creative ideas in business don't require the "genius" of a Shakespeare or Tolstoy or, for that matter, a Thomas Edison or Henry Ford. Ideas come from reading your customers and prospects and, like Robin Cook, figuring out what they have in common.

Ever notice how the best ideas come from people who (a) say they've "sort of seen this problem before" and (b) manage to fine-tune their solution a few degrees so it works again? Creativity in business is often nothing more than making connections that everyone else has almost thought of. You don't have to reinvent the wheel, just attach it to a new wagon.

In our business, for example, the fundamentals of representing and managing athletes haven't changed in twenty-five years. Our "creativity" was to take the techniques that worked with Palmer, Nicklaus, and Player in golf and then apply them to sports such as skiing, motor racing, tennis, running, and more recently to nonsports such as classical music, publishing, and broadcasting. Much of this wasn't achieved personally by me but by creative executives in our organization who followed, and happily improved on, my example.

Sometimes the most creative aspect of an idea is not how much it's different but how much it's the same.

Get Mad, Get Even, or Get Better: Which Would You Do?

Few setbacks in a business career are more painful than getting passed over for a promotion. In such situations it's tempting and understandable to follow John F. Kennedy's rule: "Don't get mad. Get even."

While this may be effective in electoral politics and cathartic in personal affairs, it's usually self-destructive in business. In my experience the people who keep trading an "eye for an eye" eventually lose sight of what's really important in their lives.

I learned a sure-fire alternative to getting mad or getting even several years ago from a friend. He had become obsessed with getting an equity stake in a medium-size family-owned retail chain where he was a senior vice-president. Though I didn't fully endorse his desire for equity (I think a minority position in a privately held company is a 24-hour ego trip that you can't sell or use as collateral), the idea had clearly taken on a life of its own in his mind. He didn't want much, just a few percentage points. "Being an owner rather than an employee," he said, "is very important to me."

He approached the three brothers who owned the company and they agreed to let him buy a 5 percent stake. At the last minute, however, the brothers balked. They gave no specific reason. To make up for this setback and to show that they desperately wanted to keep my friend happy, the owners doubled his salary and bought him a Mercedes sedan. I was happy for him. But he was miserable.

He loved his job. He didn't want to quit. He felt betrayed and confused (though he appreciated the irony of quitting because someone doubled his pay!). Since he hadn't offered the brothers an ultimatum, I pointed out, quitting to save face really wasn't an issue. Perhaps his timing was off? Or the brothers suspected his motives? Or they weren't convinced of his commitment?

Faced with the choice of getting mad or getting even, my friend chose a third course: he got better. He didn't sulk or change jobs. He made up his mind to show the brothers they were wrong.

In the ensuing months he worked his buyers mercilessly. On each purchasing contract, he fought over nickels and dimes as if they were his own. In short, he behaved like an "owner." Profits soared. A year later he approached the brothers about 5 percent of the company. And they agreed to let him in.

Now he has all the risks and headaches of an entrepreneur. But he's very happy.

The Qualities of a Champion

Because of my association with champion athletes, people often ask me if a competitive streak on the playing field helps you in business. I prefer to divide the question into two answers, one for ordinary athletes, another for the elite.

I think business people who were athletes in high school and college and continue to compete informally as adults usually derive a benefit in their business behavior. Whether it means winning a point or winning a sale, they seem to have the discipline, stamina, and courage to come out on top. They also mesh well within an organization. People who competed in team sports such as football or basketball are particularly effective in a corporate hierarchy. They're team players who know instinctively when to obey the rules and when to bend them.

Major sports personalities—professionals, world-class champions—are a different story. The reason? They have no business patience. They're used to instant results. They play a tennis match and know if they've won or lost three hours later. They get instant adulation every time they sink a putt or put the ball through the hoop. That sort of quick score and automatic applause is usually missing in the business world. In business, patience and an eye on the long term are more highly prized skills.

Five Winning Attributes

On the same subject, I'm often asked what qualities I admire in the champion athletes we represent and how those qualities translate into business success. Here are five winning attributes:

1. Arnold Palmer's honesty and integrity

I remember being teamed up with Arnold in a rainy pro-am tournament. Because the greens were covered with puddles, the rules permitted pacing off a new putting position an equal distance from the pin to avoid putting through water. Throughout the round I watched Arnold pace off new putts, always taking bigger steps when going away from the hole to his new position than going toward the hole. He was turning 18-foot putts into 25-footers. I thought he was being too scrupulous, and I asked him about it because I knew he wanted to win as much as I did. He told me, "If one person in the gallery thought I was taking advantage of the situation, then the putt just wouldn't be worth it." That kind of integrity is a big reason why corporations and businesspeople want to be associated with Arnold.

2. Chris Evert's mental toughness

I don't know anyone mentally tougher than Chris. She has tremendous discipline and can keep her mind focused on a situation without letting emotion interfere. She does this on the tennis court and off. You always know where you stand with her. In business this is the way you want to deal with someone. I would much rather get a direct "yes" or "no" decision from someone than a "maybe" that doesn't resolve anything.

3. Bjorn Borg's stubbornness

Bjorn is stubborn in a healthy way. Once he makes up his mind to win a point or a match, he usually succeeds. He refuses to break. That kind of inflexibility is not always right in business, but it comes in handy when times are tough and you need to assert yourself.

4. Gary Player's thoughtfulness

Gary is a genuinely nice person who always goes out of his way to say something positive. Under the most trying golf course conditions, I've heard him find a way to be enthusiastic—about the fairways, the galleries, the hospitality, and the tournament officials. That sensitivity to people's feelings and that talent for making them feel comfortable is priceless.

5. Jack Nicklaus's maturity

Jack (whom we no longer represent) was very successful at a young age. I think he believed in his twenties that he could win in business as easily as he won on the golf course. Unfortunately, that wasn't the case. Jack made some costly decisions. But since then he has learned to be a businessman, to delegate, to hire experts who know more about specific opportunities than he does. That's a very mature (and profitable) attitude.

Four Syndromes That Can Kill a Career

Nearly everybody in business has some sort of personality "complex" or "syndrome." Most are trivial and hard to detect at first. But if you work with someone long enough, you begin to recognize—and compensate for—their quirks and defects.

Then there are the people whose personalities are impossible to ignore. For example, there are the executives with Expert Syndrome, who must have the first and last word on any topic. There are the Machiavelli Disciples, forever scheming for power. There are the Mavericks, whose recurring theme is "I did it my way."

Tiresome as these types may be, they're often very successful because (a) they know themselves and (b) their character flaw is designed to promote, not hinder, their career.

Then there are the people with more subtle personalities. Their character flaws seem minor but, ironically, wreak much more havoc on their careers. For example:

1. The Love-My-Warts Syndrome

Some people feel so secure that they are willing to expose their weaknesses as well as their strengths. In fact, they revel in it.

I know an executive who is a fabulous manager. He motivates, his people are loyal, and he keeps an incredible number of balls in the air. But he has two major flaws: he meddles and he talks too much. The weird part is he is aware of both but goes out of his way to flaunt them, as if they were two perks he's awarded himself.

I can't help thinking that this what-you-see-is-what-you-get attitude will haunt his career. Eventually, someone above him won't want to see or, worse, won't get it.

2. The Overcompensating Syndrome

Just as some people feel compelled to display their warts, others overplay their strengths. They keep telling you how good they are at a certain job—until you're bored with the tune or suspect they have no other tricks.

I know a very talented woman who owns a medium-size public relations firm. She's creative and remarkably persuasive one on one. By most criteria she's a success, yet her business has not kept pace with the competition. When I asked three of her employees what she was doing wrong, they answered in unison, "Overcompensating." If she had twenty minutes to make a sales proposal, she'd take twenty-five minutes and spend most of that time on details and minutiae to prove her expertise—when all the client wanted was to say hello.

Apparently, as a businesswoman in the male-dominated 1950s and 1960s, she had had to spend a lot of time promoting herself and going the extra mile to prove her worth. She hasn't realized that times have changed, that now *she's* a chief executive, and that her achievements speak for themselves.

3. The Glass-Is-Half-Empty Syndrome

If there's a good news–bad news side to every situation, then you can count on someone to tell you that the glass is half empty. Every company needs at least one gloom-and-doom character, if only to provide balance and rein in some of the sillier enthusiasms of their colleagues.

Unfortunately, vital as these corporate pessimists are, no one wants them around all the time. That's why they are frequently (and unsuspectingly) shunted to secondary projects, out of the mainstream, where they can be seen but not heard.

If I recognized this in myself, I'd go out of my way to change—or at least bite my tongue.

4. The Hermit Syndrome

These are the people who want to do quality work but prefer to do it alone. They often have some great technical skill—for example, engineering, tax law, computer programming—that they believe allows them to shut out the rest of the world.

You can't accuse them of being mavericks or not being a team player. On the contrary, they're very accommodating. They'll agree to anything as long as you leave them alone. Eventually they get their wish.

They'll always have a good job, because they're skilled. But that skill never takes them as far as they expect. They're usually stranded (and probably frustrated) in a company's middle ranks, toiling away behind closed doors.

Ten Ways Careers Get Stalled

Few things in business life are as puzzling as executives whose careers suddenly stall—even though they are very good at what they do. When these executives don't go as far or as fast as expected, I usually look for clues around, rather than within, them.

Like the investment adviser who makes millions for his clients but can't balance his checkbook, many capable executives turn out to be "street stupid" about their most important client—themselves. While they have been diligently doing their job and meeting their company's goals, they have failed to look above or around them. They neglect the superiors and colleagues who very often have the most influence over their corporate fortunes.

Just because you do your job well, or even brilliantly, doesn't guarantee a steady, rapid ascent up the corporate pyramid. Fairly or not, other factors are involved. To succeed in today's overcrowded executive marketplace, you need to be as insightful about yourself as you are about your job. In particular, you need to sharpen your instincts about bosses and peers.

Here are ten personal pitfalls I've seen stall the careers of even the ablest executives.

1. Not knowing why you were hired

Executives at every level exist for one reason, and one reason only: to make their bosses look good. If you don't believe this, ask your boss. If you're the boss, ask your company's shareholders.

2. Following up too slowly

Hesitation is commendable if it curbs some expensive impulses, but it rarely works to your credit when the boss is concerned. Failure to act immediately on a boss's commands lingers in the boss's mind and usually taints your reputation. For example, if the boss says, "Smith's not working out. Get rid of him," you might, in a noble moment, rush to Smith's defense. But authoritarian bosses tend to regard such behavior as insubordination, not nobility. Stall too long on Smith's departure and you may soon join him out the door.

3. Ignoring the Peter Principle

The Peter Principle says that everyone eventually rises to their level of incompetence. Nearly everyone knows this principle, but few think it applies to themselves. Street-stupid executives, in particular, reach their level of incompetence faster than they should. For example, employees customarily regard a promotion as cause for celebration. But not all promotions are in your best interest. A bad promotion, one that isn't suited to your talents, only speeds up the Peter Principle in your life. I've seen this happen frequently with super salespeople. They are so productive management feels compelled to promote them—to sales manager. What amazes me is that so many of these salespeople accept the promotion even though they have no interest in managing other people. Everyone ends up getting hurt in this arrangement.

4. Ignoring the corporate culture

Abused as the idea of "corporate culture" has become, it is a fact of life at many companies. You don't wear turtlenecks when everyone wears white shirts. You don't seek the spotlight when teamwork is the rule. And you don't punch in at nine and out at five if everyone else is putting in twelve-hour days. If you must be a nonconformist, why not start by outperforming everyone else?

5. Wanting to be liked by everyone

The best executives are respected (certainly) and liked (maybe). That's the way it should be if you want to continue making tough—and correct—decisions. Decisions should be dictated by the *situation,* not by your sympathies and personal feelings.

6. Failing to protect yourself when a new boss appears

Organizations make changes at the top to make the organization better, not to make life difficult for you. Many executives find this hard to believe; they take the arrival of a new chief personally. They resist the new boss, who in turn resists them. Guess who usually loses in this scenario? Simply put, the arrival of a new boss signals big changes. Don't ignore or underestimate them.

7. Going public with your private thoughts

Many a career has been short-changed when executives take the wrong colleague into their confidence. If you must gossip about your peers and superiors, save it for your family at home. Cutting remarks have a scary way of filtering up to the boss to undercut you.

8. Behaving inconsistently

Responding predictably to certain situations doesn't necessarily mean you're boring and unimaginative. On the contrary, the majority of day-to-day crises call for solid judgment rather than creativity and finesse. Few things are as disturbing to those above and below you as volatility. Blowing up one day over a setback and taking it in stride the next can brand you as unreliable.

9. Blaming bad news on someone else

There's no harm in admitting you made a mistake—but don't make a habit of it.

10. Asking employees to do something you won't do yourself

You can't ask people to put in long hours if you're not there beside them. Also, you can't expect them to do things your way unless you show them by example day in and day out.

The Seven Most Dangerous People in Your Company

Most people fear their openly ambitious peers, the lean and hungry types who are up front about where they're going and how they plan to get there. Actually if the ambitious people are as talented as they think they are, they can be your most valuable allies. You can hitch your wagon to their star and accompany them to the top. Better still, you can emulate their good points and rise above them.

The truly dangerous people in your company never clue you in on their ambition. They have a secret agenda— unknown to you and perhaps even to themselves—where the top priority is self-preservation. They are not the cream that rises to the top; they merely aim not to curdle. They exist in every organization. Here are seven dangerous types:

1. The "I'll do anything for you" pal

He makes the promises that he thinks you want to hear. But he cannot keep them. He says he can connect you with a potential client, and as you scurry to assemble a presentation, he's assembling an excuse for failing to deliver. There's no way to avoid getting burned once by this type, but there's no excuse for getting burned twice.

2. The know-it-all

These are the walking encyclopedias who've seen everything at least once. To them nothing is new. They have their value as company historians. But they can fool you. They have the brain of a high-speed computer, the confidence of a champion, and the intuition of a snail. The only phrases missing from their vocabulary are "I need help," "I was wrong," and "I don't know." They have many informed opinions, but ask them for advice and the precedents they cite will often lead you astray.

3. The "I agree" boss

He has an encouraging word for every proposal, because he doesn't want to stifle creativity. His favorite phrases are "I agree" and "Let's develop that." And that, unfortunately, is the end of it. His agreeability is indiscriminate—and therefore meaningless. Act on his go-ahead and you are wasting your time. Your files will fill up with aborted projects that he remembers dimly, if at all.

4. The confidant

He meddles, he talks, his currency is gossip. When he tells you "I can keep a secret," he can't. The tip-off: for every piece of information he elicits from you he feels obliged to share a secret about someone else. The danger: If he's willing to broadcast their confessions, what's he telling them about you?

5. The obsessive

Bosses love him. He works long hours, swoops in on every detail, and sets high standards for himself. Of course, he makes it easy on himself: he is obsessive only about details that don't matter. Whether he's counting paper clips or accounting for every minute of his day, he runs a tight ship, even if it isn't going anywhere. He thrives in bureaucracies and often becomes your boss. That's when his obsessions become your obsessions. Watch out.

6. The strategic incompetent

He becomes helpless when it's most convenient for him and inconvenient for you. He's the one who can't work the coffee machine or the copier (and asks you to help), who simply can't learn to use computers (and slows down your system), who just can't get along with a "small" client (and shunts them to you). He's available for every "sure thing" and absent when it counts.

7. The articulate incompetent

His greatest talent is for getting hired. His second greatest talent is aiming his silky banter at your blind spots. He rarely gets found out—until it's too late.

This is hardly a complete list, and I don't mean to suggest that organizations are overrun by schemers and incompetents. But if, as some management experts estimate, 10 percent of the people in a company are troublemakers and 70 percent of the people in that company are their unwitting victims, then you want to be among the 20 percent who are unaffected by these dangerous types. Half the battle is identifying them. The other half is avoiding them.

How to Manage the Boss in the Real World

A slim volume on the subject of "How to Manage the Boss" appeared a few years ago with the audacious title *The Greatest Management Principle in the World.*

Although I can think of several business goals more vital than how to manipulate the boss—for example, maximizing profits, outsmarting the competition, creating new products, and hiring the best people—I can see the author's point.

It's hard to argue with much of the textbook advice on *How to Manage the Boss:* give the boss solutions, not problems. Remember the boss is a human being. Play to the boss's weaknesses, not strengths. Never underestimate the boss. Never criticize the boss. Protect the boss from surprises, good or bad.

Unfortunately, not much of this applies to most of the chief executives I deal with on a regular basis.

These successful men and women insist on hearing problems immediately (in fact, they usually spot trouble long before their subordinates do). They can be inhumanly tough at times, basing decisions on cold facts rather than fuzzy human emotions. They know their weaknesses as well as anyone and delegate around them. They don't mind being underrated and often use it to their advantage. And they don't last very long by ignoring criticism. As for bad surprises, I don't know anyone who enjoys them, but they come with the territory.

There are two areas, however, where most bosses, including me, welcome good management from below.

Be sensitive to the boss's time

There is nothing more irritating than someone who wants ten minutes of your time and ends up taking an hour. Or the employee who brings up a subject requiring several hours of discussion as you are dashing out the door to catch a plane. Or the executive who takes long, chatty telephone calls while you wait in his or her office. The executive who respects my time has earned my eternal respect.

Be sensitive to the boss's other commitments

Sometimes employees are so eager to make a sale, that they fail to step back and consider the deal from the boss's perspective. A transaction that enhances their reputation and enriches their pocketbook might not be convenient for the company or gratifying to the boss's other clients.

Several years ago, a friend of mine who had a profitable and widely-known relationship with Allstate Insurance was distressed to learn that one of his executives was wrapping up a similar deal with an Allstate competitor. It took several months of delicate maneuvering to undo the executive's "achievement." My friend decided that the Allstate relationship was more important than the quick cash and potential conflicts of the second deal. The overzealous subordinate should have known that all along.

Confrontation Without Tears

People in business have trouble with confrontation because they confront out of emotion. A situation upsets them and they instinctively feel the need to lash out. They let their gut instincts take over when, actually, their mind should be in control. As a result, their confrontations tend to fail: while they're busy letting off steam, they ignore confrontation's true purpose, namely to prevent the distressing situation from happening again.

To win at confrontation, consider these five points:

Timing is everything

Effective confrontation usually has very little to do with emotion and everything to do with timing. In tennis, you don't go for the winner when you're off balance and your opponent is in good position. You wait for positions to reverse in your favor. On the golf course you don't decide to shoot for an eagle when it involves a reckless thousand-to-one shot over the trees. Instead, you wait for the right moment to get set up and then go for it.

I try to be very selective about confrontations. I wait until the timing is best for me. I also don't go off half-cocked, unsure of my facts. If a business partner has been less than honest about royalties owed to one of our clients, I will not apprise him of my suspicions, no matter how much they may upset me. I will wait for absolute proof of cheating rather than confront him when he still has several exits from the alley in which I want to trap him.

Don't prolong the ordeal

Confrontations should be short and sweet. They should make their point and then be forgotten. They should not smolder into long-running feuds.

If a subordinate has done something really stupid, I tend to explode very quickly and get over it just as fast. I probably overdo this hot-and-cold routine. I will literally become furious with somebody and within seconds forget about it. I will say to them, "What you did was dumb. You made a mistake, but we all make mistakes. Now let's move on to something else."

This frees me to tackle the next project unencumbered by emotion. As far as I'm concerned, the confrontation is history (although I might secretly hope the tirade lingers a few minutes longer in my employee's memory).

Contain your emotions

I remind myself constantly to "compartmentalize" my emotions, not to let them overlap as circumstances change. The attitude or tone of voice I adopt in one tense exchange or meeting may be totally inappropriate for the topic or meeting that follows.

I know many top executives who have short fuses. They are very demanding of themselves and others; as a result, they tend to be disappointed a lot. They anger quickly, perhaps believing that it is an important part of being a leader. (I've heard this referred to as "Theory F" or Managing by Fear.)

Where these executives go wrong is not in their hotheadedness but in their inability to compartmentalize. By letting their frustrations spill over from one situation to another they become more vulnerable rather than more authoritative. They become easy to read. Someone sensitive to their moods can get almost anything from them simply by pushing the right buttons at the right time.

Watch out for innocent bystanders

Carrying over your anger from one situation to another is deplorable when dealing with the same person. It is inexcusable when dealing with different people.

If I've scheduled consecutive meetings with two executives and the first meeting has sorely tried my patience, there's no reason for me to be mad at the next executive who walks into my office—especially not for his predecessor's offenses. Yet, people do this all the time.

Confront the good times

Confrontations laced with anger are usually destructive; inevitably someone says something they'll regret. Levelheaded confrontations, on the other hand, can be surprisingly productive. Again, timing is crucial.

I've found that the best time to confront the staff over their indiscretions is not when business is bad but when business is a little too good. If a valuable employee has just made a costly mistake (and knows it), the last thing he wants from me is a confrontation about his stupidity. In his moment of dejection, he needs encouragement. The time to knock him down a peg or two is after a string of successes, when he's feeling cocky and could use the reminder that he might not be as good as he thinks he is.

Taking on the Boss

There are plenty of occasions in business when you need to assert yourself, but not, it must be emphasized, by going toe-to-toe with your boss.

Confrontations with the boss are rarely decided by who's right and who's wrong. The determining factor usually is who brings the most chips to the table. And the boss, by definition, holds one chip the subordinate doesn't: the one that says you're fired. It amazes me how many overzealous executives forget this.

An article in *Manhattan Inc.* described a confrontation

that occurred a few years ago at the highest levels of Petrie Stores, a billion-dollar public company largely owned by Milton Petrie.

Soon after his eightieth birthday, Milton Petrie hired Michael J. Boyle, a 38-year-old wunderkind, as chief executive and heir-apparent of his company. Petrie gave Boyle a seven-figure salary, stock options, and complete authority.

A sad but familiar succession scenario followed. Petrie, who founded the company in 1929, wanted to give up control with grace and dignity—and he preferred to do it very slowly. Too slowly for the ambitious Boyle, who within weeks was wondering aloud when Petrie would move out of company headquarters. According to Petrie, Boyle "let the job go to his head."

By the third month, the two men were on a collision course. "He handled himself stupidly," Petrie later explained. "In meetings Boyle would say, 'I'm the boss and my judgment prevails.' The last straw was when I was dressing him down one day and he said to me, 'If you didn't own 60 percent of the stock, I'd take you to the board of directors.' And I said, 'Mike, you're fired.'"

Boyle's chances would not have improved even if Petrie had owned only 49.9 percent of the stock.

Employment Contracts: How Good Are They?

From what I read and from what other chief executives tell me, it has become fashionable for senior and mid-level executives switching jobs to ask for employment contracts. I can understand an executive's need to guarantee a job and salary in writing, particularly when anyone's career these days can be stalled by a corporate merger or reorganization. But employment contracts are tricky. They can damage an employer-employee relationship as easily as they can cement it. And over the long term they can limit rather than improve an employee's financial gains.

Consider an employment contract from my perspective as an owner of a business. An employment contract requires me to pay for an employee's services and to continue paying that employee even after I conclude he or she can't properly deliver those services. The employee, even in the worst of times, is locked into an escalating salary arrangement. That's not a smart arrangement for me.

It's also an unfair arrangement. The employee is more free to break the contract than I am to enforce it. If an executive wants to leave the company in midcontract, I usually have no choice but to say good-bye and wish him well. If his heart's not with us anymore, I won't jeopardize our organization by insisting he fulfill his commitment.

If you're an employee, you should also be wary of employment contracts. In exchange for an insurance policy if things go badly, you are giving away the potential rewards if you or your company hits a home run.

As a general rule, if you don't need a contract, don't ask for one. It can backfire on you. It can sour a potentially good relationship. While you're pressing for corporate perks, up-front bonuses, and lengthy severance pay, your prospective employer could lose his enthusiasm for you and look elsewhere.

As a business owner, I'm inclined to suspect the sincerity and motivation of someone who needs a piece of paper to feel secure in our organization. I prefer that people prove their commitment and loyalty to the business before I prove my commitment and generosity to them.

We pay our people well once they prove themselves. We can also be generous with attractive perks. Executives should be reminded of this largesse when their compensation is reviewed.

If a valuable employee wants an employment contract, I would try to dissuade him. For example, if an employee wants to lock in a three-year salary structure of, say, $50,000 in year one, $60,000 in year two, and $70,000 in year three, I would point out that this arrangement may look munificent now but stingy three years down the road, especially if the business continues to grow the way we expect.

I would also try to determine what's really important to this executive. Is he hung up on form, a fancier title, showier fringes? Then let's deal with that. Does he want to defer some income for tax purposes? Let's figure out a plan. Does his sense of self-esteem require a big salary increase to, say, the $100,000 level? I might give him the raise, but then I would be far less generous in subsequent years or with collateral benefits.

If he wants a small equity stake in a privately held business, I would point out that this may be less valuable than it seems. Do his shares give him a say in the business? How does he establish the shares' market value? To whom can he sell them?

Of course, there are situations when an employee has the leverage to get a contract. In the computer industry, for example, where ventures come and go and the competition for talent is fierce, good managers can easily get salaries, bonuses, stock options, and severance pay down in writing.

Employees also have an advantage in industries where ideas and creativity are at a premium. If a contract is the only way to secure an employee who can boost business significantly, as long as the contract is handled discreetly and doesn't endanger the integrity of the organization, an employer's flexibility on the issue may be his smartest move.

Salary Discussions I Can Do Without—and Two That I Can't

As an employer I've been in enough salary discussions to be familiar with nearly every argument for increasing an employee's compensation.

Employees will bring up the strangest things. They boast about increasing profits (and conveniently omit anyone else who contributed to the growth spurt). They complain about unfair quotas (which they agreed to the year before). They'll mention their kids' college tuition (which is good for a little sympathy but nothing else). Sometimes, out of helplessness or frustration, they'll argue for a raise because they "deserve" it.

Unfortunately, most salary discussions aren't like baseball arbitrations, where pitchers can cite increased attendance on the days they took the mound and hitters have clear-cut statistical goals.

Nearly everybody thinks they're underpaid, and those who think they're overpaid aren't going to mention it. The fact of the matter is that most people are underpaid in the beginning of their career and overpaid at the end. In between, they sometimes get confused about what they're really trying to accomplish at work.

The pleasure factor

I was in a salary discussion not too long ago with an employee who pointed out that his best friend in college was making more money than he was. I pointed out that asking me to subsidize his envy was hardly a persuasive argument.

I also told him that you can always find *someone* who's earning more than you. You can cherry-pick your examples. Ten years ago the big salaries were in Silicon Valley, before that in engineering. Now they're on Wall Street doing mergers and acquisitions and leveraged buyouts. Tomorrow it might be lawyers or marketing consultants.

Keeping everything in balance, you have to figure out what kind of life-style you have and how much pleasure you get out of your job. If the work is something you might do for free, consider how lucky you are to be paid well for it.

The long-term factor

As I've already said, it's not always advisable to jump from company to company in search of constantly bigger paychecks. If you fail to look ten years down the road it will often catch up with you.

When we promote employees to an executive position, we know that by virtue of that title and position they have an added value to our competition. When they are lured away, I tell them the questions to ask are: where will you be in ten years? Will that new salary continue to grow, or could you be earning much more with us in a year or so? Will the new company still be in business (you'd be amazed how often they aren't)?

We've never lost an executive we really wanted to keep and it isn't because we pay more—some of our people have been offered astonishing amounts to leave us—but people see where we're going and decide to stay. Employers and employees should not lose sight of this long-term factor.

The Double Life of Salaries

I once overheard two young office workers at another company complaining about their paychecks. "My boss can spend more on a business dinner than I make in a week," said one of them. "Yet when I ask for a tiny raise, he says he doesn't have the money."

To the untrained eye, most compensation policies don't make sense. I've seen chief executives who take great pleasure in giving an executive a five-figure raise and yet they'll agonize and procrastinate when their secretary asks for $20 a week more.

Unfair as this may seem, there's an explanation: in many companies salary increases have a double life.

The big increases in compensation are seen as *corporate*

statements; they are benchmark figures for other company executives to be aware of and aspire to. Since the money often doesn't come out of one particular budget (and therefore doesn't tarnish an individual's reputation for holding down expenses), the big raises are often made gladly and with a flourish. The giver looks good, the recipient feels good, and the company benefits from all this goodwill.

At a company's lower levels, the raises are smaller and sometimes more *personal*—and therefore more problematic. Ultimately, power rather than money becomes the issue. The salary review is usually done one-on-one and requires the boss to *yield* to the subordinate's modest request—in effect, to give up some authority. Is it any wonder that some bosses (with fragile egos) resent this?

Four ways to prove you're worth it

For anyone caught in the office worker's bind, the trick obviously is to depersonalize your salary request and show that you are a corporate asset. Four pointers:

First, ask for what you really want, not what you think your boss is willing to give. Before you try reading his mind, read yours. Who knows, you might get what you want without a struggle.

Second, remember that the company pays for the raise, not your boss. This should ease some of his pain at parting with the money.

Third, outline all your positive achievements during the past year. If you don't, who will?

Fourth and most important, prepare a list of everything you expect to achieve in the coming year. This is more crucial than the first three points combined. It's the one thing most subordinates forget and most bosses don't expect. You'd be surprised how thinking a year ahead will impress your boss—and make him reluctant to lose you.

How to Find Your First Great Job (or What Every Graduate Wants to Know)

I'm often invited to speak at campuses on the subject of "What Every Graduate Should Know." So I prepare a talk about reading people, listening aggressively, creating impressions, the sort of personal stratagems that can give young people the edge in business.

Yet when I arrive on campus I find that I'm talking above the students' heads. My talk should really be titled, "What Every Graduate *Wants* to Know," or more bluntly, "How to Find a Great Job."

I also notice that the students are incredibly curious about the inner workings of my organization. What they're really asking me, I now realize, is: what's it like on the inside? How do I as an outsider get inside?

The answer is self-evident: start thinking like an insider.

To me this means concentrating less on factors already within your control (your credentials, interests, appearance) and more on the factors that common wisdom suggests are beyond your control. From my perspective as an employer, here are six factors that recent graduates have more control over than they think:

1. Persistence

As I write this, we're looking to hire someone in one of our divisions. It so happens that within the week I have received two unsolicited résumés that were near perfect for the opening. This sort of coincidence occurs so often in business I'm no longer amazed by it.

I'll probably end up hiring one of these two candidates, and most executives I know would do the same. The reason: It's more convenient than going through the 2,000 as good or better résumés we receive each year. This may not be the textbook way to hire the best people, but it's a fact of life. At many companies, hiring decisions often follow the path of least resistance, especially at the entry level.

The moral: If you really believe in your own credentials and you're not sending a mass mailing to a thousand companies, be persistent. Aim for a very specific job at a specific company. And don't take the standard rejection letter—the one that says we don't have an opening at the moment for someone with your skills—as a final verdict. Thank them for the letter (giving your name a second exposure within the company). Then go back to them in two or three months. There's no guarantee that the employer will remember you specifically for the next vacancy, but you can be sure you are far ahead of the 200 résumés buried in some file.

2. Get lucky

Persistence, properly and tactfully applied, usually leads to luck. The trick to getting lucky, of course, is to know when you have been—and to act on it. Most people are lucky every day, but only the perennial successes seem to recognize this. They regard life's twists of fate—dialing the wrong number and getting the company chairman or sitting next to a talkative passenger on a plane—as opportunities rather than inconveniences.

Years ago, during a flight from Chicago to Des Moines, a young Harvard MBA got into a conversation with an older gentleman in the next seat. The MBA, an eager but guileless sort, did most of the talking. He told the man of his unhappiness at work. Joining Proctor & Gamble straight out of business school, he said, was a mistake. Marketing wasn't his strong suit; investing was. The older man listened in silence as the MBA passionately outlined investment strategies that would double his money in a year. When the plane landed, the two men exchanged business cards and the older man said, "Look me up if you're ever in Baltimore."

The MBA thought nothing of this casual remark until he got home and looked at the card, which bore the name of the legendary investor T. Rowe Price. Realizing that the gods had smiled upon him, the MBA made sure he was in Baltimore within 48 hours, where he indeed "looked up" Mr. Price. Today he runs several T. Rowe Price investment funds and helps manage the company.

3. Bring something to the party

With recent graduates, most employers look for signs of achievement—such as athletic or scholastic prizes or election to leadership positions. Failing these impressive credentials, try to bring some business with you.

If a recent graduate wanted to join our team sport division and knew a great athlete at a major university, he'd have a leg up on everyone else in my mind if he could join our company with that athlete signed as a client. This applies to anyone, no matter how young or inexperienced, in any business.

Bring a little something to the party (or indicate that it will happen soon) and few employers will care about your scholastic achievements—or the lack of them.

4. Endear yourself to the boss's secretary

Pierre Cossette once told me how he discovered and managed the actress Ann-Margret in the early stages of her career. Ann-Margret appeared in his reception area one day, but Cossette told his secretary he was too busy to see anyone. Ann-Margret, a student at Northwestern University at the time, got talking to the secretary and somehow learned they belonged to the same social club. Because of that link, the secretary buzzed her boss again and pleaded, "Pierre, won't you see her? She's really nice . . ." All because she made a good impression.

Most young people either fail to appreciate the secretary's power as gatekeeper to the executive suite or neglect to turn that, through a warm personal comment, to their advantage. I'm convinced that my secretary could persuade me to see anyone—or, conversely, prevent me from hearing their name—depending on the impression that person has made.

5. Select a company before it selects you

You never have more control over the hiring process than at the beginning—when you decide who you allow to accept or reject you. Yet this is the precise moment when many graduates get careless.

Instead of selecting future employers with the same obsessive care they used four years earlier in applying to colleges, many graduates scatter dozens of résumés around the country and, because it's a buyer's market, place themselves at the market's mercy. Worse, they favor quick results over long-term self-interest, focusing on starting salaries and job titles instead of geography or a company's profitability or how many layers of management will block their advancement.

In the late fifties, after William and Mary, Yale Law School, and two years in the Army, I had to look for a job. The first thing I did was consult a national directory of law firms. I studied law firms in cities I wanted to live in, paying particular attention to the age of the partners in each firm. I was trying to find firms where many of the partners would be retired in ten years, which would seem to give me a good chance, assuming I performed well, of being higher up than I would at a randomly selected firm. Then I wrote to a lot of law firms and went to a lot of interviews.

6. Spend the cash

After spending thousands of dollars on a college education, can you afford *not* to invest a few hundred dollars more for travel and lodging in pursuit of the right job?

Working for Nothing

When young people ask me how they can find a job they will really like, I tell them quite candidly, "Work for nothing. If you're as good as you think you are, the situation will only be temporary."

I tell them about a young woman a few years ago who was so eager to join our Toronto office she offered to work for free. Whether she knew it or not, she was pushing all the right management buttons, because (a) everybody thinks they're overworked or understaffed, (b) nobody has the budget to do anything about it, and (c) when confronted with an enthusiastic freebie, who can say no?

Not long after she joined us and had proved herself, her boss (partly out of guilt) began paying her out of petty cash. She received lunch money, parking money, a per diem, even room and board with an executive's family. She's still with our organization, only now she gets a paycheck like everyone else.

For recent graduates (as well as people in their thirties who can afford to contemplate a career switch) working for free may be the smartest way to get a foot in the door of the ideal company. For one thing, no manager will turn down a free addition to the staff. Even if it doesn't work out, the cost is nil. Second, after a few weeks of watching you work hard, even the most coldhearted employer will feel guilty or succumb to pressure from your new colleagues and offer a token salary. Then you're on the payroll and on your way.

Third, you have nothing to lose and everything to gain. An

opportunity at a top-flight company is invaluable. The experience will look good on your résumé. You'll find out first-hand if you've chosen the right business. You'll learn from the best. You'll make contacts that could pay off years later.

What Really Happens to Résumés

The trouble with most résumés is that, after you send them out, you have no idea what happens to them. We receive and file away more than 2,000 unsolicited résumés a year. I do one of four things with a résumé.

One, I throw it away, which is rare.

Two, I answer with a polite rejection in a form letter saying we have no openings at the present time.

Three, I send it to someone within our company with one of three notes: (a) "Why don't you respond to this?" which means "Do whatever you want"; (b) "This seems pretty good," which means "Try to see this person and let me know what you think"; (c) "This is an exceptional résumé," which means "I really want you to see this person."

Four, I call the job seeker myself.

Résumés are important—if only to get you a face-to-face interview—but they're not that important.

A whole industry has been built around the preparation and production of the mythical "perfect" résumé. Most of the advice is useful: address an individual, not a title; seek a specific job; be brief; avoid irrelevancies and flattery; make it easy for them to take the next step.

I sometimes think you're ahead of the competition if your résumé does nothing to *unsell* your candidacy.

The most glaring gaffes, in my opinion, are spelling errors. The traditional spelling of my name, for example, is McCormick; the correct is McCormack. A job candidate would have to show up with a lot of credentials to overcome misspelling my name—not because I'm personally offended by the error but because it indicates a carelessness I'd prefer to keep out of our organization.

Gimmicky, exquisitely designed résumés on creamy stationery don't impress me. In fact, in Europe half the applications we receive are handwritten. If they're legible, we won't rule out a candidate because he or she doesn't own a typewriter.

Make a Big Impact with Little Opportunities

If you have limited access to somebody and it's important to your career, short-term or long-term, to be impressive during your limited access, you have to figure out something that makes a lasting impression should your big shot arrive.

I noticed this in my Army days at Fort Lee, Virginia. The Army had very structured inspections then to review the troops. Inspections essentially were a soldier's only chance to stand out. If you could impress the inspectors—for example, by having the shiniest shoes—they would single you out and make you the colonel's orderly, which would exempt you from guard duty and give you a day off.

There was a game aspect to all this, and I was determined to play to win. Unfortunately, I didn't have much latitude. Sometimes inspectors checked out your shoes, and my shoeshining wasn't all that great. Sometimes they would pass you by, saying nothing. Sometimes they would ask you to recite the general orders, but this was a simple memory task and I couldn't recite it better than the next guy.

However, I *could* learn the chain of command more completely. I could memorize all the officers' middle names, from the commanding officer on down, on the off chance that the inspector would ask me for the chain of command. And lo and behold, he did.

So I fired off the commanding officer's middle name, which the inspector probably didn't know himself. He looked surprised, demanding another one. After rattling off a few more middle names, I was named colonel's orderly—because I had made a major impression in a split-second opportunity.

I think this applies in many business situations. If you happen to be in the airport when the chairman of the board offers you a ride to the office, you should be prepared to make the most of those thirty minutes in the car. (Likewise for a three-hour plane trip or a twenty-second elevator ride next to a CEO you've been trying to reach for months.) Resorting to small talk or silence because you didn't expect to be there is no excuse.

Fine-Tuning a Code of Ethics

In 1987, during the height of the insider trading scandals in the American security markets, John Shad, the former head of the Securities and Exchange Commission, whose job is to police Wall Street, gave Harvard University $30 million to establish a program on ethics in business.

Of course, this noble gesture presented Harvard's professors with the problem of how *ethically* to spend that much money studying the Golden Rule. After all, ethical business decisions in their most simple state boil down to "Do unto others as you would have them do unto you." You've heard this since kindergarten. It still applies in 99.9 percent of all relationships. Probably more.

Here are four other rules to help you fine-tune your sense of right and wrong:

Rule 1. Let people off the hook

As a lawyer, I like to think "a deal is a deal." But life isn't so cut and dried. People often agree to do things and then for reasons beyond their control are unable to do them. If you let them off the hook, are you being a nice guy or a fool?

Obviously, if you intend to do business with them again, the choice is not that tough. I've let people off the hook for various reasons—because circumstances have changed, because new information has altered their desire to complete the deal, and on occasion because their boss has overruled them. Rarely have the long-term benefits from such decisions made me feel foolish.

One-shot deals are a tougher call. Years ago a friend sold his $100,000 house to an executive who was being transferred from Iowa to Ohio. A few days before the closing, the buyer's father died, forcing him to remain in Iowa to take care of his mother. These clearly were extenuating circumstances. My friend let him off the hook. There was no long-term benefit in it for him, but it was the right thing to do.

Rule 2. Don't abuse the power of omission

Omission is a legitimate tool in business, particularly in selling. The best salespeople seem to include all the information they need to close the sale and leave out anything that might jeopardize it. If there's any confusion, they reason, it's because the questions went unasked, not unanswered.

This is part of the gamesmanship of business—and subject to abuse.

In the 1960s, we set up a series of televised "golf challenges" sponsored by the Lincoln-Mercury division of Ford and produced by MCA. During the discussions, MCA implied to Lincoln-Mercury that the thirteen shows would be played on California's finest courses, including Pebble Beach in Monterey and Olympic in San Francisco. The final contract, however, mentioned no specific sites, only "some leading courses in California."

Once they started budgeting the shows, MCA's producers decided that they could save money and increase profits by limiting all matches to southern California. This infuriated the Lincoln-Mercury people to the point that MCA chairman Lew Wasserman had to get involved.

"Forget the contract," said Wasserman. "If you gave Lincoln-Mercury reason to believe that matches would be filmed at Pebble Beach and Olympic, then you better go there."

Rule 3. Tell people when the meter is running

Ever have a friendly lunch with a lawyer or consultant only to receive a hefty bill for the hour or two you were exposed to his "services"? What's irritating and less than ethical about this is not that one friend is billing another but that he failed to mention that (1) dining with you was "work" to him and (2) his meter was running.

Rule 4. Establish your ground rules and don't waver

Being ethical doesn't always mean giving in to the other guy's point of view. Statements can be interpreted in different ways by different people and sometimes sticking to your guns is the only proper decision.

In 1984, when Walt Disney Productions was the subject of takeover rumors, wealthy investors Sid Bass of Texas and Irwin Jacobs of Minneapolis bought millions of shares in Disney. According to John Taylor in his book about the battle for Disney, *Storming the Magic Kingdom,* at one point when the two tycoons met, Jacobs considered buying Bass's shares. Bass, however, wasn't selling. He liked Disney's newly installed management and planned to keep his shares for at least five years.

"I think I'm going to make a lot of money," Bass told Jacobs. "That's why I'm doing it. I think you ought to do it too. Let's both buy a lot of Disney stock."

Some time later, Bass bought 1.5 million more Disney

shares. Jacobs, apparently under the impression that Bass had suggested they work in tandem and buy stock together, immediately called Bass and asked, "We're entitled to half the stock, right?"

A lesser man might have been intimidated by Jacobs or at least tried to accommodate his interpretation.

But Bass knew exactly what he had said and politely disagreed. "We're not giving you half the stock," he told Jacobs.

The Three Most Stressful Situations in Business

People often ask me how I cope with the constant tension of trying to sell our proposals to tough-minded businesspeople or negotiating multimillion dollar contracts for our clients.

I tell them that sales presentations and contract renewals are not tense situations. They're big situations that I'm prepared for. Like most executives, I thrive on them. I look forward to them. They're not some painful experience I have to "cope" with.

The tensest situations in business actually stem from the little things. And they most often involve people who, in some emotional way, are little human beings. You can't prepare for them, but you can file them in the back of your mind and act accordingly when they come up. Here are two needlessly tense situations:

1. When you forget the small details

The businessperson who first said "No detail is small" must have been an expert on tense situations—because that's where most conflicts begin.

I once knew a fairly junior marketing man at a large West Coast company who was doing lots of business with various elements of our company. He asked one of our West Coast executives for basketball tickets. The tickets weren't properly delivered, and when he finally got them, they weren't very good seats. As a result of this little error, the marketing man, in a very immature way, not only exploded at our executive but effectively blocked some significant business with our company.

There's an unprintable name for people like that—and obviously we can now figure out why he's a junior rather than senior executive. But you have to deal with people like that. You particularly have to tell yourself that, if you're about to close a big deal with someone, don't mess up some incidental detail.

2. When you do someone a favor

We once represented a golfer for whom, by anyone's criteria, we had done absolutely stunning work. One time as he and his family went off for a European vacation, he asked someone in our office to book a rental car in Rome. For some reason, the reservation got lost and he had to wait three hours at night at the Rome airport with an angry wife and screaming baby before he could take a two-hour taxi ride to their hotel. His wife kept badgering him about how our company couldn't do anything right.

That tiny mishap, which we had done as a favor and which was totally out of the mainstream of our responsibilities or obligations to our client and was, at the same time, not our fault, negatively affected what should have been a fantastic relationship.

Doing favors for people in business is nice, but not if they're poorly executed. What starts out as a friendly gesture somehow becomes an obligation, to the point where you're almost better off saying you can't do it.

The Good and the Bad of Doing Good

You can never have too many contacts in business. Everybody seems to recognize this now, especially the younger generation crowding—and competing to get out of—the ranks of middle management. I can't think of a better way to give your career an extracurricular boost than voluntarism—giving your time and talent to hospital boards, church committees, or civic organizations.

Voluntarism remains one of the best (and least used) ways to meet people. Of course, there's a right reason and a wrong reason to get involved.

The wrong reason to volunteer

Two types of people get involved in charitable organizations: the *givers,* who join up because they really want to do good, and the *takers,* who very obviously sign on to meet people and to use the people they have met.

While there's nothing wrong with being in the second category (most people will admit to falling somewhere in between), the trouble starts when the takers get impatient. They want the payoff before they've delivered the goods as a volunteer.

If you really want to do something for yourself, you should wait a long time before even suggesting doing business with anyone within your volunteer organization.

The right way to volunteer

Getting involved in a not-for-profit organization—from big civic projects like the United Way to tiny causes like a theater group—is quite simple. First, you pick a cause that's close to your heart. Second, you volunteer. Third, you work hard.

I cannot overemphasize the last item. The chairpersons of local charities are usually the area's business leaders. In business or charity, these leaders look for results, not promises, and they remember (if not immediately reward) those who deliver.

By far the best way to distinguish yourself as a volunteer is to raise money. If you can do this by writing a personal check, congratulations. Equally as good, though, is the ability to identify potential donors and to organize events that get them to open up their checkbooks.

In the early 1960s I joined the Cleveland Junior Chamber of Commerce and was able to secure the services of Gene Littler and Gary Player for a golf exhibition that was of significant benefit to the organization. The event was an aesthetic and financial success. It gave the organization unprecedented visibility on local sports pages, and it raised money. Right away I was perceived as bringing something to the organization. I was a giver rather than a taker. Although I never did business with my Junior Chamber of Commerce contacts, I think I could have quite easily after that.

The lesson: don't start selling *yourself* in a volunteer organization unless you've built up a nice equity stake of achievements. I admire people who can use their situation, insights, and intuition to tilt a transaction in their favor, but I don't like seeing someone try to take the edge when he or she has done nothing to earn that advantage.

It Isn't *Just* Business with the Japanese

Enough praise has been lavished in recent years on the Japanese for their high-tech ingenuity, their management techniques, and their talent for motivating workers. But as our company's Japanese activities continue to grow dramatically each year and I spend more time there, I marvel more and more at the personal qualities of Japanese businessmen.

1. Politeness. No matter how adverse the circumstances, a Japanese businessman will never lose his composure. The Japanese are just as clever as we Americans in creating ways to ruin a transaction, but unlike us, they will never let anger be one of them.

2. Patience. I pride myself on never forcing the time frame of a deal, but the Japanese are Zen masters at this. They are perfectly content to wait years for a deal to come through or a business plan to bear fruit.

3. Thoroughness. The Japanese are so thorough that sometimes when we have licensed them to copy a design— such as a tennis shirt or a piece of equipment—they'll even copy the unintentional flaws in the original item. In the long run, this quality is more good than bad.

4. Punctuality. In the same way that they are patient, the Japanese have a reverence for time—yours as well as theirs—that makes them uncomfortable with lateness or missed deadlines.

5. Long-term loyalty. American business, it has frequently been pointed out, is still trying to impress Wall Street with next quarter's earnings. But it goes deeper than that. American executives seem to think that they have a limited amount of time to make their mark on their company, and if they're young enough, they'll tailor that impact to win promotions or land a better job at a bigger company. On the whole, I think American executives of publicly traded companies are more self-oriented than company-oriented. This is not all bad, of course. But I admire Japanese workers for being *so* company-oriented. They are committed for life to one employer. And when a good situation arises, they'll celebrate first for the company, then themselves.

6. Honesty. I think I would be less likely to get a dishonest royalty report in Japan than in any other country in which I do business.

The Five Attributes of a Leader

The whole idea of getting ahead is to help you attain a position of leadership. Leading people, as opposed to following them, of course, demands a whole new set of talents.

John Keegan, a British military historian, believes that great battlefield commanders such as Alexander the Great and Napoleon possessed five essential attributes of leadership:

1. They show the troops they care.
2. They tell the troops exactly what they want.
3. They convince the troops they'll be rewarded if they fight, punished if they don't.
4. They know when to attack.
5. They share in their troops' danger.

At the risk of making business sound too much like warfare, I think Keegan has a point for any manager who aspires to be a leader. Here's how Keegan's five attributes can apply in business:

1. You have to persuade the troops that you care about them

This requires action rather than words, in the form of a personal gesture that treats people as human beings rather than revenue producers.

On one level, this could mean permitting a valuable executive to take a vacation at the company's expense, or bring a spouse along on a business trip, or borrow your ocean-front condominium for the weekend.

On another level, it means unwavering loyalty, even when it runs counter to economic common sense. I remember a few years ago when a CEO I know was going through a downsizing crisis at his company. The hungry young executives on his staff were urging him to get rid of several executives who had been with him for twenty years. Their best years were behind them, argued the Young Turks, and their salaries could be used better elsewhere.

The CEO knew they were probably right. But he couldn't bring himself to abandon associates who had been loyal to him for so many years. He kept them on and rode out the down cycle.

I believe he grew, rather than shrunk, as a leader in the eyes of his Young Turks for this gesture.

2. You have to be able to tell people exactly what you want

A leader will give his employees the big picture: "This is where we'll be in five years."

A more effective leader will also mention the little details. Clear details, not "vision," are what employees carry with them from day to day.

For example, I recently suggested that our golf division consider signing up Dave Martz. Martz is the golfer who *didn't* win the tour's long-driving contest. His drives were very long but crooked. But I believe people at exhibitions and corporate outings would love to watch him just hit the ball.

That's a very small detail in our golf division's overall scheme, yet bringing it up, I think, makes more of an impression about how much I care than a dozen of my lectures about the big picture. And it conveys exactly what I want.

3. You have to convince employees that they will be rewarded if they fight and punished if they don't

In military life, this means honors and decorations for exceptional conduct. In corporate life, it means titles and compensation (or the denial thereof) and the feeling that they're being handed out with consistency and fairness.

The most effective leaders rarely surprise their employees with promotions or demotions. They are constantly reminding them what's expected of them and how they're doing. There's nothing more counterproductive and cruel than letting someone go through the year thinking they're doing a great job when you actually think they're failing.

4. You have to know when to attack

In business this means timing: when do you take a soft or hard line, when do you become aggressive or passive, when do you really pay attention and when is it better to relax?

The surest sign of a leader is his or her ability to say, "Do it now!"—and it gets done.

Knowing when to attack is also the easiest leadership quality to detect in junior employees. Few things catch my attention more quickly than a forceful memo from a lieutenant urging us to attack a flank now. If I agree and we win the battle, that lieutenant will soon be a captain.

5. You have to show the troops that you share their dangers

In military terms, this means being present on the battlefield. In business, this means leading by example.

Have you ever noticed how the most respected bosses are those who can do every job in the company—from the warehouse to the executive suite—and are not afraid to show it? That ability to get their hands dirty, not only to impose risk but to take it on themselves, is the source of their authority.

One of the more fortuitous things I did in the early years of our business was to bring along one of our executives to a meeting with a Fortune 500 company and walk out with our first consulting contract.

I think that first example—where I could literally show an associate that you *can* walk into someone's office, ask for the order, and come out with a deal—is one reason that executive has obtained so many contracts since.

5 | Getting Organized

Time Management to Tilt the Calendar in Your Favor

At a certain point, I think most successful executives come to terms with the rudiments of efficient time management. They're actually quite simple:

1. Have a system. Any system.
2. Stick to it.
3. Write everything down.

Unfortunately, the world is complicated and does not always yield to your simple terms. Here are a few time management exercises that I practice religiously, which have helped make the world a little more responsive to my needs:

1. Factor in the power factor

I know an executive who gauges his corporate power vis à vis other executives by whether he must accommodate their schedule or they must accede to his. Nothing delights him more or does more to confirm his self-importance than getting other people to change their plans to fit his.

I'm not sure I agree with his *attitude,* but I see his point about recognizing the power factor. The more honest you are about your ability to influence other people's schedules and, conversely, their power to influence yours, the more likely you are to be well organized. Too often people delude themselves about how much autonomy they really have— and that can throw even the simplest organizational system into turmoil.

When I first started at the law firm of Arter & Hadden in Cleveland, my time was never my own. I couldn't tell you where I would be two weeks ahead because at any moment the firm could assign me to a case in a new city. I didn't delude myself about my status and I planned accordingly.

Similarly, a few years later when I was working for Arnold Palmer and our other clients, my schedule was clearly built around their needs. Because we were in a fast-breaking day-to-day business, I had to be ready to go anywhere at a moment's notice. A client would win the Masters in those days and you had to capitalize on that quickly. You couldn't do that if you had scheduled yourself to be in Europe that week or stayed in Cleveland to attend to the usual priorities.

By the above executive's standards, I now have power. I have the luxury of being able to schedule meetings more or less at my convenience. This hasn't made me any more organized than when I was a junior associate in Cleveland, just a little more comfortable.

2. Schedule far in advance at your peril

There's a tremendous advantage to always knowing where you're going to be. To be able to be definitive with someone who wants to know when the two of you can get together makes you look buttoned-up and in control.

But you pay a price when you lock yourself in weeks and months ahead. Circumstances change and you often find yourself spending as much time trying to extract yourself from a situation as trying to arrange it.

In 1987, for example, I scheduled my semi-annual trip to Japan in April at a time when I thought my wife, Betsy Nagelsen, would be there playing a tennis tournament. Because of changes in the world of tennis, Betsy had to play in a different sequence of tournaments. By that time I was totally committed to a Japanese schedule. And so I ended up in Japan when she wasn't and she was in Japan when I wasn't.

Of course, if I had waited until the last minute to arrange the trip, I wouldn't have been able to see half the people I wanted to meet in Japan.

3. Leave empty blocks in your day

Executives, particularly when they first move into senior positions, often have a misguided notion about the empty blocks in their daily calendar. They regard the unfilled hours as a sign that they're not doing enough or that they're falling behind. I've even been in offices where an executive made excuses for the blank sections in the diary on his desk.

I think I'm as "on the go" as the next executive, but I've never been embarrassed by the empty blocks in my daily schedule. They are not a sign that I'm slowing down; on the contrary, they help me pick up speed.

If you looked at the legal pads that I use to organize each day, you would find two substantial gaps on each sheet: one in the late morning, the other in the middle of the afternoon. I wake up very early and use the hours between 5 and 7 A.M. for dictation, reading incoming faxes, and internal company matters. By 10:00 I've generally had one or two breakfast meetings and several other meetings as well.

Thus, the "wild card" time in the late mornings and late afternoons gives me a chance to phone people about topics that may have occurred in the previous hours or to schedule meetings at other people's convenience. I need these hours to react rather than initiate. And I find that they help propel me and the company forward.

The occasions when I could truthfully say to a visitor, "My afternoon is totally yours," have always been moments of great pleasure rather than guilt. In my mind, they prove that I'm managing my time better than ever.

4. Mapping out the near future

Because the bulk of my time involves meeting with people, it's crucial for me to take time deciding with whom I'm going to spend the rest of my time. I have a very specific method for doing this.

For example, when I'm preparing my New York schedule around the US Open tennis championships I determine that there are 45 people I want to see during that period, and perhaps another 20 fringe people that I might like to see if I have the time.

I'll divide those 45 people into three categories of priority. Group A are the 15 high-priority people I need to see whenever they can make it. Group B are slightly lower priority but I will also accommodate my schedule to see them. Group C are the next priority of people I want to see, but if I miss them I can live with it.

I then try to fill my schedule with people from Group A. If I know them well I'll have my office call theirs. If they are less familiar to me, I'll call them myself. If five of the 15 "A" people are not available, I then put those people on an even higher must-see priority the next time I'm in New York. (I don't let people fall through the cracks just because we cannot connect the first time.)

After I fill my schedule with "A" people, I then do the same with Group B and then Group C and finally with fringe people and social contacts. If my secretary is making the arrangements, I'll even prioritize each category from 1 to 15 and single out which people I prefer to take to lunch and which days I'm free.

(Scheduling tip: In setting up meetings with busy people, always offer them several options and be careful to say, "These are the three *best times* for me," rather than "These are the *only good times* for me." If the other party is not available then, you can still come back with alternative times—and insure a meeting no matter how busy you both are.)

I've been using this ABC priority system for years. For one thing, it forces me to focus on who and what is important in my business life (which many people never take the time to do). More important, taking control of my time and orchestrating the overlapping relationships and discussions has an exponential effect on the results. The sum of my New York meetings will actually be greater than its parts.

A Week in My Life

Indulge me while I review a typical business week in my life. I include my diary here not to impress you with names and places and how busy I was, but rather to draw a few lessons about getting organized.

The week began and ended in New York.

Sunday, New York

8:00 A.M.: Prepared for three hours with my attorneys for a deposition in a lawsuit against Allegheny International, where I was a director.

12:30 P.M.: Met in the New York office with our international television executives to review recent developments relating to international TV rights to the National Football League (a client).

3:00: Dictation to my secretary who had arrived from Cleveland.

7:00: Dined with Pat Ryan, managing editor of *Life* magazine, and Ray Cave, then editorial director of Time Inc., in Little Italy.

Monday, New York

5:15 A.M.: Dictation.

7:15: Breakfast meeting at Essex House with United States Tennis Association officials and our executives to discuss TV and marketing developments.

12:30 P.M.: Lunch with the head of our tennis division to bring me up to date on client activities.

2:30: Packed for Stockholm trip.

3:30: Briefed by the head of our publishing division about lunch at week's end with former British Prime Minister Edward Heath.

6:30: Hosted dinner in our office for Masaaki Morita, chairman of Sony Corporation of America, and his family. We all went to the finals of the Nabisco Masters Tennis championships at Madison Square Garden, where Ivan Lendl beat Mats Wilander.

Tuesday, New York–Stockholm

5:30 A.M.: Dictation.

7:15: Worked on newsletter.

9:15: Two-hour interview with Walter Bingham of *Life* about what the Olympic Games will be like in the year 2000. (My opinion: They'll be totally open to professionals.)

Noon: Hosted lunch for Pete Rozelle and Val Pinchbeck of the NFL to present our TV plans in Europe.

3:45 P.M.: Met with Sony executives.

4:15: Courtesy visit from George Allen, former coach of the Washington Redskins and head of the President's Council on Physical Fitness.

5:00: Flew with my wife, Betsy, to Stockholm via Copenhagen for the Nobel Awards (our client).

Wednesday, Stockholm

Noon: Arrived at Grand Hotel. Quick nap.

3:00 P.M.: Attended reception for Nobel laureates at the Swedish Academy.

5:00: Attended reception announcing the opening of our Stockholm office.

7:00: Dinner hosted by Baron Stig Ramel, director of the Nobel Foundation.

Thursday, Stockholm

Squeezed in some Christmas shopping, visited our Stockholm office for first time, had lunch with my wife, and met briefly with *Newsweek* publisher Gerard Smith about the *Newsweek*–Nobel association and their advertorial.

4:00 to 11:00 P.M.: Attended the Nobel Award ceremonies at Stockholm's Concert Hall, followed by banquet and ball for 1,300 at the Town Hall. Met the King and Queen of Sweden. My first time in white tie and tails.

Midnight: Had a drink with Caterina Lindqvist, top Swedish tennis client, and her fiancé, one of our European executives.

Friday, Stockholm–London

7:00 A.M.: Early flight to London.

Noon: Luncheon in our London office with officials of the

European Broadcasting Union (EBU) to discuss future European TV rights to various sports properties.

2:00 P.M.: Drove out for meeting with Wimbledon committee.

5:00: Returned home to meet Michael Grade, former head of the BBC, for a pleasant discussion about his new post as chairman of Britain's Channel 4.

7:00: Hosted thirtieth birthday party for my son Breck, at the White Elephant restaurant.

Saturday, London–New York

6:00 A.M.: Dictation.

8:30: Interview with *Golf Monthly* magazine on the "state of golf."

11:00: Interviewed by ITV News film crew on Royal Family's public image.

11:30: Drove out to Salisbury for lunch at Edward Heath's home.

4:30 P.M.: Administrative meetings in London office about our European operations.

7:00: Flew Concorde to New York.

8:00: Enjoyed a pizza with my wife on Manhattan's East Side.

What's most interesting to me about the week is that I didn't close any deals or actually sell anything. Still, I'd characterize any week in which I dealt with clients such as Wimbledon, the NFL, the USTA, the Nobel Foundation, Sony, and *Newsweek* as being very productive.

This is the kind of week, I've learned, where you sow the seeds of even greater success. I also noticed some points about pacing yourself, getting lucky, and influencing other people.

Pacing

Not every week in my year entails eighteen-hour days and meeting heads of state. I pace myself over twelve months.

In a typical year I'll have seven or eight very busy three-week periods, during which I try to raise the level of my game (much like a champion athlete who can "peak" for major events). I plan it this way, and I'm prepared to be exhausted (and exhilarated) at the end of each day.

Afterward, I slow down or take a brief vacation—both to reward myself for working hard and also to remind myself that it's impossible to continue nonstop at your absolute best week after week.

Luck

One of my highlights in Stockholm was meeting with the managing director of a major international company with whom we should be (but have not been) doing business. I think I accomplished more in my brief chat with this CEO than our executives have in fifteen years of knocking on this company's doors.

Was this luck or skill? I can't say. But over the years, my crowded itinerary has taught me that showing up is often 90 percent of the sale and the more I travel the luckier I get.

Influencing schedules

The week went like clockwork because I planned well and, frankly, I am at a point in my life where I can probably influence other people's schedules more than they can influence mine.

It wasn't always so, but there comes a time in everyone's career when their status changes. Suddenly you're not "a nice young man" any more, scrambling for ten minutes with a decision maker and answering questions like "Who are you?" and "What's this about?" People are more eager to meet you. They call you up. Invite you to lunch. Offer you opportunities you never expected.

It's a subtle evolutionary process, which many people don't notice. But being aware of your increased influence, and using it, is one of the greatest time management tools you have.

Time Bombs That Can Blow Up Your Carefully Structured Day

I run my business life from a yellow legal pad, with one sheet devoted to each day and with a vertical line drawn down the middle. "People to call" go on the left side, "things to do" go on the right. I also carry index cards in a coat pocket to jot down bulletins for people I regularly speak with and also write down information to be transferred later to the appropriate page on my legal pad.

I mention this not to convert the world to my way of managing time. What works for me might not work for you. Yet I have never known a successful person in business who didn't operate from some personal organizational system.

The system can be simple or complex. Some people list what they want to do that week on a scrap of paper and work their way down accordingly. Others have bulging "Filofaxes" and "Dayrunners"—elaborate systems with cross-references and refills—that they're constantly thumbing through and updating.

But all the systems in the world won't get you organized unless you come to grips with the little time bombs—the fallacies you and others build into your system—that conspire to mess up your carefully structured day.

Savor the easy tasks

If you have eleven things you want to accomplish during the day—for eight of which you know exactly how much time is required, two of which you think you know, and one of which you're not sure because it could get involved—which would you tackle first?

Many people tackle the last one first and never get anything done. (Perhaps they regard an open-ended challenge—as opposed to an achievable one—as the only challenge worthy of their time.) I always try to get the eight achievable tasks done first. It gives me a pleasant sense of accomplishment and the proper momentum for the tough parts on my agenda. In my mind, easy tasks are to be enjoyed, not ignored or taken for granted.

Plan backward to keep moving forward

It's not life or death for me to be on time. But I take pride in knowing how long it takes to get things done. I attach the same thought and care to budgeting my personal time that I do to projecting accurate financial budgets.

I apply this to even the smallest details. For example, if I have an eight o'clock breakfast meeting with someone at my office, I don't take my wake-up hour casually.

Like most people, I have a fairly predictable morning routine, made up of necessary tasks and pleasant rewards. I know, for example, that I need thirty minutes to get dressed and ten minutes to get to the office, but I also want fifteen minutes for exercises, twenty minutes to read the paper, ten minutes to read overnight faxes, thirty minutes for dictation, and five minutes to think about that eight o'clock meeting.

That's two hours of time which, working backward, tells me I have to wake up no later than six o'clock. To get a later start means I sacrifice something, usually one or more of my rewards. That kind of loss is no way to start the day.

Don't be a time hero or the hero's victim

People want to be time heroes. They are constantly trying to do too much in too short a period of time, as if heroically trying to do two hours of work in one hour—and predictably failing—makes them heroic. It doesn't. And these sort of people can destroy your schedule. They're always running behind at your expense.

How often has somebody told you they'll meet you after work at 6 P.M. but first they must make two phone calls and run across town on three errands? And then, as you suspected, they show up at seven?

Before I'll be a victim of somebody's poor organization, I'll calculate their time and say, "Wait a minute. How can you get all that done by six? Why don't you just do it all and agree to meet me at seven? Why make both of us feel foolish?"

For the sake of sanity, don't expect to go through life without having some serious disappointments and disruptions in your schedule. For example, people often cancel appointments. However, if you detect a *pattern* of cancellations with certain people, you may be as much at fault as they are.

Are you too obliging? Are you disciplining them by voicing your displeasure (preferably with humor)? I remember one sales executive several years ago telling me after two unavoidable cancellations: "You realize, Mark, every time you put me off, my price goes up." Since he had something we really needed, even in jest this statement caught my attention.

People cancel appointments for two reasons: (1) *Something else came up,* in which case you shouldn't let them off the hook without a new date. Or (2) *What's important to you is less important to them,* in which case you're either wasting your time or have a lot more selling to do.

Prioritize your phone calls

For one day, try this experiment. Limit each phone conversation to five minutes or less, no matter who it is. You'd be surprised how sharply this can focus your phone manner and what you'll learn about other people's manner on the phone.

Because some people are brisk on the phone, others more leisurely, I give a lot of thought to the order in which I talk to people on the phone.

If you have thirty minutes for seven phone calls, six that can be dealt with in two minutes each and one that may ramble, you're far better off saving the long-winded call for last, knowing that the six quick calls are behind you. This is less frustrating than initiating a potentially lengthy call and wondering how you're going to get the six calls done in the next half hour.

The ideal "to do" list is unreadable

I love making lists—not because I need to remind myself how busy I am. I simply get a keen satisfaction and tactile thrill out of scratching out tasks that are done.

To me the true sign of an organized executive is not how many projects he or she can enumerate on a "to do" list at the start—as if that's a legitimate symbol of their importance—but rather how many are crossed off at the close. My ideal "to do" list is unreadable at day's end.

Taking Control of "Transition Times"

Most executives agree that no element of business life is more important than time. It's the only thing there's a limited amount of.

People who deal with me on a regular basis know that I have a heightened sense of time and that maximizing the 168 hours in a week is a high priority for me.

However, I don't think I am a prisoner of time. I won't, for example, rush a delicate negotiation that's running longer than planned simply to save five minutes on my schedule. Five minutes as an isolated increment of time is not that important.

But if you can save five minutes twelve times a day, you've saved an hour. And an hour is something you can work with. You can go jogging or play with your children or take a nap or read a book in an hour.

There are lots of periods in each day that are wasted time. But in my mind the most galling are what I call "transition times"—the period between the end of one transaction and the beginning of the next. The time at which an associate and I finish our business and the time it takes for us to leave each other's presence is something that most people in all walks of life have trouble with.

On social occasions, transition times are almost like a ritual. How often at a dinner party have you seen people (a) decide to leave, (b) wander into the next room, (c) stop and chat, (d) loiter by the door, (e) promise to get together real soon, then (f) renew those promises out by the car? The period between everyone thinking "I'm finished with this beautiful evening" and everyone actually heading home can take twenty to thirty minutes.

Of course, that's one of the pleasures of a relaxed social life (and one of the rewards of organizing your business life). But if you let them, similarly "relaxed" transitions can occur half a dozen or more times during your workday, and the stolen minutes or hours are hard to recover.

Being aware of the value of transition times is half the battle. The other half is letting people who abuse these periods in on your secret—without being rude.

For example, I try to make fun of my crowded schedule. I try to be blunt and at the same time poke fun at myself for being so. To time-thieves who outstay their welcome, I might say, "I'm afraid I'm going to have to kick you out," and be sure to laugh.

The easiest situation is when the other person has something to do and says he can only see you for, say, half an hour. When he lingers past thirty minutes, I will say, "I'm sorry you only had a half hour for our meeting. But I scheduled something after you." There's no excuse for wasting time with people who claim to be busier than you are.

The best situation, of course, is when a scheduled thirty-minute discussion gets resolved in fifteen minutes. If someone gives me the gift of time, I won't waste those extra fifteen minutes thanking him for it. I'll return the favor—and let him go.

How to Dodge the Overprotective Secretary

More and more I am running into secretaries who are literally not informing their bosses about calls. Perhaps they need the ego boost of trying to control their boss's schedule. Perhaps they believe that insulating the boss proves they are loyal and effective. Perhaps they believe they know it all.

I'm not really sure what their "game" is, but unless their intuition is as good as that of their boss (in which case they are in the wrong job), I'd wager that they shut out two opportunities for every nuisance call they block. This misplaced loyalty is not only a disservice to their boss but infuriating to callers.

Over the years, the best way to dodge overprotective secretaries has been to (a) acknowledge their "gatekeeper" role and (b) include them as a co-conspirator in your plot to reach their boss. Unfortunately, the tenaciously protective breed sometimes encountered is no longer so easily manipulated. Getting around them calls for more aggressive tactics. For example:

1. Call the boss at home

A situation once came up where, because of my friendship with a CEO, I knew that this busy man would want to talk to me. And yet his secretary made it impossible for us to get together. "He's booked up for at least three weeks," I was told.

So I called him that night at home. He turned out to be happy to hear from me, and on hearing my reason for calling, even happier. "Great. What time next week can we have lunch?" he asked.

I'm continually puzzled why otherwise smart business-people hesitate to call executives at home. I wouldn't make a habit of it, but if you have an extraordinary opportunity to discuss, your gesture will be regarded as extraordinary, not intrusive.

2. Go through the chairman

Sometimes calling the chairman is the only way to get past an overprotective secretary. This is the corporate equivalent of the irate citizen who calls the White House to complain about poor postal service and suddenly is talking directly to the president.

Ironically, it's often easier to get a company chairman on the phone than a midlevel manager. It's not that the chairman has nothing to do. But he—and his secretary—usually have a better understanding of the value of certain calls. (That's one reason he's the chairman.)

When Dennis Conner, the yachting champion and one of our clients, visited our New York office shortly after his America's Cup victory in 1987, he decided to call the head of marketing at a Fortune 500 corporation. Conner got the marketing chief's secretary, who said he was in a meeting and offered to take a message. Dennis identified himself and said he'd only be at our number for thirty minutes. Twenty-five minutes later, no call back.

Dennis isn't the type to pull rank but he has a champion's instinct for getting quick results. So he phoned the company's chairman. The chairman's secretary answered, Dennis again identified himself, and immediately the chairman was on the other end, saying, "Hi, how are you. Congratulations. Great win in Australia. What can I do for you?"

"Well," Dennis explained, "I think I have a lot of ideas that would be good for you. The problem is I'm trying to get a hold of a guy who works for you, but I can't get through."

"You stay right where you are," said the chairman. And within thirty seconds the marketing chief was on the line for Dennis.

Obviously, Dennis Conner's celebrity didn't hinder him in this case. But even without this factor, most company chairmen I know would have done the same thing, no matter who was calling.

Breaking Through to Superbusy People

One of the biggest changes in personal time management in recent years is how far ahead today's decision makers actually make their schedules.

As recently as five years ago, senior executives (the ones who had control over their own schedules) rarely locked up their calendar more than three or four months in advance. If I wanted to meet with the chairman of a large corporation in April, I could set up that meeting quite easily by calling up in February or March. Today, I might have to make that appointment the year before.

I'm not particularly pleased by this turn of events. But that's the way of the world. Executive life is more complicated. This is how I adapt.

My point is: Most people have not adapted. Either they have not recognized the new breed of superbusy executives or they are not very clever about how to make this breed yield to their timetable. Three suggestions:

1. Invite people early—very early

The easiest way to get people to yield to your schedule is to get to them very far in advance.

A friend of mine (who is one of the busiest people I know) was invited to be a guest on a very elegant tour of the jungles of Venezuela. Ordinarily, this is the sort of event my friend politely declines. But the tour's host was shrewd: he sent the invitation 18 months in advance—which is sufficient lead time even for a head of state.

To my friend, 18 months down the road was so distant and unthreatening that he said yes. Predictably, as the tour date gets nearer, my busy friend is having second thoughts about the commitment. He's too honorable to back out, of course, but if the host invited him today I suspect he would have a reason not to go.

2. Reach them in their "off-season"

Everyone has an off-season—a period during the year when they are not that busy.

In our business of athlete representation, the off-season is obvious. If you want to pursue some off-the-field activities with a Herschel Walker, you schedule it between February and July, when Herschel is not playing football. The same with baseball players, who tend to make their speeches, conduct their clinics, and open their restaurants sometime between October and March.

The off-season isn't as clear-cut in business. But there are pockets of inactivity in everyone's calendar that you can take advantage of.

For example, New York is allegedly a ghost town during the month of August. Everyone is on vacation or stealing away for long weekends or stalling until September by saying, "Why don't we meet after Labor Day."

Yet for more than a decade, my busiest and most productive time in New York is the two weeks before Labor Day. I'm in town for the US Open tennis championships and I see practically everyone I need or want to see—because, I suspect, no one else is calling on them.

3. Make them set the date

If you've ever tried to put together a major meeting or conference built around two or three superbusy individuals, you can appreciate the difficulties of not only getting them to attend but getting everyone to agree on a specific date. One solution, we've found, is to let one of the key players set the date.

We'll say, "We're trying to gather several industry leaders for a conference in Scotland sometime in 1990. Since you're the main attraction, what date is good for you?"

The key, of course, is giving the busy individual an entire year—in this case, all of 1990—to play with. The larger the window, the more likely people will jump through.

(This approach has the added benefit of locking him in to that date—because you are accommodating his schedule. Only a churl would back out after you've bent over backward for him.)

The same logic applies in scheduling sales calls with busy people. Don't force them to fit your schedule. Yield to theirs and then pin them down.

Unfortunately, most people get this wrong.

If they're making a business trip to, say, Los Angeles, they'll warn a prospect, "I'll call you when I get to town." That's too vague. When they arrive and call, the prospect is either busy or gone and they never get the meeting.

The right way is to call ahead and say, "I'm planning a trip to California next spring and want to see you when I'm out there. Is there a particular week that's best for you?" That forces them to set the date and is far enough in the future to pin them down.

What "Talk To" Files Tell Me and My Employees

Ever since our organization grew beyond five employees, I have maintained "talk to" files for each of our executives. There are several dozen such files now in more than a dozen cities.

I literally toss any document to or from or about that executive into a file and keep it there. Some date back to the 1970s. Then the next time I see that executive I'll go through his or her "talk to" file to refresh both of us.

Often, the executives' reaction is, "I can't believe you still have that!" And they're right. Most of the documents aren't useful or relevant. But it's like going through a family photo album. You run across some interesting memories and occasionally an idea that's more appropriate now than it was then.

For example, if an executive says, "Let me do this, Mark, and I promise we'll have a $2 million profit center in two years," I'll keep that memo rather than rely on my memory two years down the road. Similarly, if I ask someone to do something, I'll include that request in their "talk to" file.

I think this has helped me get a tenuous grip on one of the more irritating aspects of running a business—the feeling that too many things are falling between the cracks. I used to believe that things only fell between the cracks in small companies, where too few people were responsible for too many projects. But as our company has grown to nearly 800 employees, I'm convinced that the cracks get wider with each expansion.

When a company's layers of management increase and each executive's responsibilities become more narrow and specific, that's when the new or undefined projects get lost. For some reason, everybody thinks that "the other guy" is handling it. My "talk to" files at least let me check up on things when no one else is doing so.

I've made "talk to" files an integral part of my note-taking and time-management system. When my legal pad and my pocket-size index cards are combined with the "talk to" file, I have all the things I need for any meeting.

I'm even prepared when someone shows up unannounced. Thus, when an executive says, "I have to see you," I might pull out his "talk to" file and say, "Wait a second. I've got a few things for you too."

The system is not cumbersome. After a few years, though, the folders for the senior executives got so big that I had to split them up into a fat "historical" file and a slender "current" one.

I don't know any other CEOs who do this quite my way. But in our company it seems to be having an impact. Now when I see our executives in Cleveland, New York, or wherever, many of them show up with their own "talk to" files—for me.

Getting On and Off the Phone

Every phone conversation, no matter how brief or interminable, has a beginning, middle, or end. Nearly everyone can handle the middle portion, where the heart of most discussions takes place. It's the openings and closing that throw them.

I know an executive who face-to-face is one of the most genial and lively persons you'd ever want to meet. But you'd never know this by his telephone voice. He speaks in a monotone so dull and relentless that, if you didn't know him well, you'd think your phone call was causing him physical pain.

This is unfair to him because talking to him is invariably worthwhile. He seems to pick up steam as the conversation goes on. After twenty minutes or so, when you're ready to hang up, he's animated and creative; *he* doesn't want to get off.

This can be maddening if you don't have the time to bring him up to speed. I wonder if he realizes how much more impressive and effective he would be—with strangers and friends—if he put a little energy into his opening "Hello."

He'd be better off if he paused to anticipate each call. This has worked for me. I wasn't even aware I did it until someone pointed it out. Before making or accepting a call, I put my hand on the receiver and pause for a few seconds before picking up. This lets me collect my thoughts and decide what I want to accomplish and how I can do it with my voice.

If the person on the other end is calling about a serious or delicate subject, I'll pause to decide how I want to come across. I might tell myself not to distract the caller by being artificially chirpy or, in some cases, by pretending I'm 100 percent glad they called. On the other hand, if I know the caller needs my advice or encouragement, I'll make sure that my first words are conveyed with energy and enthusiasm.

You'd be surprised how your opening line on the phone can set the tone for everything that follows. It is often the difference between getting your way or settling for theirs.

Getting off the line

Ending a phone conversation is just as important.

I sometimes think Larry King has the best phone technique in America. As the very successful host of two daily call-in shows on the CNN cable network and the Mutual radio network, King literally makes his living on the phone. He is a polite, funny, agile interviewer who somehow can simultaneously ask guests very tough questions and make them feel pampered.

But I really admire King's phone manner with chatty or rude callers. If a caller rambles on, wasting precious air time, King asks, "What's your point?" That almost always brings callers back to reality. If that doesn't work, King moves to the next caller with a punch of the button.

I think most people wish they could be that blunt—or had the courage to cut off callers so abruptly.

I know at least one executive who emulates King by pretending to be all thumbs around phone buttons. If an insensitive caller is boring him with endless details, he'll simply cut them off by punching a button. When they call back, he'll either make himself unavailable or apologize for the mishap and resume the conversation according to *his* agenda. I don't fully endorse this technique, but it gets the message across when the usual methods don't.

Leisure Time: The Most Poorly Managed Time of the Day?

Ever notice how tenaciously executives fight to get an extra week or two of vacation time into their employment contract—and then never take the time off?

Executives who treat their leisure time cavalierly or say they're too busy to take days off are fooling themselves. They don't appreciate the restorative powers of a long ski weekend or an afternoon squash game.

They think of relaxation or free time as the time when nothing's going on. They tend to fill their free moments with trivialities. They trap themselves in a spiral of busyness that usually leads to disaster either in their personal life or their business efficiency or their health. It is crucial to force yourself to take time off. But it requires discipline.

I always *schedule* leisure time, whether it's one hour or several days. I put relaxation time on my calendar in as ironclad a position as any other business appointment. If I decide to take an afternoon nap and put it on my schedule, that hour or two is inviolate. I simply will not toy with it.

I frequently schedule four days in Hawaii and tell my secretary I don't want to hear from anyone. I need four days of nothing to do. If I have the urge to call the office, I want it to be my choice, not someone else's.

Because I run my own business, I find it's better for me to take mini-vacations of two to five days. Two or three weeks away would leave me with such a backlog that the thought of it would ruin the last half of my holiday. As a result, I take more time off than my associates think.

Plan your leisure time and vacations and lock them in tightly. If you don't, your time is like an empty closet—it just fills up.

6 Communicating

How to Write Persuasive Memos

A surprising benefit of writing *What They Don't Teach You at Harvard Business School* has been its effect on my writing. Trying to express my thoughts on paper to strangers, I found, was a bracing discipline. It wasn't easy, but it was worth it. It forced me to read other people's writing—their books, articles, memos, correspondence—with a fresh eye.

I quickly learned that before you can persuade somebody, you have to grab their attention. And you can't do that with jargon, clichés, and digressions.

In our organization, I get "copied" on virtually every document. Consequently, I have a profound appreciation for short memos. My favorite memo is one sentence in length. My second favorite is two sentences. And so on. My executives know this. If they want to win me over, they better do it quickly. Lengthy memos don't impress me; they worry me.

The business memos I admire (and the ones that can

make a difference in someone's career) obey the following rules about clarity and simplicity:

Try to express, not impress

In most memos, writes William K. Zinsser in his invaluable book *On Writing Well* (Harper & Row), "the main villain is pomposity. Executives at every level are prisoners of the notion that a simple style reflects a simple mind. Actually, a simple style is the result of hard work and hard thinking; a muddy style reflects a muddy thinker or a person too lazy to organize his thoughts."

Keep it short

Short words, short sentences, short paragraphs work. Trust me.

Think: Are you on offense or defense?

Business memos usually have two purposes—either to project your ideas onto the company or to protect you from other people's ideas. Make your choice before you write a word. Whether you're advancing your cause or defending your turf, your readers won't be clear about it unless you are.

Deliver a clear message

I once read that the eight toughest memos to write deliver these messages: (1) This is how you do it. (2) I want to sell you. (3) I goofed. (4) I have some bad news for you. (5) I did a great job. (6) Dear Boss, you're wrong. (7) This is my demand. (8) This is how you rate. I would read a memo that began with any one of these sentences.

Get in and get out

Weigh every word against your readers' time and attention span. Too many writers write for themselves, using their memos to duplicate their thought processes. People don't need a blow-by-blow chronology of how you thought a problem through—and they certainly don't want to read about it. They want the nugget that inspired the memo, and they want it fast. If you have a way to cut costs, announce it in sentence one. If you're asking for a new computer, say so at the start. Don't drop your bombshell at the memo's end—it may blow up in your face.

Be yourself

With the best memos, I don't need to see the signature to know who sent it. The writer's identity is there on paper. Unfortunately, for most memo writers it's easier to abandon personality. Instead of trusting their unique way of expressing ideas, they mimic the safe, familiar language of memo-speak ("It has been determined that to facilitate increased productivity goals . . .").

Adding personality to a memo is not easy. But you can start by heaping on the personal pronouns such as "I" and "you" and "we" and "our." These are short but very specific words.

The only personal touch to avoid is humor. I say this even though I believe humor is one of the most valuable business tools. But jokes are best delivered face-to-face. On paper humor is dangerous because you can't predict how readers will take it.

Know your readers

Tailor your memo, if only slightly, for your intended readers. This isn't a license to toady to your boss or bully your underlings. But don't forget that readers have preconceptions about you: your boss expects to be *informed,* your peers want to be *included,* and your subordinates need to be *instructed.* Everyone, of course, should be treated with respect; you never score points at someone else's expense.

Use bullets

Use this visual device, setting off items as I have below, for the following reasons:

- To organize your thoughts.
- To simplify complex subjects.
- To highlight the main point.
- To break up the page visually.
- To give readers a breather.

Use a thesaurus

The quickest way to improve your writing is to use more colorful verbs. You'll find hundreds of vivid verbs in a thesaurus (the use of which is nothing to be ashamed of). Sprinkle fresh verbs into your memos and your language will have precision and action. Whenever possible, use active verbs ("I recommend") rather than passive verbs ("It is recommended"). Eliminate the passive voice and you'll silence the biggest source of bombast in memos.

Neatness counts. A lot.

Only sloppy executives send out sloppy memos. Perfect grammar and perfect proofreading display professionalism and courtesy to the reader. Even if your suggestions are shot down, you will earn credibility.

Great One-Line Memos

Three memos you should be writing or reading more often if you feel besieged by paperwork:

1. "I will meet with Jones if you think it is worthwhile." This is the kind of memo that is always better to send than to receive. That open-ended phrase "if you think it is worthwhile" is very provocative. It forces your subordinates to be considerate of your time. More important, it can inspire them to heroic efforts to make the meeting worth your while—often in ways that you might never have imagined if you tried to dictate a course of action in a lengthier memo. This is the ultimate memo for people who like to delegate.

2. "I need to see you for five minutes." The key here is the specific reference to time. Most successful executives I know will schedule time with any staff member as long as they know their time won't be abused. When someone writes to see me "for five minutes," my first thought is do they really mean five minutes or is it more like fifteen? If the memo is honest and realistic, I will block off time for anyone—whether they ask for thirty seconds or three hours.

3. "I must have an answer by November 2." This is a deadline memo. The more specific it is, the more likely your deadline will be met. Write "I need that report by the first of November" and people may generalize the date into the first week of the month. Worse, they may read no sense of urgency into the memo at all.

Great one-line memos have one thing in common: they say very little, but the little they say cannot be misinterpreted.

A Tale of Two Memos

Very often the differences between a successful piece of correspondence and a disastrous one are so subtle as to escape detection. The only people who notice are the ones who have to read them—and by then the damage may be done.

Consider the following two messages on the exact same subject of tax withholdings on a client's prize money. Two executives in our Cleveland headquarters sent them by fax on the same day to the same executive in our Tokyo office. Although they seem to convey the same message, in effectiveness they are worlds apart. At the risk of hanging our corporate laundry in public, I think the memos are instructive. The first one reads:

> I do not understand why tax was withheld from the last client prize-money payment. It is important that tax should not be deducted. Please arrange to have the client's prize money remitted without deduction of tax.

Memos like this worry me. For one thing, the first sentence makes a bad impression. It is either an admission of ignorance or, if intended facetiously, arrogance.

The second sentence states the obvious. Our Japanese accountants know it's their job to reduce a client's tax liability. No one likes to be lectured to, either face-to-face or by fax.

The third sentence is bossy but not very commanding. It tells the receiver to do something but not how to do it. It is also vague (what precisely does "arrange" mean?). And it is not particularly shrewd about the law. Withholding taxes is required by law, regardless of whether those laws please the person who sent this fax. Even factoring in a little brusqueness for an in-house communication, this memo is not inspiring. I'd understand if it was ignored.

The second fax, sent by a more experienced executive the same day, reads:

> I received the remittance of client's prize money for the U.S. versus Japan team matches. I noticed that prize money at 20 percent was deducted. Isn't this unusual? I thought that usually we were able to avoid this withholding tax obligation. This particular client needs all the cash flow he can get, so if there is any way to avoid this tax withholding, we would really like to do it. Is there a way? Please let me know if there is anything I can do to help the client avoid this tax withholding.

There is no peremptory tone here. Everything is suggested rather than ordered, and yet it commands a response. Phrases like "I noticed" and "I thought" soften the blow and add a personal touch (I hear the voice of a human being here). The writer *thinks* rather than *knows* that there is a problem and has politely left the door open for the reader to solve it. The writer also remembers to say "please" (a small but not insignificant point).

I particularly like the fifth sentence. Note how the writer enlists our Japanese office's sympathy by confiding that the "client needs all the cash flow he can get." A bond is formed by sharing that simple secret.

The congenial tone makes this fax effective. Questions like "Is there a way?" suggest a willingness to cooperate. The fax doesn't treat a fairly routine problem, mandated by law, as if it were the fault of its recipient.

Writing Proposals That Get Read

I still write many of our company's sales proposals. I should probably delegate more of this but, frankly, a proposal over my signature has a greater chance of being read at a company that doesn't know us well. Here is a short course on writing proposals:

1. Keep it short. Before you mail your 24-page master-piece, ask yourself: When was the last time you got as far as page 24 of someone else's proposal?

2. Give them your best ideas, not all your ideas. I often think a proposal is judged by the worst idea in it; at least that's the one someone at the prospect's company always seems to pick on. You never get a second chance to send a first proposal. Save your off-the-wall suggestions for later when they know you better.

3. Canvass your colleagues. When it comes to propos-als, I think it's foolish to work alone. So I brainstorm before I write. I'm always asking our executives for a dozen ideas each that would be appropriate for a new prospect. I then cherry-pick the best suggestions and drop them into my proposal.

4. Create a "proposal relationship." My favorite pro-posals are the ones I don't have to write. Instead, an associ-ate writes me a memo on what XYZ Corp. should be doing and I send it on to the company with a cover letter saying, in effect, "Here are some of our internal thoughts that you might find interesting." It gives our proposal the aura of "inside information"—and always gets read.

The "Let's Not Bother the Boss" Syndrome

It is a paradox of business life that people will always prefer to tell the boss good news rather than bad news. And yet, to the boss, the bad news is infinitely more important.

This is understandable if the employee's immediate self-interest is at odds with the company's good interests.

Ironically, this situation only gets worse as a company gets more successful. It's human nature that as a company grows and its organization gets more complicated, the employees more easily fall into the syndrome of "Let's not bother the boss about this. We can work it out ourselves." While this is admirable initiative on the employees' part, I could understand if their boss would at least like to sign off on the decision.

Street-smart executives are aware that, on occasion, they are victims of "Let's not bother the boss." They try to minimize this (1) by keeping an open door and (2) by treating bad news on equal terms with good news (and vice versa).

To the best CEOs, bad news is not a signal to practice power and intimidation. Most know that *not blowing up* is a sign of strength, not weakness. It's also the surest way to get subordinates to confess.

One very demanding CEO I know started off a staff meeting by half-joking, "Okay, what *haven't* you done for me lately?" This worked like truth serum for the attendees, who admitted to a series of minor screwups that stunned the CEO.

In a way he was glad. As he told me later, "The only thing worse than someone saying "I told you so" is someone who should have told you so—and didn't."

"Let's See, What Did I Do Wrong?"

I was meeting with a chief executive at her offices recently when we were interrupted by an important call from one of her senior managers. I gathered the manager was anxious to know what happened on one of her recent sales calls.

After a few seconds of small talk, she said, "Let's see.

What did I do wrong?" And rather than recounting all the triumphs of the day, she reviewed her errors—which turned out to be few in number and in consequence. I found this "What I did wrong" technique intriguing and worth repeating.

For one thing, it was a gentle backdoor way to allay her manager's doubts and fears. Anyone who can joke about the few things that went wrong must be confident that considerably more things went right.

Second, it demands action. By bringing up what went wrong, you practically force yourself to discuss measures to correct them.

Third, it's a great timesaver for both parties. I don't know how many times I wish someone had the courage and courtesy to simply tell me what went wrong rather than waste my time with a self-congratulating blow-by-blow account of all the things that went right.

Letters I'll Ignore

When it comes to writing business letters, I heed the Law of Diminishing Returns: the longer the letter, the less likely it will be answered. I know this is true because of all the long letters that *I* ignore.

You'd think that the people besieging busy executives with long letters, some with very good proposals, would learn this by now. But they don't.

Perhaps they think a long letter will impress the reader (it won't). Or that a good idea needs to be explained in five pages (if it's really good, ten words will do). Or that length will convince the reader they have every angle covered (usually the opposite is the case).

Length isn't the only reason letters go ignored. Here are three more:

1. Asking the reader to do too much

People who write letters that require the recipient to do too much have a good chance of getting ignored.

A business acquaintance in London once wrote to me about his thirteen-year-old son who wanted to get into the sports business. The father was seeking my advice but in such a way that he was literally asking me for a four-page letter mapping out his son's future. That's too much work (not to mention that it's really *his* responsibility). I ended up writing a one-page letter, but that sort of request is very close to what I'll ignore.

Make your requests simple ones. This can be nothing more than "Think about it" or "Read this and call me to discuss it." If you give your readers easy things to do, they're more likely to do them.

2. No return address on the letterhead

Not everyone, I've discovered, writes on corporate letterhead. They often write on personal stationery, with only their name engraved on the sheet and the return address on the envelope. Unfortunately, envelopes have a way of getting lost or tossed out, leaving the reader with a name, an interesting proposal, and no way to pursue it.

If your stationery doesn't have a return address (and it should), tell people how to contact you in the body of the letter.

3. Organized with too much logic, not enough care

Many people are too logical. They organize their letters as if they were step-by-step proofs, saving the punch line for last. This may work in mathematics, but there's no guarantee it will grab or hold an executive's interests.

I once received a letter from a young man looking for a

job that was a model of careful organization. It began: "I have now decided that you truly are as busy as you claim to be." To me, that opening is too intriguing to ignore. And so I continued reading for two pages about his efforts to contact me, his family background, and his career plans. He closed by warning me, "I will try your office every day to try and meet with you."

I may not have a job for that young man, but he certainly commands my attention.

Different Strokes for Different Folks

People often overlook the importance of rank or position in determining how to communicate with others. Different people need to be communicated with in different ways about the same subjects. Your boss expects to be informed. Your peers want to be included. Your subordinates need to be instructed.

For example, senior executives in our company know by now that, in communicating with me, I only need a few sentences on most subjects. I don't need an elaborate chapter-and-verse historical summary of "How I did that deal." I want simple information on the order of (a) what was sold, (b) by whom, (c) to whom, (d) for how much.

That sort of brevity isn't appropriate or constructive with peers and subordinates. Your peers deserve more details, not only to feel included but also because they might learn something and can offer suggestions that would improve future transactions.

Subordinates, on the other hand, often have huge gaps in their understanding of your business. This is the sort of information that you gradually take for granted as you ascend in the company. It's important that you take time out to give subordinates the complete picture of a situation or relationship that started long ago.

This communication hierarchy of bosses, peers, and sub-ordinates applies in corporate sales as well. When you approach other companies, tailor your sales presentation with the following in mind:

- Bosses (CEOs, senior officers) want *strategic* answers: why should we be in this market? What's the long-term impact? What trends are we anticipating?
- Peers (vice presidents, department heads) want *tactical* answers. How much will this cost? How will it make my job easier? How will it improve my bottom line?
- Subordinates (line managers, engineers) want *technical* details. How does it work? Will it last? Does it fit?

As a general rule, there's no percentage in talking long-term strategy with technicians, and there's no excuse for boring the CEO with nuts-and-bolts details.

Learn to Speak Less and You're Only Halfway Home

As I've already said, a big challenge for many business-people is learning to speak less; this is unfortunate because, in theory at least, it's easy to do. But even if you speak less, you're only halfway home. Most people when they're not actually talking are busy rehearsing what they're going to say next. This is worse than talking too much—because you're neither making a point nor hearing one.

It follows then that the second biggest challenge is learning to listen. The key is not simply to hear what other folks are saying, but to *listen aggressively.* Pay attention to the adjectives and adverbs people choose, their intonation in responding to certain topics. If you listen to how people are saying something, you'll understand why they're saying it.

I learned this in the very early days representing Arnold Palmer.

I received a call from *Sports Illustrated* magazine. They said, "There's this country club in Valdosta, Georgia, that wants Arnold Palmer to play a golf exhibition. They'll pay him $500. They'd like him to appear four weeks from Monday, just after he plays in a tournament in Mobile, Alabama."

In those days, $500 was a nice fee. When I mentioned it to Arnold, he said, "Tell them thank you, but no. I'd rather spend the time between tournaments at home."

I conveyed the message to *Sports Illustrated*. Five days later they called back, saying, "This country club really wants Arnold and they'll pay $1,000." Again I presented this to Arnold and again he declined.

Two weeks later, I was with Arnold on a practice tee in Memphis, Tennessee, when two fellows approached us. They introduced themselves and said, "Mr. Palmer, we're from Valdosta, Georgia."

Arnold and I looked at each other.

They continued, "We really hope you can come down there to play."

"I'm not sure I'll be able to," Arnold politely told them.

"But we really want you. In fact, we won you."

"What do you mean *won* me?" asked Arnold.

"We won a contest sponsored by Campbell Soup in *Sports Illustrated* for being the country club that best promoted "Beef Bouillon on the Rocks." Our prize is an exhibition match with any one of fifteen people in various sports, and you're on the list. The magazine keeps trying to get us to pick someone else. But we want you. And we don't care what it costs."

Arnold and I looked at each other again.

As it turned out, Arnold went to Valdosta for considerably more than $1,000. But I went away from that experience knowing that I had not listened aggressively. I hadn't asked myself, "Why does *Sports Illustrated* care if Arnold Palmer plays an exhibition match in Valdosta, Georgia?" If I had I might have picked up some valuable information, or at least started to appreciate that forces other than Arnold's popularity were at play.

Why We Misread Body Language

You probably know that body language, the unconscious visual clues that people send out, can be very telling. But there are two problems that make body language less telling than you think.

Problem No. 1: You can't predict with any certainty what body language means.

I have met with people who, at crucial points in a negotiation when they intend to get serious, will unknowingly "lean into" the conversation, or unconsciously push aside their papers to give me their undivided attention. Yet just as often, I have seen people at similar points lean back in their chair and strike a relaxed pose.

Problem No. 2: Although body language is supposed to be unconscious, some people consciously use it for effect—and get it all wrong!

Public speakers, for example, will raise their voice to get their audience's attention, even though whispering might be more effective (and less annoying). Young executives will talk rapidly and make shotgun decisions to appear more authoritative, even though a less frenzied pace is usually more impressive.

(Whenever I see someone posturing or misusing body language for effect, I'm reminded of the words of Boston Celtics coach Red Auerbach: "It's not what you tell them that's important. It's what they hear.")

It's not that I don't think there's a message behind body language. There usually is. But you have to resist hasty conclusions, conventional interpretations, or reading meanings where none exists. And you have to fold your insights into an overall context of more reliable observations.

The vocal factor

In any dialogue you should be keying in on the other person's emphasis and intonation. After all, there is a difference between "I'd really like that" and "I'd *really* like that"— although not enough people trust their ears or intuition when they hear it.

You should also consider the wide range of adjectives and adverbs that people choose to describe their reactions. With some executives, you can even ascribe some significance to them. I can think of at least one British executive whose clipped responses are shorthand for something else:

> "I might like to do that." (I'm noncommittal.)
> "I would really like to do that." (Tell me more.)
> "I'm prepared to do that." (So, move on to the next topic.)
> "I can think of nothing I'd rather do." (Done deal.)
> "I don't want to do that." (Are there other options?)
> "I won't do that." (Close the door on your way out.)

The sequence factor

You also have to measure a person's responses in sequence. How does what they're saying now compare, in terms of emphasis or enthusiasm, with what was said before?

I once suggested an idea to an executive in his office and he rather coldly responded, "That might be nice." A half hour later his assistant rushed in to where we were sitting with some fabulous news. The executive said nothing except, "That's nice."

A flag instantly went up in my mind, and I began to recalibrate his levels of enthusiasm. If "That's nice" was how he reacts to a major bulletin, then perhaps in his frame of reference "Might be nice" was a giant "Yes."

The time factor

Never underestimate the importance of time in affecting your perception of a message. People tend to equate a project's significance with how much of their time it requires or how much other people devote to it—when very often the opposite is the case.

If you attend a speech scheduled to last sixty minutes and the speaker only talks for thirty, you very likely will feel cheated. Even if the speaker has covered the material succinctly and spared you thirty minutes of hot air, you will feel shortchanged; a topic vital to you has somehow been diminished.

The same thing happens when people go into a one-hour meeting with the boss and it ends on a positive note in fifteen minutes. No matter how encouraging the boss's verbal statements and body language, some people take their curtailed stay as a sign that they and their ideas are of minor importance.

Their preconception about time has forced them to misread the clues and the situation completely.

Ending the Endless Conversation

To busy executives few business situations are more stressful than being trapped in a conversation that should have ended minutes earlier—but didn't. Even seconds seem like hours if you have other things to do but are too polite to cut the other person off.

Many trapped listeners resort to body language—they squirm, tap fingers, scribble notes, reach for the phone, nod their heads in agreement—but the effect, at best, is unpredictable. Someone too dense to pick up your verbal clues is not apt to read the nonverbal ones.

Here are three lines that should bring a swift conclusion to dialogues that have overstayed their welcome.

1. "You'll have to get me out of this conversation." This is a euphemism for "Enough!" but few people feel stung by it. If you frame the ending of the discussion as a favor they can do for you, most people will be very happy to oblige.

2. "Let me see if I can help you get where you seem to be going." This is an interruption that both implies "I understand" and "I can help you." Use it when people interminably restate the same idea in different ways. If you promise to help them, few will mind the interruption.

3. "Tell me what you think we should do." Most people prefer to talk about problems because it's easier than finding solutions. They claim they need to discuss a problem but actually want to conjecture about every permutation that *could have* happened *if* they had done this or that. These people are reliving the past (at your expense) and avoiding the future (also at your expense).

This phrase works as a challenge. It asks for a solution, and either forces the person to rise to the occasion or rise to leave.

Perfect Pitch: Finding the Words That Sell

I continually marvel at how nomenclature can make or break a deal. Some people have perfect pitch in describing their ideas. They carefully select the perfect word that crystallizes the concept and closes the sale. Others are tone-deaf. They heap words upon words into meaningless piles, hoping that a gem will emerge on top.

You find the tone-deaf in government, politics, the military, and any other bureaucracy. These are the people who refer to tax increases as "revenue enhancement," who can describe an airplane crash (with a straight face) as "controlled flight into terrain," and who consider Mafia leaders as members of the "career-offender cartel."

Businesspeople are just as blatant about not saying what they mean. I still don't understand why greeting cards are now called "social-expression products" or why automobiles no longer break down but "fail to proceed."

I'm sure there are tricky moments when this sort of doublespeak can come in handy. But selling situations aren't one of them.

The problem in selling is that doublespeak *obscures* rather than *enhances* your message. People won't get excited about your proposal if they can't understand it. And they certainly won't give you their money if they think you're serving up euphemisms rather than simple facts.

Adding one word

Sometimes adding one simple word to your proposal can make the difference between triumph and disaster.

A literary agent I know sold an excerpt of a book to a mass-circulation magazine. This is common in publishing. Prepublication excerpts are called "first serial rights," magazines bid competitively for these rights, and the sale often enhances an author's income by four or five figures.

Unbeknownst to the agent, the author offered the same rights for considerably less money to a friend who published a tiny but prestigious professional journal—thus jeopardizing the larger magazine sale.

The agent solved the dilemma by adding one word to the traditional phrase. The small professional journal, she told everyone, was obtaining "first *professional* serial rights."

She created a new category that no one could argue with. And that was that.

When euphemisms work

Of course, some people, for perfectly legitimate reasons, don't respond to simple language. They need to be sold with a euphemism.

I know a businessman who once came up with a recreational program for the US Army. He believed it dovetailed with the Army's "Be all that you can be" recruiting image and would show the Army in a "fun" light. He pitched the idea to an ad agency executive, again stressing the "fun" aspects.

The agency executive stopped him in his tracks. "I like it," he said. "But go easy on the 'fun' part. You have to understand that serious military officers aren't looking for 'fun' programs. They prefer the phrase 'quality of life.' That's what they need to hear."

Simple words for complex deals

The most crucial time for the precise and simple phrase is when you are selling a complicated or revolutionary concept.

When we helped negotiate the sale of US television rights on behalf of the organizing committee of the 1988 Summer Olympics in Seoul, Korea, one of the thornier aspects was the thirteen-hour time difference between Seoul and the East Coast of the United States. This meant that noon events in Seoul would air live at 11:00 P.M. in New York. As you can imagine, the greatly reduced audience at that hour didn't improve our bargaining position with the three major American networks.

But Barry Frank, the head of our negotiating team, solved the problem with the three simple words: "Seoul Olympic Time."

He suggested extending Korean daylight savings time to include the two weeks of the Olympic Games, calling it Seoul Olympic Time. This would create a fourteen-hour time difference so that all morning events could air live on American prime time.

That terse but elegant phrase altered everyone's perception of how special the Games were.

How to Handle the Press on Your Terms

A chief executive was complaining to me about how his company was always getting skewered in the press. "If we're not misquoted," he said, "then the facts are distorted and the tone is very negative."

I asked him who was responsible for his press relations.

He said, "Oh, no one. We have a policy of never talking to the press." Which, I guess, explains everything.

It would be nice to write off this CEO as a neanderthal in the ways of modern media, with no one to blame but himself. But I know plenty of smart executives who actively court journalists, hire publicists, and maintain a clipping service to track every mention of their name—and they fare no better in the press.

The point is, the press doesn't like you to be too familiar or too remote. Somewhere in between is a media policy that works. Here's how to get there.

Don't argue with the press

It raises the dialogue to fever pitch, and the quotes always come out more hostile, more combative than you intended.

Members of the press are like any other profession. Some are honorable and bright. Some are dishonorable and dim. But they have a unique weapon unknown to other professions. They always have the last word. And you can't argue with that.

Give them as much (or more) time than they need

You can't blame reporters for getting the facts wrong or disliking you if you only give them one hour when they ask for three.

Keep your secrets for as long as you can

I've never been a great fan of press attention, especially the kind initiated by publicists. I find that any business strategy works better the longer you keep the competition unaware of it.

If you're big enough within your industry, your secretiveness can actually damage your competitors—or at least distract them. IBM, for example, never comments on any new product in development. As a result, a cottage industry of experts has arisen to read the meaning of IBM's "refusal to comment." The experts are rarely right, and even if they were, I certainly wouldn't base my company's future on them.

If you must talk, have a strategy

Even though we never solicit publicity, we have still had some nice attention. In the sports business, if you do your job well, people will want to write about it.

If you must blow your own horn, at least have a strategy for doing so.

In the mid-1970s, when I more than anyone else knew the scope and significance of our company, *Sports Illustrated* approached us about an article. I decided to go overboard in cooperating with them, to ensure that they positioned us accurately as the dominant company in our field. That's when they called me "the most powerful man in sports."

At the time, the article was an eye-opener to many people in and out of our industry. They said, "We had no idea you were doing all these things," because until that article there was no way they could.

Of course, there are other times to keep quiet about how well you're doing. If we represent 100 basketball players, we will lose more from telling the world that secret than we can gain. We have the fleeting ego gratification of announcing "We're big!" But a shrewd competitor can sell against that fact. He can woo clients away by saying, "They handle so many basketball players, you're just another number." (This may be unfair to us but not unpersuasive to some clients.)

I'd rather let the world think we have thirty basketball clients even if we do in fact have 100.

Make them pay if they don't play

We were accused years ago of charging for our clients' interviews, which infuriated the press. I think parts of our company did that on occasion out of a well-intentioned desire to protect our clients. After all, a magazine might ask for three or four days of a young athlete's time for interviews and photography. And time is the most precious commodity an athlete has.

But having dealt with the press the past three decades, I have a new theory: charge them if the interview or photo session *doesn't* appear. I've come to this conclusion because so often a periodical will seek more and more of a client's time by promising a cover story—while they're saying the same thing to a dozen other celebrities. This is their privilege, I guess. But charging them for not living up to their promise is a great way to find out if they're sincere.

How to Look Good on TV

Going on TV has its rewards. It's the most powerful way to promote or defend your business (and, not incidentally, your career).

But it's not as easy as it looks. I've seen the most polished CEOs, confident executives who wouldn't blink in front of print journalists or angry stockholders, crumble on TV. The little things that may make them effective CEOs in real life—the calculated silences, the eyes that dart around a room, the talent for finding out more than they reveal—are deadly on TV.

Before you go into "show business" you should know as much about the TV business as your own. Here are seven points to consider:

1. TV hosts have their own agenda. You should too

Don't expect nice-guy treatment on TV. Newscasts need drama and controversy to hold the viewers. Questions can be tough, pointed, even hostile. If I don't like a question, I'll ignore it and give an answer that fits my agenda. An even better approach: make a point of rephrasing the question to your liking, then answer it. Most interviewers will admire your spunk. Politicians have been doing this to them for years.

2. Be a little paranoid

Before you let a show's producer woo you into the studio, ask three questions: What's the show about? What do you expect me to say? Who else will be on? If you don't like any of the answers, decline the invitation.

3. Keep cool

TV, as Marshall McLuhan said, is a "cool" medium. It favors calm, avuncular, nonthreatening Walter Cronkite types. Many TV producers, however, believe the best way to prove a topic is controversial is to have two or more people argue about it. You should remember this before you agree to lose your cool on the air as a verbal combatant. At the least, make sure there's no confusion about which side you're on.

4. Don't stop talking

Just as nature abhors a vacuum, TV abhors silence. The only thing worse than saying something boring or fatuous is saying nothing at all. If you stumble or drop your voice midthought, your host will interrupt you instantly. And you'll have lost your forum. The best TV performers learn to speak in forty-word "sound bites" that sum up their views and invite a response. It's a good idea to memorize a sound bite or two.

There's nothing worse than freezing on the air. I've been doing BBC television commentary on the British Open for twenty years, yet I still rehearse two or three filler phrases— a comparison with a past event such as "Gee, seeing this threesome reminds me of . . ."—to keep my vocal cords working in case my mind isn't.

5. Be prepared

Know your facts and don't stray from your area of expertise. President Reagan, for example, prepared for press conferences with mock questions from his staff. Before he faced the nation, he knew exactly which questions he'd answer and which he'd duck. He also arrived with impressive statistics that supported his position.

6. Beware of trick questions

Interviewers are clever people. They'll ask you hypothetical questions ("What if your company leaves town?"). They'll ask for a simple yes or no on issues that demand more than a one-word discussion. They'll set up false premises, ask you to speculate on what the other guests are thinking, give you a choice between X or Y when what you really believe is Z, anything to make the show lively. Before I'll answer a trick question, I'll gently point out the fallacy to host and audience.

7. Three fundamentals

(1) Look at your host, not the camera. Let the studio crew worry about photographing you. (2) Don't refuse makeup. You'll look ghostly under the harsh TV lights without it. (3) Sit still. Your heart may be pounding and your palms dripping sweat but the audience won't have a clue unless you squirm, talk with your hands, or clear your throat too often.

Where Do You Get Your Information?

An executive I know recently read in *The Wall Street Journal* that a major conglomerate was shutting down one of its midwestern plants. He immediately called the company and offered to take some of the plant equipment off their hands. Within a few days, a deal was struck.

Nothing unusual here, really. This sort of "distress sale" wheeling and dealing goes on all the time.

But what struck my friend as unusual was that *he was the only one who called the company.*

"You'd think," he said, "that out of 2 million or so *Journal* readers, at least one other person besides me could use good machines at 10 cents on the dollar!"

I'm not surprised. Most of us in business absorb information constantly from all directions, but only a handful are bold enough to act on it.

The sad part in all this is that it doesn't take any particular genius to realize that a shuttered plant means bargains on equipment. But you do have to discipline yourself about unsolicited information; you must register *and* act on it.

In our organization we are constantly circulating published articles, memos about meetings, comments on industry rumors—and urging people to check out this item or call up that person.

Over the years we've developed a good sense about our sources of information. Here's how I would rank five of the most common sources of information and whether or not we should act on them.

1. Friends. Friends are your most important source of information, not only because they'll always steer you straight but if they're outside your industry, they'll often see connections that wouldn't occur to you. Perhaps more important, if they're knowledgeable in your area, they can give you a blueprint of who, what, when, where, and why that can save you months of wandering in the wilderness. They're usually flattered that you asked.

One of our executives recently came up with a program that he wanted to sell to a major financial services company. Before he called on the financial giant, however, he spoke to a close friend who ran that company's advertising agency. He didn't ask his friend to make an introduction or arrange a meeting with a decision maker; he only wanted information—which his friend was happy to share. That advice saved our executive weeks of knocking on wrong doors.

2. CEOs. Chief executives, if you can get to them, are excellent sources of information. I can learn more from spending five minutes with a CEO than I can in five hours with his or her staff. (That's not a swipe at subordinates; it's praise for CEOs.)

I don't know how many times I've sat through meetings at other companies listening to that organization's experts explain all the reasons we *can't* do a certain project, and then the CEO walks in at the end and within minutes offers the one reason we *can*.

3. Consultants. A tough call. The good ones are independent. They tell you what you should know, not what they think you want to hear. The bad ones, who are trying to keep their job, will always require a second opinion.

4. Competitors. You can learn a lot from your competition (and their suppliers)—if they're reckless or stupid. I particularly enjoy industry gatherings, where competitors—perhaps under the impression that we are confidantes—often tell me more about their business than I tell them about mine.

5. Media. I tend to be very selective with the information I hear and read in the media.

For one thing, it's not particularly exclusive; the whole world, in theory, knows it the same moment you do.

Also, at best it's second- or third-hand information, customarily provided by competitors, consultants, CEOs, even your friends.

Finally, it's not particularly reliable. I've seen too many inaccurate reports—on topics where I know the facts as well as anyone—to believe otherwise.

Personnel changes at other companies are the most valuable information the media provide to our organization—because one of the best times to sell to someone is when they are joining a new company or have just been promoted. That's when they're eager to make an impact. If you follow personnel changes in the business pages or trade press, you'll find that contacting those people who are coming or going can be a very worthwhile exercise.

Rating the Medium, Not the Message

How would you rank the following eleven forms of business communication in terms of effectiveness (starting with the least effective)?

Handout
Advertisement
News Item
Brochure
Mass-produced letter
Typewritten letter
Handwritten letter
Phone conversation
Large group discussion
Small group discussion
One-to-one conversation

If you left the above list unchanged, you'd have what market researchers call the "Ladder of Communication Effectiveness," arranged from least to most effective. Here, in a slightly revised and ascending order, is how I would grade each method—and why:

11. Handout, Grade F: Flyers are virtually worthless. They're distributed on one street corner and deposited in a trash can at the next.

10. Mass-produced letter, Grade D minus: You'll never convince me that mailing 1,000 letters to have 990 ignored is effective communicating. Yet in some direct-mail circles, this 1 percent response is considered great.

9. Advertisement, Grade C: Quick! What's the last great advertisement that you can recall?

8. News Item, Grade C: High readership, high credibility, but hard to control.

7. Brochure, Grade C: Great for image building and selling the pre-sold.

6. Typewritten letter, Grade C plus: The standard form of communication. Essential as a means of self-protection. Effectiveness is inversely proportional to its length.

5. Handwritten letter, Grade B minus: This personal touch is memorable when you're writing to someone you know. Debatable when you don't.

I've met many executives socially, but I don't know them well. Yet I suspect they'd take notice if I wrote them a letter in longhand. I know it would make an impression if they communicated that way with me.

4. Large group discussion, Grade B: A favorite of self-perpetuating bureaucrats: the less certain they are of what exactly they want to discuss, the more people they invite to discuss it.

Large discussions are fine for *handing down* decisions, less so for *making* them. They also require ruthless follow-up.

3. Small group discussion, Grade B plus: The preferred method of making internal decisions. To me, an acceptable small group is three people. The ideal is two.

2. Phone conversation, Grade A minus: As they say, the next best thing to being there. Keep this in mind the next time you debate whether to write or call.

1. One-to-one conversation, Grade A plus: Not only the best form of communication, but in my experience better than all the other forms combined. Keep this in mind the next time you debate whether to bring an associate or go alone.

7 Getting the Job Done on the Road

The World According to Clerks

If you travel as much as I do, you quickly realize how much of your life on the road is at the mercy of clerks. You also begin to appreciate how important the face on the other side of the counter can be.

Yet many people don't.

Perhaps you've witnessed the following scenario in your travels. A man arrives at an airport ticket counter to learn that he's been bumped from an overbooked flight. He will do anything to board that plane. Unfortunately, in his desperation, he turns stupid. Instead of pulling back and considering his options, he begins to push—real hard.

He tries to bully his way on to the plane. He berates the ticket clerk (who is really not at fault), hurls invective at the airline, demands to see the supervisor, and generally makes a fool of himself. The entire exercise makes him feel good for a moment but so thoroughly alienates the ticket clerk (who no doubt has seen such behavior many times) that the man can wave good-bye to his plane.

The fact is, ticket agents, maître d's, waiters, and hotel clerks don't have a great deal of power (at least not in the sense that they can say "Jump!" and people jump). But within their narrow territory, clerks have a great deal of discretionary power. They are the ones who decide whether you get a good seat on a plane or even board at all; whether you enjoy your meal at a quiet table in the corner or suffer by the kitchen door; whether you sleep in a comfortable room at the lowest price when your reservations are lost or are left to find lodging on your own.

For those few routine moments when your life intersects with a clerk, he or she can be the most important person in the world as far as your comfort and sanity are concerned. Here's how to get them on your side:

Flatter them

This is the simplest rule to remember. But it's the one that many people forget, especially when they're tired or harried or behind schedule (and, ironically, most in need of a friendly hand).

I can see why. Some people are no good at small talk. Others can't fake sincerity. Still others regard check-ins, check-outs, and ticket purchases as routine nonevents. Nothing unusual is supposed to happen; no unnecessary words need to be exchanged. And so, they walk up to a counter, announce their name, and expect everything to fall into place.

But it's the routine aspect of the whole system that should make you want to do something out of the ordinary.

The more interested you are in the person across the counter, the better off you'll be. Find a reason to say, "Where'd you get that suntan?" or "That's a beautiful bracelet you're wearing." It may mean a better room, a better car, or whatever else you are trying to get.

Better yet, ask a question that indicates your respect for that person and his knowledge. For example, "You look like you'd know the good restaurants in this area. Where should I go tonight?"

Deferring to another person's judgment is a great way to elevate their opinion of you.

Let them display their power

A woman I know is really skilled at getting people to relate to her. She's got plenty of time for people. She's friendly, funny, and interested in them. She's always asking questions rather than talking about herself. She's not manipulative. She simply likes people and gives that extra 5 percent to get them to like her. As a result, she's constantly getting people to do incredible things for her—because when somebody likes you, they'll go out of their way to prove it.

This is borne out time and time again in some of the most mundane (but potentially frustrating) situations. For example, say you order the luncheon special at a restaurant. You get a hamburger, French fries, salad, apple pie, and tea for $9.95. The menu warns you, ominously, "No Substitutions." But you hate apple pie. Instead, you ask for cherry pie. If the waitress likes you, she will take pleasure in demonstrating to you that she has the authority to overrule the menu. That's her power position. She'll say, "Don't worry about it," and bring you cherry pie.

Make them negotiate

In Mediterranean countries, everything is negotiable. Shopkeepers and sales clerks enjoy haggling and, in fact, lose some respect for you if you *don't* bargain with them. They think you are a fool.

Negotiating in retail stores is not as common in English-speaking countries. But in a curious way, I think that sales clerks will respect you—and will do more for you—if you are willing to try to talk them down in price. It indicates to them that you are nobody's fool.

This is true whether you are angling for an extra scoop of

ice cream in a candy shop or haggling over expensive jewelry. If you state your terms firmly but nicely, a sales clerk will enjoy arguing with you—and often concede.

One of the wealthiest men I know is a master at winning sales clerks over by his eagerness to negotiate. A few years ago, while watching the St. Patrick's Day Parade on New York's Fifth Avenue, he walked into the showroom of a very prestigious jeweler. He examined a pair of earrings and then asked the sales clerk, "Have you got anything a little bit nicer?" The clerk showed him a diamond and emerald necklace with matching earrings. The price: $375,000.

He said to the clerk: "You've got two things working against you. One, we're alone here so there's nobody for me to impress if I buy the jewelry and nobody to embarrass me if I don't. Two, I don't really need to buy it. But I'm willing to give you $225,000 for this jewelry."

The clerk grew huffy and imperious. "That's silly, sir. Who do you think we are?"

My friend was polite. He said, "Here's my business card. Here's my hotel. I'll be there for four more days."

Two days later, the clerk's supervisor called my friend. "I understand you were looking at our diamond and emerald set."

"Yes," he replied.

"We can let you have it for $300,000."

"I really appreciate your call," he said. "But I told you that I don't really have to buy it. I'll give you $225,000 for it."

Two days later the store called back and gave him the jewelry for $225,000.

It amazes me how this man could make this haughty establishment act like a Teheran rug market. But the moment they agreed to negotiate with him, it was inevitable that they would cave in.

The Danger of "Junk Travel"

In many businesses, particularly multinationals, executives can come up with an excuse to be almost anywhere in the world anytime they want to be there. This can lead to the sort of abuse that I call "junk travel," contrived trips that are more recreation than business.

An executive in our New York office once told me he was planning to meet an official of the World Ski Federation (our client) in Kitzbuhel, Austria, over a winter weekend for business and, I assumed, some skiing. By coincidence, I knew the official was in New York at the time and, oddly enough, was also planning to fly to Kitzbuhel that weekend. I gently pointed out that Austria was a long way to go for a meeting when the two of them happened to be only a few blocks apart at the moment.

I think everybody manipulates the company for his or her personal ends a little bit. It's a matter of degree, which you can gauge on a scale of zero to ten. "Ten" is the dangerous employee who's creative energies are channeled to ripping off the company. "Zero" is the employee whose worst offense may be a company subscription to *Sports Illustrated*.

In between it gets complicated. And every boss has to handle "junk business" case by case. You have to know your people. Some, for example, love to travel, some don't. The first group you have to question constantly. The second group you might have to encourage to get out more often. You also have to consider which executives secretly regard their trips as perks and which ones are doing a good job so they are justifiable perks.

I particularly look at annual business conferences in exotic locales with great skepticism—even though I know they're put in those locales to attract attendees. Such conferences have a way of turning into junk travel.

I have a grudging admiration for the Frenchman who created a television industry conference called MIP in Cannes, France, which convenes each April. He played this "junk travel" issue like a violin. He set up the conference and attracted the entire industry because everyone wanted to be on the Riviera in April. Executives at one Australian TV channel, for example, would contend they had to go because the competition would be there—and at each competing channel people were making the same self-fulfilling arguments to their boss. Our executives presented a similar case.

Within a few years, the MIP conference had snowballed into a huge unquestioned "must," an industry ritual where our company alone was spending $40,000 to send six people to sunny France for a week. After asking ourselves, "What business specifically resulted from this conference?" we now don't go at all!

The biggest danger of "junk travel," though, is not the petty expense-account abuse but the way it blinds some people into making "junk deals." A few years ago a venture capitalist I know watched helplessly as one of his partners invested a huge sum of the firm's money in the stock of a high-tech company in Denver, Colorado. The partner was not acting on a shrewd hunch or careful analysis of market trends. All he wanted was an excuse to visit Denver five or six times a year so he could piggyback a skiing holiday on each trip. The lure of the ski slopes so beguiled this fellow that he held on to the stock even as its price plunged from 72 to 3.

Getting Your Money's Worth from Hotels

Countless magazine articles and travel guides presume to rate the best hotels in the world's business capitals. For the busy international traveler, the bottom line is not how many stars are beside the hotel's name, but whether the hotel's staff know you and treat you well. Once you find such a hotel, stick with it on subsequent visits. The service will get better. In the hotel business, at least, familiarity breeds contentment.

Assuming that the hotel's staff is nice to me, I have three criteria for choosing a foreign hotel:

1. Twenty-four hour room service. This is very important if you've been flying across time zones and your inner body clock says you are hungry or thirsty at 3:30 A.M. local time. Even in some of the best hotels, room service shuts down after midnight.

2. Laundry and valet services that return your clothes better than you left them. This is crucial on an extended business trip with a crowded schedule, especially if you travel light. Valet service varies widely from hotel to hotel, country to country. There are certain countries—such as Japan—where you're never afraid to send your best clothes to be laundered, and then there are others where your main concern is if they come back at all.

3. Efficient telephone service. Because I travel so much, I have to conduct a lot of business on hotel telephones. I try not to sabotage myself by staying at a hotel with a slow, outdated phone system.

I also make a point of tipping the hotel's telephone operators. All travelers know to tip the bellboy, maids, waiters, headwaiter, and concierge, but tipping the operators makes you memorable and can inspire extraordinary service. Once at London's Carlton Tower, I was out when an overseas call came in at a critical point in a negotiation. The operator knew me well and sensed the call was important. She called the doorman and asked him if he had any idea where I had gone. The doorman had overheard the restaurant I had mentioned to the cab driver. She then relayed the message to me at the restaurant.

Tips, by the way, don't have to be cash. They could be tied in to your business. Because my business is sports, noncash tips such as tickets to a major sporting event or free sporting goods equipment add a personal touch that often means more than money.

Efficient phone service applies to outgoing calls, which means touch-tone dialing and direct connections to most of the world. It also applies to incoming calls, which means both an alert staff and fast switchboard activity. It's one thing to be known and chased down by the hotel staff, but all that diligence can be undone by a sleepy switchboard. If someone is calling me in the hotel and it takes fourteen rings to answer, and then more rings while the call is transferred to the concierge, three-quarters of the time the caller will hang up in frustration.

A Code for Frequent Flyers

Frequent flyers automatically knock airlines and airports these days. Complaints, delays, and near misses are at all-time highs. Horror stories about canceled flights and sitting on the runway for six hours continue to play in the national press.

But you won't hear me complaining, and I've been flying more than 200,000 miles a year for the last twenty years. When I think back to 1967, I'm actually grateful that I can go directly to the gate, that I can breeze through customs and immigration in most foreign cities, and that baggage claim is relatively quick and reliable.

It's not that I haven't had my share of delays and missed connections. Believe me, I have (mostly at Dallas–Fort Worth now that I think about it).

But I don't go looking for trouble. I choose my airlines carefully. I make a point of knowing which ones in which cities have the most flights, the most nonstops, the most delays, and the most backup planes; which ones are closest to baggage claim; which ones have more than one-class carriage; even which ones are lenient about carry-on luggage.

Here is my Code for Frequent Flyers.

The airlines want to help you. Let them.

I try very hard to get to know the customer relations people at each airport. All airlines have these "special services" people to assist VIPs and not-so-VIPs. They're amazing people. They can get you upgrades to first class. They'll tell you about empty seats in first class so you can make sure you're next to them. They'll walk you through customs and immigration if you're in a hurry.

You don't have to be a movie star or the chairman of Chrysler to get this royal treatment. But if you travel a lot, you do have to work assiduously and cleverly at developing relationships with the customer relations people.

Join the VIP clubs

I belong to most of the airline clubs. They come in handy when you arrive early or are delayed and need a place to relax, work, or even conduct a meeting.

Run early rather than late

This is the most obvious advice—and virtually impossible for many people. They have to make an adventure of showing up at the last minute. They need to race through airports.

I don't. I'd rather get there an hour early than endure the discomfort of driving through heavy traffic wondering if I'll make my flight.

I've been told that Helen Gurley Brown, the savvy and serene editor of *Cosmopolitan,* finds traffic delays so disturbing she arrives at the airport *two hours* before departure (and brings along work).

Give yourself an hour between connecting flights if you have checked luggage. You can schedule connections a little tighter if you carry on everything. And I do.

The bigger the better

Stick with larger airlines with frequent flights and lots of aircraft coming in and out. Given the choice of flying from London to Los Angeles on British Airways or Varig, I'd go with British Airways (even though I might prefer cabin service on Varig) because they're more likely to have several planes on the ground ready as backup whereas Varig has only one flight a week (increasing the likelihood of getting stranded in case of mechanical problems).

I've been advised to avoid big airlines with labor problems. But I often think you need a weekly newsletter on airline labor relations to keep fully informed. In Europe, for example, the traffic controllers, ground crews, pilots, or stewardesses are apt to go on strike within twenty-four hours. There's no way to avoid these instant job actions.

The best days to fly

Statistically, the worst flight days are Fridays and Sunday nights. Tuesdays and Saturdays are supposedly the least congested. Of course, the airlines know this too, so they offer cheaper fares on Saturdays and the crowds seem to be averaging out.

The best hours to fly

If you regularly book five o'clock flights out of LaGuardia or O'Hare, don't complain if you're stuck on the runway. Eight o'clock flights in the morning and five o'clock flights in the afternoon are murderous. I try to get the first flight out at 7:00 A.M. or I tend to take something midday or very late at night. The advantage of flying midday is that you can still get a good morning's work done (if you wake up early) and you can avoid lunch (if you want to control your weight).

If you don't know when you're going, overbook

I hesitate to admit this, but I sometimes double- or triple-book flights when I'm not sure if I'm leaving Tuesday evening or Wednesday morning. Of course, I immediately cancel the other bookings once I decide. An alternative: book the flight *before* the most convenient flight; this gives you an acceptable fallback.

Don't do in the air what you can do better on the ground

I used to catch up on reading and paperwork during flights. But I soon realized I could do this more productively on the ground. Now I catch up on sleep, because there are no phones and few interruptions 30,000 feet in the air. As a result, I'm more awake on the ground.

Taking Control of Time Zones

I don't set much store by people who use "jet lag" as a business excuse. I fly over 200,000 miles a year and if I worried as much about crossing time zones as some people do, I'd never get anything done.

When it comes to coping with different time zones, I guess I do everything you're not supposed to do. But the following four rules work for me.

1. Sleep on the plane

I'm personally very lucky because I sleep like a log under almost any circumstances, including planes. As I said in the last section, if you can do it, it's better to get some rest on the plane than to find yourself nodding out on the ground.

2. Charge into the new time zone

As a businessman, I believe it's very important to get on the other time zone as fast as you can. And you do that by charging into a full day.

After the most common overnight flights—namely, the American "red-eye" from California to New York, or from New York to Europe—the natural tendency is to go take a nap. However, all the nap does is put you back on the previous (and wrong) time zone. It means you'll have trouble sleeping later that night, which in turn messes you up the following day. Ultimately, you fall asleep around 4:00 A.M. (which is 11:00 P.M. where you came from) and are exhausted when you have to wake up in three or four hours.

My thinking is always to fight like hell against the nap the first day. When I fly overnight from Los Angeles to New York I immediately take a shower and conduct a whole day of business. I usually go to bed early that night and, not surprisingly, sleep really well. The following day I am all there.

Of course, I'm not going to say that you shouldn't rest before the most important meeting of your life. In an ideal world you might give yourself a few days to adjust. But not everyone has that luxury. Plus, if something really crucial is in front of you, no time zone should stop you from rising to the challenge over a period of several hours.

3. On very short trips, ignore time

The converse of charging into the day applies to brief visits. I have gone from New York to Tokyo for a one-day visit. Because 2:00 A.M. in Tokyo is 11:00 A.M. in New York, what I try to do is begin my day at 2:00 A.M. there (which is like sleeping late here) and make international calls or go over paperwork before the sun rises. I don't try to get on Tokyo time.

4. Eat less, or not at all

As a general rule, don't eat on an overnight flight because what you're really doing is having breakfast in the middle of the night. The less you eat on planes, the better off you are (same with alcohol). Let your stomach figure out what time zone you're in once your feet are on the ground.

How to Tame a Rude Restaurant

Before you can tame a rude restaurant, you have to know what rude is. In my opinion, true rudeness is an establishment that has a double standard of "us" versus "them." They play favorites, openly catering to an elite at the expense of everyone else.

The irony here is that how well a restaurant plays "us" versus "them" is precisely what makes it "hot" with the general public (for a while at least). The "us" crowd naturally doesn't regard the restaurant as rude because they're treated royally. The "thems," however, are virtually asking to be manhandled.

Frankly, there's not much you can do to correct this sort of gratuitous rudeness, short of not dining there in the first place. The obvious responses, such as not tipping or never coming back, may work after the fact, but they won't improve the meal first time around.

Here are a few strategies to consider before your dining experience turns into a nightmare.

1. Distinguish between poor service and rudeness

The difference between rude and inefficient is not subtle. Inefficient means no ice water, lukewarm soup, forgotten drink orders, slow service, an incorrect bill.

Rudeness is a much bigger sin, and much more unusual. It's that "go to hell" attitude when you must wait an hour to be seated despite your reservation (and no one tells you why); when you ask for a bigger table and they lie that they don't have any; when you sense that the super-crisp service is a ruse to rush you out of there. It's hard to pin down rudeness, but as Justice Potter Stewart said about pornography, "I know it when I see it."

Poor service is far more common than rudeness—and far more correctable if you're willing to forgive.

2. Don't get mad or get even. Get the maître d'

If you're displeased, don't make a scene. It only inspires the staff to offend you more. And even if you do manage to unnerve your waiter into submission, you've probably done the same to your guests and your digestion.

Try a soft approach. Take the maître d' aside and quietly register your complaint. If you know someone in charge, take the following position: "I really like your restaurant. I like the ambience, the food, I've recommended it to many people. But things have gone wrong here that I think you should be aware of." Any establishment worth revisiting will listen.

3. Be businesslike

People should handle restaurant situations with the same care and sensitivity they extend to business negotiations. But for some reason, people undergo a personality change when they walk through a restaurant's door. They develop a hair-trigger sensibility. They take umbrage at the most trivial offenses—slights they wouldn't even notice if they occurred in an office setting.

A friend of mine has a very businesslike attitude about waiting for a table—and in turn he rarely is kept waiting. He isn't pushy or self-important. He doesn't name-drop or threaten or pretend to be a regular (all strategies guaranteed to have the opposite effect you intend).

He treats the maître d' like a manager under the usual managerial pressures, and he makes his intentions very clear. He'll explain to the maître d', "We have backup reservations at another restaurant at nine o'clock, but we really want to dine here. We'll stay if you can guarantee a table by nine. If it's nine-fifteen, just tell me and we'll come back another time." Few establishments will refuse someone that reasonable.

4. How do they handle complaints?

An important criterion by which to judge restaurants (or any enterprise) is not whether you have something to complain about, but how they respond to your complaint. I think any establishment can have an isolated employee who's not operating at his peak. Everyone has lapses.

How they treat that information—whether they're defensive or willing to accommodate the customer—is often more important than the information itself. If your gripes are just, the best restaurants will tear up your bill or invite you back as their guest.

5. Don't set yourself up

Nobody likes to wait, but if you show up during a popular restaurant's "rush hour" you have only yourself to blame. At places that don't take reservations, I see nothing wrong with dining at 6:30 P.M., especially when I know that thirty minutes later I'd have no chance of being seated.

Another point about reservations: If you're going to be late, call ahead no matter how inconvenient it may be. Never assume the maître d' won't give your table to someone who arrived on time.

6. Never stand in line outside

Why people wait in line for two hours outside trendy restaurants—as they do at New York's Hard Rock Café—is beyond my comprehension. It's as if they're willing to accept rude treatment even before they get inside.

7. Make friends with the management

You can deal with any restaurant, no matter how trendy or crowded, if you know the management well. This requires regular patronage and generous tipping. But to many people it's worth it. After all, there's something to be said for the fleeting glory of gliding by everyone waiting in line and getting a table at the toughest spot in town. Enjoy.

Finding the Power in the Power Lunch

William H. Whyte, the author of the fifties classic *The Organization Man,* once told *The New York Times* about what he calls "the long good-bye" at lunch. For many years Whyte has observed executives lingering outside restaurants after a meal in midtown New York City.

"Something holds them so they can't say good-bye," says Whyte. "Something is unresolved. I think most deals are made on the sidewalk *after* lunch."

If Whyte is right, I think many of these people are missing the whole point of business meals. They're taking the power out of the so-called Power Lunch. People do business in restaurants not just because they have to eat, but because the atmosphere is intimate, friendly, sometimes revealing, and tends to make people more receptive to good ideas.

Don't wait until the end

Waiting to make your points on the sidewalk after lunch, to my mind, is self-defeating for at least three reasons. One, you're no longer in the relaxed confines of the restaurant. Two, the person you're trying to persuade is most likely thinking about the next appointment. Three, agreements made as you hastily shake hands are about as firm as saying "Let's have lunch." You'll need at least three more meetings to resolve the loose ends and conflicting opinions these handshake deals create.

My experience is that people get down to business in restaurants somewhere between the end of the main course and coffee, when waiters are more likely to leave you alone. Many executives, I notice, tip off that they are ready to "talk business" by pushing their plate slightly away and clearing out a clean place on the tablecloth in front of them. Perhaps this is their tiny "power desk" away from the office. I get very alert when I see this.

There is no perfect moment to bring up key points in a restaurant. But the first few minutes (when you should be establishing everything that is to follow) and the final minutes (when you should be leaving with a warm feeling about each other) are probably the worst.

I don't introduce important business topics as we're leaving the restaurant and I'm wary when my lunch guest tries to turn the tables on me.

Lincoln Kirstein, a powerful patron of the arts in New York City and co-founder of the New York City Ballet, tells a story about having lunch with Nelson Rockefeller in the 1960s. Rockefeller was governor of New York at the time and Kirstein was successfully feuding with his brother, John Rockefeller, over control of the State Theater in Lincoln Center.

When Nelson invited him to lunch, Kirstein told him point-blank that he wouldn't come to lunch if Lincoln Center was going to be discussed. It was a closed story as far as he was concerned.

Nelson assured him, "Lincoln Center won't be discussed. I just want to see you because I'm so fond of you and I haven't seen you for a long time."

Kirstein could hardly refuse, even though he knew perfectly well what the issue at lunch would be.

As Kirstein tells it, "We had lunch and nothing was mentioned about Lincoln Center until he said that he had to go to an appointment and would I excuse him. As I stood up to go, he shook my hand and said, 'What is all this about Johnny?' And so I laughed and turned around and walked out of the place."

This was the appropriate response. Anyone who can deflect Nelson Rockefeller after he's bought him a meal is someone who understands the power in a power lunch.

P.S. No matter how you intend to behave during a restaurant meeting, there are two things you can do before you even sit down to assure that the atmosphere is relaxed and conducive to business.

First, unless circumstances demand otherwise, avoid restaurant meetings with more than one person. The psychological dynamics become more complicated and variable with each additional guest, and therefore harder for you to interpret or control.

Second, particularly in Paris, New York, and London, never make reservations for less than three (even if there are only two of you). This will at least get you out of sardine row.

The Care and Feeding of Friends and Clients

Because my professional life revolves around discussions with people, I have a lot of breakfast, lunch, and dinner meetings.

As a general rule, I dine with friends and clients primarily for pleasure, not profit. But if you become skillful at making the dining experience pleasant for yourself and others, the profits tend to follow. Keep in mind that entertaining in many ways is like playing the guitar: it's easy to do but difficult to master.

Here are some lessons I've learned over the years about the care and feeding of friends and clients.

1. Take advantage of being the host

There's something to be said for being the host rather than the guest. Along with the privilege of paying the check, you get to decide who's invited and, more important, where you'll dine. Don't abdicate these decisions to your guests or your secretary. You'll lose whatever advantage there is to being the host.

2. Know what serves you best

Given the choice, I'm most comfortable in a dining ambience that's quiet rather than noisy, roomy rather than crowded, responsive rather than difficult. And yet there are many appealing restaurants that are anything but quiet, roomy, and responsive. Save these places for intimate friends, not with people you expect to do business with.

3. For total control, try catering

The best way to insure a good table and minimum interruptions is to have the meal catered.

You can, for example, reserve a private room at a restaurant that understands business dining and, if you're so inclined, control everything from the seating arrangement to the choice of wines to when the salad is served. Every town has a few establishments that excel at this sort of thing.

Even better, you can have the meal catered at your office. Not only are you in complete control, but the experience can introduce your guests both to you and your business.

You don't need a palace or lavish corporate dining room to carry this off. Just be clear about what kind of statement you want to make.

Roger Penske, the former race car driver and now CEO of a billion-dollar transportation empire that is a paragon of efficiency and cleanliness, once invited his bankers to his Pennsylvania headquarters and served them lunch in the garage—which was spotless.

4. Be unpredictable

A little unpredictability in your choice of venue goes a long way to guaranteeing success.

Everyone gets into restaurant ruts. They select a place more by inertia than imagination, choosing the safe and familiar restaurant (which invariably is safe and familiar to their guests as well).

Next time, try to introduce your guests to a place they've (a) never heard of, or (b) would never go to on their own, or (c) would never associate with you. If the restaurant is up to your standards (and theirs), they'll be impressed.

Then, if possible, try to add some unexpected people to the mix. In our business, that might mean inviting a tennis champion like Martina Navratilova to dinner with two or three CEOs. Mixing those two elements can be refreshing for everyone. Martina might be intrigued to meet people who are as successful in business as she is on the tennis court. And the CEOs (who can dine with their fellow titans of commerce any day of the week) might find talking to a world-class athlete an eye-opening experience.

5. Pick up the check quickly and gracefully

There's something to be said for being fast at picking up the check, no matter who is at the table.

In my mind, the wealthier the person is the more I feel I should pay for dinner—not because I want some billionaire to owe me one, but because the gesture is so unexpected.

As you ascend in business, keep in mind that at a certain level you'll meet people who never get *taken* to dinner. They're so rich, they always pay. To them buying a $300 dinner is like buying a paper clip.

Frankly, a $300 meal is a little more than a paper clip to me. But even in my early days, when it would have been a major expense, I still fought to pay the check.

This can be done gracefully, avoiding any scene, by warning the captain ahead of time that people will fight over the check or by getting up during dessert and paying the bill. No one will be offended by your generosity.

6. Never discuss business

The best part about entertaining friends and future clients is that it exposes them to how you conduct yourself professionally without requiring you to sell them anything.

I noticed this a few years ago with a famous husband-and-wife team, two people I enjoy tremendously. Whenever I was in London and our schedules agreed, I would invite them to dinner. Occasionally, I would also invite a business acquaintance who I knew would get a kick out of meeting them. But I never discussed business, except perhaps to plead my ignorance about their business and ask, "How do you do this stuff?"

After ten or so evenings together, the most amazing thing happened. They began to see that how I handled myself with them was probably how I handled my business affairs. And they liked that. In fact, they were so surprised that I didn't apply any business pressure that they ended up trying to do business things *to* me.

7. The pleasant conclusion

If you do all the above properly, the end result will leave your guests thinking: "What an interesting evening. Rather than taking me to the same place I always go, where I see the same faces, here's someone who takes me to a restaurant here in town that I've never heard of, which I really liked, and introduces me to someone I've never met before."

Don't be surprised if they think you're a helluva person.

8 | Entrepreneuring

The Entrepreneur Test

In the last year or two, the glamour of being an entrepreneur has peaked in the public eye. Never has so much been written about so few. Yet the entrepreneurial urge is more valid than ever, especially in an economy with a huge appetite for new services and new technologies.

More than 600,000 people will start up new businesses in the coming year. Some, with elegant business plans and considerable corporate achievements behind them, will fail. Others, with no track record to speak of, will succeed. What frequently separates the winners and losers is how, if at all, they answered some tough questions before they ever thought about a business plan.

Here are seven questions for men and women who think they want to work for themselves.

Are you plunging or hedging your bet?

It's romantic (and perfectly doable) to plunge headfirst into a new business. Some people need that dangerous thrill to get motivated. Yet I worry about people who quit their jobs and risk their life savings on a new venture in the belief that making failure so unthinkable will somehow make success more attainable.

If you can, build yourself a comfort zone at the start. Assess your risk-reward ratio and look for ways to reduce your risk. It doesn't necessarily mean reducing your reward.

When I started my business 25 years ago, I had the hedge of being with a law firm that permitted me to work on the side. I could put my feet in the water without having to sink or swim. If the business of managing Arnold Palmer didn't work out, I could swim back to the island of the law firm. At the same time I could go progressively deeper as the situation improved. This low-risk sort of moonlighting—with your employer's permission—is an enviable way to test out an idea.

What's your idea of maximum achievement?

It has taken me years to realize that there are people in our company who really don't want to devote full time to maximum achievement. They share my business philosophy but not my personal goals.

My business mentality has always been: (1) maximize the use of my time; (2) achieve as much as I can; (3) earn as much profit as possible from it; (4) be creative; and (5) obtain the ego gratification from seeing certain projects come to fruition.

But I don't expect everyone to emulate me. Many people in the world really want a 9-to-5 sort of job. They do it very well, they earn money, they get recognition, and they have more time to do volunteer work or go fishing or build a treehouse for their son. That's perfectly okay.

There's enough room in any organization for both types of individuals. But not at the top.

Can you do better working for someone else?

Maximum achievement can often be obtained by *not working for yourself*.

This can apply to any kind of business. If you have a brilliant idea in medicine or a new tax concept, you're far better off under the umbrella of a Mayo Clinic (with its patients and research funding) or a law firm (with its steady supply of clients) than you would be hanging up your own shingle.

This is something many people, eager to be their own boss, don't think about.

What's your concept of cash flow?

Every business plan makes incredibly precise assumptions about income and outgo, but nearly everybody gets it wrong. For one thing, people often overlook how long it really takes to get the money in. Quitting your job because you've convinced a $100,000 account to join you doesn't mean you start day one of the new venture with $100,000 in the bank. More likely, you're paid in quarterly installments. Unless you've lined up other clients or trim your overhead to zero, waiting for that first payment can seem an eternity.

Do you have a business or a deal?

An acquaintance once told me, "From one business you can make ten deals, but ten deals do not make a business." As an investment banker, he never forgot that his company's enormous trading operations were the "business" and the highly profitable underwriting of securities were the "deals."

There are plenty of one-shot opportunities out there that can make you money in a short period of time. But when the one-shot deal has run its course, where's the core business that sustains your cash flow and everyone's paychecks?

Do you want to be a hero or a winner?

A recent study showed that 75 percent of the 410,000 millionaires in the US are over 50 years old and made their fortune by working 7 days a week for 20 or 30 years in relatively humdrum businesses. What this tells me is that for every "hero" who starts up an airline or computer or chocolate cookie company, there are thousands of "winners" who are doing just fine in the nooks and crannies the media ignore.

Does money matter?

Yes, it does. Many people go into business to earn enough so they and their family can live in comfort. During the lean years, this seems to satisfy them and they con themselves into thinking about how they're laying a foundation, investing in the future, building an organization, that maximum profits don't really matter. Ultimately, profits matter because you need them to turn on the lights, to repay your bank, to grow the business, and to hold on to employees. An entrepreneur does not go into business just to make ends meet.

Putting Reality Back into Business Plans

If and when you try to raise venture capital for a start-up, you'll get a lot of conflicting advice on writing your business plan.

The first thing you should realize is that business plans exist to raise money. Don't rely on them to predict the future or to run your company once you've got the money.

Naturally, then, you must write your plan to convince backers, not your family or your neighbors or even yourself.

Assuming you have a good idea for a product or service that fills a definite need (if you don't, read no further), the fatal flaw in most business plans is a lack of realism. For example:

1. Too much faith in assumptions. Just once I'd like to read a plan where someone actually put in writing that they have no idea how many widgets they'll sell in year one or year two. If nothing else, I'd know they were realistic.

2. An unrealistic absence of fear. I admire people with the courage to start up their own businesses. But I don't confuse courage with fearlessness. Fear of failure, for example, is healthy and should be mentioned in the plan. Venture capitalists know it's the best motivator during the lean years.

3. An unrealistic view of the competition. Don't use your business plan to gloat over your competition's weaknesses. Give your competitors the credit they deserve. After all, they got in the business ahead of you. If you gloss over or ignore competitive realities, a potential investor might logically wonder what else you are ignoring.

4. An unrealistic faith in money. Ideas (not money) solve problems. Money only enhances the solutions. I worry when a business plan's only strategy for finding customers reads: "$400,000 for advertising." There's not enough cash in the world to throw at the kinds of problem this start-up will face.

5. Don't fall in love with the plan. Business plans, especially the lengthy, elaborate ones, tend to be self-refer-ring and self-fulfilling. Each page refers to a previous page's numbers, as if they were etched in marble rather than scribbled on paper. Venture capitalists know immediately where the plan is heading if you've stacked the deck on page one—in their wastebasket.

What Do Successful Entrepreneurs Have in Common?

When I talk to entrepreneurs about their careers, inevitably I hear them make two statements, one of which is an outright lie and the other a bit of self-deception.

The lie is a variant on "If I knew how hard I'd have to work, I'd never have started the business." The reason it's a lie is because successful entrepreneurs do know how hard the work will be but they take the plunge anyway.

The second line, which is a contradiction of the first, goes like this: "If I knew how much fun I would have on my own, I'd have started much sooner." This is self-deception, in my view, because it assumes that the entrepreneur is the creator rather than the beneficiary of good timing. Most successful entrepreneurs I know have started their ventures when the market was ready for them and they were ready for the market—and not a moment too soon or too late. They may call it "vision," but believe me, it's luck (and they deserve it).

I advise would-be entrepreneurs to be confident but never self-satisfied. Don't think you're special and don't waste too much time asking other people if you are.

Although a great idea is crucial to the success of any enterprise, so is great execution. Yet too many people believe that coming up with a good idea for business is the end rather than the start of the entrepreneurial process. They share their idea with a spouse or friends, enjoy the praise they receive for being so clever, and then nothing. These are the same people who always need one more opinion and for whom no amount of initial financing is ever enough. I guess what I'm really saying to them is, "Why aren't you out there working on this instead of talking to me?"

When the Boss Should—and Should Not— Get Involved

A lot of the revenues in an entrepreneurial venture are an outgrowth of the relationship between the entrepreneur and top executives at other companies. This makes sense in the first years of most start-ups when the entrepreneur is usually the company's best salesman.

But as the company grows, the boss's relationship with other top-level peers can be a mixed blessing, especially if it lulls the subordinates into thinking that their boss can somehow circumvent a client's chain of command whenever problems occur.

As tempting as it is for any CEO to ride in on a white horse when the troops below meet resistance, I think it's wiser to refrain from doing so. While you may win the battle, you'll lose the war.

For one thing, there's no guarantee that you can persuade another company's CEO to go along with something that his own people don't believe in.

Second, trying to get the CEO to issue an edict to his subordinates often backfires. Human nature being what it is, the subordinates inevitably get defensive and start focusing on all the ways you can fail them rather than help them succeed.

Playing on their uncertainty

Of course, that doesn't mean there aren't advantages to be derived from CEOs knowing CEOs. In many organizations, some of our most successful deals have developed when my relationship with a CEO has been the trump card that we've never had to play.

At every point along the chain of command, people know I know the CEO. And they also know that I'm not using this connection. Or they're not sure.

Playing on this uncertainty—and finding the cracks in a company's chain of command—can give you a legitimate advantage in almost any corporate sale. For example, you might drop a line like, "I had lunch with your boss the other day," to establish that you are in a dialogue with their boss. Chances are they won't degrade themselves by asking, "Gee, what did he say?" because that implies they aren't as close to the boss as they would have you believe. Therefore, they won't follow up on that provocative little statement—and neither should you.

However, they usually will try to accommodate you, on the theory that you have their boss's ear and, depending on their performance, can speak well or ill of them.

Work up the chain

This subtle sort of dynamic is not present in every selling situation, but when it is, it can be vital. You shouldn't abuse it. Just because you've got a handle on their chain of command doesn't mean you have to whip them with it.

The key to dealing with any chain of command is to start at the bottom and work your way up, not the other way around. If you get the CEO's subordinates enthusiastic about the merits of your proposal, *they* will practically sell it to their boss for you.

Line Extension: Growing Your "New, Improved" Company

There are two ways to make your business grow. You can develop a new product or service, or you can take an existing product or service and improve it.

Developing something new is risky and expensive. But the rewards can be mind-boggling, especially if you create a unique breakthrough product or service with no competition (at least for a year or two). Just ask the people at Sony who created the Walkman portable cassette player.

The second route, improving what you already have, is a variation on what marketing people call "line extension"—taking the name or goodwill of an established product and using it on a new one.

Big, sophisticated marketers are very good at it.

Tide. Liquid Tide.

Coke. Diet Coke. Cherry Coke.

In the sports business, the Senior Golf tour is a line extension of the PGA tour. Personally, I never thought Senior Golf would succeed like it has. I thought it had the usual line-extension pitfalls: There wasn't a market for it; it would cause confusion; and it would cannibalize dollars away from the regular tour. I vastly underestimated the millions of golfers over 50 for whom the older champions still had tremendous appeal.

What's interesting to me about line extension is that it can be a good model for growing a service business.

Growing by extension

In a way, the growth of our entire organization has been a steady string of line extensions. We managed only golfers for many years. When we were sure of our expertise, we extended our reach into tennis, skiing, and motor sports and later running, gymnastics, skating, team sports such as baseball and football, and even classical music.

We do certain things very well, and we don't apologize for all the things we cannot do. Just because we know a lot about golf or tennis doesn't mean we should be manufacturing golf clubs or tennis racquets.

One caveat: Marketers are always creating products and branding them as "new and improved." In a service business, I've found, you can grow a "new" company or an "improved" one, but you can't do both.

Given the risks and costs of starting from scratch, I would first opt for improving what you already have.

Acquiring Businesses That Will Help You Grow

Most of the growth of our organization has been developed internally. Our growth stems from the following axiom: We stick to what we do best but apply it in areas no one else has considered before. That's why, for example, we now offer the same financial management services to corporate executives that we have been providing all along to our superstar athletes.

But in recent years we have identified very specific areas such as publishing, classical music, and team sports that dovetail with our proven expertise. And we've also found that it's sometimes quicker and more cost-effective to enter these fields by acquisition.

The trick, of course, is to acquire businesses for the right reasons—not because you want to be bigger or can't resist a "bargain" or happen to be flush with cash. Some points to keep in mind:

1. Don't push too hard for miracles

Some acquisitions give you a quick infusion of cash. Other acquisitions take longer to make their presence felt on the bottom line. You might buy a company to get a technological jump on your competition or to introduce new concepts to your employees or even to prevent your competition from making the acquisition. None of these reasons translate into profits in the short term. And a couple of years after you close the deal, you'll need patience and discipline to remember why you made the deal in the first place.

About ten years ago, the CEO of a hydraulics distributor I'm familiar with acquired a small company that specialized in electronic controls. From the start, it ran in the red and the CEO's senior managers badgered him to unload it. Fortunately, he didn't expect miracles and he never forgot his long-term reasons for the acquisition. Now that electronic controls are a significant part of hydraulics design, this CEO looks like a genius.

2. Find the synergy

An acquisition is doomed unless both parties contribute something to the deal. The fit has to be natural.

When we decided a few years ago to represent classical musicians, we had very compelling reasons to do so as I mentioned earlier. Classical musicians were earning more and more money; like athletes, they perform their art with no consideration for language; they perform internationally and need the same tax advice as athletes who travel from country to country; their career longevity is impressive; and their concerts could benefit from the same methods we developed for promoting and sponsoring sporting events.

We also studied the competition and sensed that at the larger artist management firms, the top people were probably representing Steven Spielberg or Paul McCartney or Paul Newman; they were not in the classical division.

All we lacked was a knowledge of who was a good violinist and who wasn't. So we found a company that was small, ambitious, and reputable. We brought them our international clout and financial and promotional skills, and they brought us their clients and expertise.

3. If you "buy" management, don't let them go

In many deals, the management that comes with the company is considered expendable. You see this often in large industrial mergers where within a year the acquired managers go elsewhere and the acquiring company moves in its own team.

I don't go along with this, perhaps because in a service business like ours, we acquire talent, not factories or oil reserves or inventory.

Be sure you know whether you're paying for management talent or the physical plants they managed. If you want good managers to stay, make them feel at home. Integrate them into the rest of the company. Make them officers if you have to. But don't make them feel like a visiting team.

Coming in Loud and Clear to Your Employees

One of the best investments in time and energy an entrepreneur can make in growing a business is to issue a "State of the Business" report for all employees.

I've known several CEOs of privately-held companies who do this annually.

Obviously, it's a great device for telling employees where the business has been and where it's going. You can inculcate your employees with your values. Plus, you earn their trust by sharing confidential information with them. Employees tend to shoot straight with the boss when they *know* he's shooting straight with them.

"State of the Business" reports come in all shapes and sizes. There are no rules about length or style, what you can or can't say. I've seen two-page documents that said it all and 200-page documents that went nowhere.

I've seen reports that, to an outsider, were nothing more than dry company histories. But to observant employees, they spoke volumes about why the boss said no to some ideas, yes to others. The report was like a road map to his ego and hang-ups.

I've seen reports that were almost laughably candid about the CEO's mistakes over the years. But that candor, I think, prevented employees from repeating those mistakes.

I've seen reports that read like corporate Rolodexes. They literally listed every account and relationship the company ever had, along with the executive responsible for each. This served the dual purpose of squelching rivalries while at the same time opening up people's eyes to new connections and prospects.

I've seen documents that were thinly veiled operations manuals. Only this time it was the CEO very bluntly telling employees how to sell, how to dress, how to hire, how to network.

The best reports read like casual letters from the boss. Warren Buffett, the legendary Omaha investor who controls Berkshire-Hathaway, a closely-held public conglomerate, writes a year-end "Letter from the Chairman" that is so pithy and down-to-earth that *Fortune* and *Business Week* frequently reprint it.

While few CEO's can match Buffett's humor, style, and insight, here are some practical considerations for writing a "State of the Business" report:

• First, put your thoughts in writing (not in a speech) and make sure everyone gets a copy of the document. Your ideas won't make half the impression if you save them for a speech at the annual Christmas bash.

• Second, tell the truth, warts and all. This isn't a glossy annual report to shareholders where you accentuate the positive and bury the rest in footnotes.

• Third, don't use the report to exorcise your demons or settle intracompany scores. The idea, after all, is to galvanize, not antagonize, your employees.

• Fourth, abandon the idea if it becomes cumbersome or impractical. You might find that it is time-consuming or that your company has grown to the point where you can't be sure who exactly is reading this confidential information.

• Fifth, stress confidentiality. I know the chairman of a private but very open-minded company, where nearly all the employees seem privy to company secrets, budgets, and profit-and-loss figures. I asked him how he could let everyone know so much. Wasn't he worried about this information leaking into the wrong hands?

"Why on earth," he asked, "would anyone be interested in how we make and spend money?"

Perhaps he was being disingenuous or perhaps he had tremendous faith in his people. But that cavalier style is not for me. I happen to place a high premium on confidentiality in business because I'm basically a private person and, more important, we have many high-profile clients to consider.

Four Reasons Why Your Business Should Not Be Like Mine

The concept of a company like IMG, which represents athletes, manages sporting events, and creates television programming, is fairly unique—virtually impossible to duplicate today.

We also started out 25 years ago with some self-imposed "handicaps" that work for us but might not work as well for every company. For example:

1. We grow slowly or not at all

I have always insisted on slow growth—or none at all. We're not a publicly owned company; we don't have to contort ourselves to show steady earnings increases from quarter to quarter. We don't have security analysts to placate.

My real reason, however, is more basic. We are a personal services business, no different than a dentist or a law firm. We rely on people rather than machines. Each one of our employees has to be picked and trained carefully. If we went from 10 clients to 100 clients in two years, it would be impossible for us to acquire and train the staff to handle clients with the quality and professionalism we would want them to have.

The nastiest risk in any personal services business is that, at some point in the growth curve, people forget the word "personal." They go berserk the moment they have a little success, thinking that their talents can be cloned ad infinitum. That is the fallacy of duplication.

Restaurants are the most obvious example. A restaurateur succeeds as much for his personal "touch" as for his cooking. He knows his patrons, ushers them to their favorite tables, recites the specials of the day, recommends wines. His virtuoso performance is part of dining at his establishment. After a while, perhaps when he's bored by his success, he decides to take his show on the road. He figures if he's making $1,000 a week at one restaurant, he'll make $10,000 a week at ten restaurants.

Unfortunately, it never works that way. He can't be everywhere and he can't hire people to do what comes so easily to him. I have met many smart people who began with one restaurant, branched out to several, and ended up with one restaurant again.

2. We're international

The smartest thing I've done in business was to go international. I spend half my time overseas, and half our employees are there. Given the global nature of sports, I'm sure that ratio will get bigger before it gets smaller.

Going international is one idiosyncracy where businesses

should probably be more, not less, like mine. Yet, surprisingly, most executives still believe the only game in town is the one at home.

This kind of parochialism often leads to the most peculiar reasoning.

Fifteen years ago, when a friend of mine was interested in distributing Perrier in Australia, I approached the Perrier people in Paris on his behalf.

"What about the Australian market?" I inquired.

The international marketing director replied: "We do so little business there, I've never even been to Australia."

I pointed out that maybe Australia is such a small market *because* he's never bothered to go there.

But his astonishing statement, with its Catch-22 logic, is typical of how many people regard the international marketplace. To them a market they haven't seen is a market that doesn't exist. They treat it as a fact to be accepted, not an opportunity to be exploited.

Have these people ever considered that what might be a tough fight in their own backyard is often a cakewalk in another country?

3. We don't seek publicity for its own sake

There are certainly many companies with products and services that need to be publicized. We are not one of them.

Our only job is to provide good service—on the theory that if we do that well, the word of mouth will take care of itself.

I don't have much patience with people in our company who are always waving articles about our competition in front of me, saying, "We've got to counteract this." Doing excellent work, I tell them, is the best counterpunch of all.

4. Our expertise is narrow—by design

In our company, we do a limited number of things very well. We don't apologize for all the things we cannot do, or rush into new areas merely to fill some real or imagined void.

Basically, we represent athletes. And remarkably, every year there are more athletes to keep us busy.

As I often tell associates, if you find yourself playing in a big apple orchard, and there's nobody in the apple orchard but you, and there are still a lot of apples on the tree, there's no point going into a peach orchard. We are still playing in the apple orchard, happily and vigorously.

Epilogue

Do I Follow My Own Advice?

As a reader, you may be wondering if I really believe and practice all the advice I write. Are street smarts necessary in every situation? Am I always aggressively looking for clues to gain an edge? Do I have to extract the maximum profit from every relationship?

Yes and no. Yes, I believe the advice I write. No, I don't always put it into practice—because most of the time I don't have to. An overwhelming majority of the transactions and relationships in business are fair, uncomplicated, and straightforward. You provide a benefit for someone and they do something nice in return. This is the classic win-win scenario, which I firmly believe in.

I doubt if our clients and customers—both individuals and corporations—would have stayed with us over the years if they didn't feel they were winning as much or as often as we were. But I don't let the fact that we're both doing well stop me from trying to do as well as I can.

Unfortunately, not every transaction goes by the book. Like everyone else, I have run into people who don't keep their promises, who don't pay their bills, who aren't committed to quality, who scheme for every negotiating edge and then exceed it.

In those situations, I find that being street smart—for example, knowing how to read people, massage relationships, or assert my own agenda—is not ruthless. It's absolutely necessary.